PEACE
WITH FREEDOM

MAURICE
TUGWELL

KEY PORTER BOOKS

Canadian Cataloguing in Publication Data

Tugwell, Maurice.
  Peace with freedom

ISBN 1–55013–128–1

1. Peace 2. Liberty 3. Canada — Politics and government. I. Title.

JX1961.C3T84 1988   327.1'72'0971   C88–094283–5

The publisher gratefully acknowledges
the assistance of the Ontario Arts
Council.

Key Porter Books Limited
70 The Esplanade
Toronto, Ontario
Canada M5E 1R2

Printed and Bound in Canada
88 89 90 91 92 6 5 4 3 2 1

PEACE

WITH FREEDOM

CONTENTS

INTRODUCTION

"Peace" can mean different things to different people. Is mere survival peace? Can there be peace when human beings are deprived of human rights? If not, what rights are essential before peace can exist? And what price are we prepared to pay to ensure that future generations of Canadians enjoy the kind of peace that matches our answers to these questions?

Our answers are likely to be influenced by our Western political and cultural heritage, by our Constitution, and by our experiences and expectations as citizens of a lively and developing democracy. For most Canadians, peace is surely more than the absence of war. The word has a positive connotation, implying a definite, attestable contribution to human happiness. The preamble to the United Nations Charter reinforces this view when it urges us "to practise tolerance and live together in peace with one another as good neighbours."[1] "Peace" and "goodwill" are firmly linked within our conception of what is morally right and politically desirable. Peace speaks of trust, of mutual respect, and of people living free from the threat and reality of war.

Expressed briefly, peace as most Canadians have understood it, enjoyed it, and taken it for granted, is *peace with freedom*.

This type of peace is threatened. Anti-democratic groups on the one hand and confused apolitical forces on the other promote the peace of submission and rigid ideological conformity as a preferable or at least inevitable alternative. The external threat, centred on the Soviet Union, is military, ideological, and subversive; the internal threat to peace with freedom is part-subversive and part-idealistic. The latter element, loosely referred to as the Canadian peace movement, argues or at least implies that to maintain peace with freedom requires a high risk of nuclear war between East and West, with terrible consequences for mankind. No one would question those consequences. The false assumption lies elsewhere: in the notion that we must choose either survival by submission or annihilation. Either the peace of the prison cell or the peace of the grave.

The real choice, surely, is between retaining control of our future through the careful, rational management of national and international affairs—so avoiding both prison and grave—and that collapse of spirit and intellect that leads to self-deception and surrender. Remember too that the totalitarian prison cell more often than not leads to the grave, so peace on these terms does not guarantee survival.

"Peace with freedom," then, implies support for the Western democratic tradition and a determination to defend it from external and internal threats. Defence is not a warlike activity, but a response to a warlike threat. The same can be said of efforts to prevent warlike threats from developing into warlike acts—what we call deterrence. Freedom and peace call for clear heads and stout hearts. These do not threaten anyone.

Clear heads recognize that wishful thinking is the enemy of peace, because it clouds the intellect and distorts reality. It can become the smoke screen behind which an enemy might advance. For this reason, clear-headed Canadians, and Western publics generally, should be watching recent developments in the Soviet Union with interest, hope, and no little caution.

Hope is always needed, since without it there can be no future worth the name. And it should encompass a readiness to recognize and encourage any signs of real change in the world Communist system, especially in the Soviet Union. However many times our hopes may be raised, only to be dashed as each new "reform" turns out to be hollow, we must not close our minds to the possibility that one day things may *really* alter.

Indeed, when the secretary general of the Communist Party of the Soviet Union admits that the free economic system of the

West has worked better than his own, as Mikhail Gorbachev has done,[2] he admits by implication that the economically based Marxist theory that forms an important ingredient of his legitimizing ideology is false. This is significant, and welcome. So too is the policy of glasnost, the tabling of selected subjects for more open debate within Soviet society. Designed no doubt to rekindle intellectual support for the Communist Party, as well as to impress the West—objectives that are not useful to peace or freedom—glasnost may yet change patterns and induce secondary changes that are useful.

There is also cause for hope in the concept of perestroika. The word is evidently a disguise for a thoroughgoing purge of the entire Communist system—the party and administrative apparatus in the USSR, the client or clone states that are Communist, and the nonruling Communist parties in the West and Third World. Some analysts see perestroika as a mobilization for renewed political warfare, while others see it as a survival exercise. In these forms, it is unlikely to contribute to peace with freedom. But like glasnost, it may conceivably begin a wider process of change within the Communist system; its very existence is evidence of the failure of orthodox Marxism-Leninism.

New political thinking forms the third element in the Gorbachev reform package. It has been described by Alexander Yakovlev, head of Soviet propaganda, as "not just a package of specific ideas and proposals. We see it as an appeal to be guided by reason and by the experience and knowledge that have been gained and proven correct."[3] This may sound innocent enough in isolation, but in the same article Yakovlev stressed the importance of the "new strategic parity that we have literally wrested from history"—meaning the massive Soviet military build-up. The Soviets are obsessed with power; understandably, because power is all that communism has to offer. They are convinced that the dominant military power will inevitably rule the world. "New thinking" is evidently coded language for Western acceptance of pre-eminent Soviet power.

The Soviet term for the balance of strength is the *correlation of forces.* Within this concept, they assess every imaginable asset —military strength, training, morale, civilian attitudes, ideology, economic power, allies, and so on. *Nothing* is overlooked. They are conviced that a change in the correlation of forces in their favor accounted for the West's willingness to endorse the Helsinki Agreement of 1975; today they boast that "partisans of realism [meaning proponents of surrender] in questions of peace and war are getting more numerous among leading circles of some Western states, which also reflects the shift in the correlation of forces."[4] There is, alas, a great deal of evidence from Soviet sources that indicates that "new thinking" is a complex politico-psychological operation designed to lull the West into a condition of gradual surrender, one that will not be recognized for what it is until the process is irreversible. If this part of the Gorbachev "charm offensive" is a trap, it would be reasonable to view the remainder with caution.[5]

In his book, *Perestroika: New Thinking for Our Country and the World*, Mikhail Gorbachev asserts that "neither the Soviet Union, nor its perestroika pose any threat to anyone,"[6] and he complains that "again and again we are accused of wanting to implant communism all over the world."[7] Yet throughout the book, Gorbachev constantly stresses the importance of a "turning to Lenin" for inspiration and guidance. He even makes this the title of a chapter.

If we turn to Lenin, we find: "We are living not only in a state but in a system of states, and it is inconceivable for the Soviet Republic to exist alongside the imperialist states for any length of time. One or the other must triumph in the end."[8] This is the essence of the Leninist "who-whom?" philosophy, which asks "Who, the capitalists or Communists, will destroy whom?" Within a revolutionary strategy, and especially one driven by Marxism-Leninism, which insists that history has already decided that communism will be the "who" and democracy the "whom," it is possible to deny warlike intention while simultaneously working flat out to destroy the rival system.

Turning to Lenin also reminds us of his 1920s reform period—the New Economic Policy. The analyst and former US

State Department official George Kennan has described the Soviet leadership's attitude toward the West during that period:

> We despise you. We consider you should be swept from the earth . . . We reserve the right to do what we can to bring this about . . . to do everything in our power to detach your own people from their loyalty to you . . . and to work for your downfall in favour of a Communist dictatorship. But since we are not strong enough to destroy you today . . . we want you during this interval to trade with us; we want you to finance us. We want you to give us the advantage of full fledged diplomatic recognition.[9]

Déjà vu?

If, as they claim, the present Soviet leadership has returned to Lenin, peace with freedom is still under attack; indeed, all the more so with the threat now so well camouflaged.

This book is about the internal component of the threat. Since the internal is partly a manifestation of the wider Soviet threat, however, this too will receive attention.

CHAPTER I

SAFEGUARDING PEACE WITH FREEDOM

"A spectre is haunting Europe—the spectre of communism." So began Marx and Engels' famous Manifesto.[1] Nearly a century and a half later, the Communist spectre, materialized in Russia, has taken possession of Eastern Europe, China, parts of Asia, Africa, and the Western Hemisphere, and continues to haunt the rest of the world. The internal restructuring of the Soviet Union is accompanied by a global political and psychological offensive, by a continued military build-up that far exceeds any possible defensive requirement, and by renewed efforts to consolidate recent acquisitions in the Third World.

There appears to be a determined attempt on the part of the USSR to break out from all the constraints that have hitherto limited her actions, including the restraints imposed by Western—particularly NATO—defence and deterrence policies. Before examining that part of the Soviet offensive that has to do with "peace," it may be useful to review briefly the West's response to the Soviet threat and the military strategies that have supported the response.

The choice for the democracies has always been quite straightforward: to resist or to surrender. Various compromise positions have been advocated, such as appeasement, buying the adversary off, or declaring oneself neutral or nonaligned. There being no state of war, however, a declaration of neutrality has no real meaning, nor is there any reason to suppose it would provide security in the event of war. Nonalignment, a term usually applied to Third World countries, suggests an unconcern over Western political and social values, a desire to not take sides

between democracy and totalitarianism. It comes close to nonresistance. As for the various forms of appeasement, these tend
merely to delay the choice between resistance and surrender, or
to provide a bridge from the first to the second. So it is that the
serious options come down to two: surrender (a course reluctant-
ly adopted by a number of central European nations in the years
immediately following World War II) and resistance. The latter
course can be followed by each state separately, or taken collectively. Nations such as Sweden and Switzerland resist separately.
It is misleading to speak of them as neutral, although the media
does this all the time, because they share our Western values and
political principles. One does not accuse a neighbor of being
neutral in the fight against crime simply because he prefers not
to join some scheme like Neighborhood Watch.

In 1949 many of the European democracies, together with
Canada and the United States, adopted collective resistance.
They formed the North Atlantic Treaty Organization (NATO).

The West's initial lead in nuclear technology provided NATO
with an economical means of deterring Soviet aggression and
stopping it should it nonetheless occur. NATO strategy has always
depended in part, and often the larger part, on the United
States' strategic nuclear forces, and more recently on medium-
and short-range nuclear missiles.

As an alliance dedicated solely to defence, NATO's military
concerns have been to prevent the Soviet Union and her Communist allies—the Warsaw Pact—spreading outward across the
non-Communist world. The focus has been Western Europe, the
military choice between preparing the alliance for war: creating
huge standing armies; putting the economies on something ap-
proaching a war footing; waiting for the enemy to attack; and
applying relatively modest manpower and material resources to
defence while using nuclear power to deter war. The first option,
based on fighting a defensive war, would commit the alliance's
resources to *war fighting*. In a nuclear age, it would invite nuclear
war. The second, while by no means ideal, at least recognizes the
dangerous consequences of war in the nuclear age and is design-

ed to prevent such a catastrophe. It is called the strategy of deterrence.

Deterrence means thinking through the possible reasoning of an adversary and the way in which alternative courses of action might appear to him in advance. It also means doing this on his terms, not your own. The deterrer seeks to ensure that, whatever military action or political bullying a potential aggressor might contemplate, he could not foresee any likely situation in which victory is obtainable without costs so unacceptable that the word victory *loses its meaning. Nuclear weapons combined with modern means of delivery have transformed the notion of deterrence from a pious hope to a reality.*

To be effective, deterrence strategy has certain requisites. The deterrer must have the physical means to inflict unacceptable damage on a potential aggressor. Moreover, when the adversary also possesses strategic nuclear forces, the deterrer's means, including the decision-making apparatus, must be capable of absorbing a first strike by the enemy and *still* doing the job. Next, the leaders of the deterring nation or alliance must demonstrate their commitment to the strategy; the adversary must believe, or at least fear, that the threat inherent in deterrence would in the last resort be carried out.

Extended deterrence carries the threat of nuclear attack beyond deterring the adversary's strategic nuclear forces. It serves warning that even a "conventional" military attack on one's allies may eventually be met with a nuclear response. This is NATO's strategy: to resist any aggression without nuclear weapons for as long as possible, then if necessary to use "battlefield" nuclear weapons, with the possibility of "escalating" to an all-out nuclear war as the last resort. The concept throughout is to cause the opponent uncertainty in light of an unacceptable risk factor. It is called the doctrine of flexible response.

Such a strategy commits NATO to the first use of nuclear weapons should the aggressor launch an invasion that could not be stopped by conventional means. Without this commitment, the alliance would be back to preparing to use its weapons to wage war, rather than preventing it. Member nations would have to go onto a war footing if they were to have any hope of survival.

First use is therefore a cornerstone of war prevention. A policy that made Europe safe for conventional war would invite such a war. And there are other arguments to show why abandoning the first use policy makes no sense. Any NATO declaration that it would not be the first to use such weapons would not be believed by the Soviets; nor would we accept such an assurance from them. It would weaken deterrence without gaining trust. Even if they did believe us, the outcome would surely be a renewed Soviet conventional build-up and a refusal to negotiate the reduction of conventional forces. Finally, in a book published in Moscow in 1987, Soviet military writers discussed selective nuclear strikes against NATO nations as a way of forcing them to quit the alliance at an early stage of any conflict.[2] Such notions might well be encouraged by a NATO no-first-use declaration.

First use should not be confused with first strike. Whereas first use relates to the use of nuclear weapons against a non-nuclear invasion, first strike is a contraction of the phrase "would-be disarming first strike" aimed at enemy strategic nuclear forces. As an adjective, *first strike* has several meanings. Strategic weapons that are so exposed that they could not possibly survive an enemy attack qualify for the term simply because their vulnerability makes them useless for any role other than a first strike. More recently, rocket systems of great accuracy, particularly those that deliver several independently targeted warheads, have been called first strike on the grounds that they are especially suitable to destroy an opponent's weapons in a pre-emptive attack, even those that are well protected. Finally, critics of nuclear deterrence apply the term *first strike* to virtually any weapon they happen not to like, as a form of denigration.

When one side receives an opponent's first strike and nevertheless succeeds in replying in the same coinage, the response is called a second strike. Second strike capability is essential to a stable deterrence. Second strike weapons are those suited to absorbing a hostile attack but remaining functional.

Stability is the key to peace in a nuclear-armed world, and to a considerable extent stability depends on balance. This has always been recognized by Western and Soviet leaders and specialists in the field. Consider this excerpt from the 1961 McCloy-Zorin Agreed Principles between the superpowers:

> All measures of general and complete disarmament should be balanced so that at no stage of the implementation of the treaty could any State or group of States gain military advantage and that security is ensured equally for all.[3]

Lord Louis Mountbatten's Strasbourg speech has been selectively quoted by peace activists. This is what he actually said about balance: "To begin with we are most likely to preserve the peace if there is a military balance of strength between East and West."[4]

It was to stabilize the strategic balance that the West entered into arms control negotiations with Moscow. It seemed at the time that if both sides agreed to a concept of "mutual assured destruction" (MAD) then, as the USSR achieved parity with the United States in strategic nuclear weapons, a balanced sufficiency of such weapons would be stabilizing. Unfortunately, Western publics often misconstrued arms control for disarmament, which in turn implied a partial solution to the East–West confrontation itself. Arms control is really a symptom of conflict—albeit a sign that both adversaries wish to keep the conflict within bounds—rather than an exercise in conflict resolution. Because the process of arms control negotiations seems to have a calming effect on Western publics, it has tended to cater increasingly to the demands of public opinion rather than the needs of a stable balance.

Canada is firmly committed to NATO, its deterrent strategy (together with the policy of first use), and arms control. The country also contributes to North American Aerospace Defence (NORAD), in surveillance, warning, attack assessment, and defence against air attack. Canada permits the United States to flight-test unarmed air-launched cruise missiles over her territory because of its similarity to Soviet terrain and because, as a component of the strategic deterrent, such weapons contribute to stability as well as deter aggression. Since the Soviets use similar weapons as part of their strategic forces, an unstable situation might develop if theirs worked and ours did not. Hence the need for tests. An incidental benefit arises from the opportunity for our air force to practise intercepting such missiles, as if they were hostile.

CHAPTER II

SOVIET VIEWS ON PEACE, POLITICS, AND WAR

"History is on the side of Socialism. The Socialist countries advance confidently towards victory over capitalism."

Marxism-Leninism on War and Army (Moscow: Voyenizdat, 1972)

"The apologists of capitalism stubbornly refuse to accept the fact that history has long taken away the banner of rights and freedoms from the West and justly handed it over to another social system. History does not reconsider its verdicts, and this is the reason why all plans of social revenge have fallen through . . . The development of Socialism and its achievements convince us that . . . it holds the future."

Gennady Pisarevsky, Soviet spokesman, September 1985[1]

These restatements of what Marxists call historical determinism remind us that it lies at the root of what people in the West often call the Soviet threat. According to the determinist theory, Soviet Marxists possess and even control the timetable of history. The philosophy rests on the unfounded assertion that man once enjoyed a golden age referred to as primitive communism. Later, he was reduced to slavery, from which condition he progressed to feudalism and thence to capitalism. Next he rose to socialism, of the sort claimed to exist in the Soviet Union, and finally he will reach a kind of heaven on earth or second golden age: communism.[2] Observers are divided over whether the Soviet ruling class still believes this superstition or merely acts as though it was not in doubt. Either way, it remains absolutely vital to that class that the core beliefs are never publicly challenged by anyone living under Soviet communism, because the myth legitimizes its leadership role.

Marx wrote that "violence is the midwife of progress." Thus, to assist determinism and demonstrate the power of the myth, any amount of violence in any form is justified, because Marxist or "just" wars obey the laws of history. Likewise, the dictatorship of the proletariat and the monopolizing of power by one party, the Communist Party of the Soviet Union (CPSU), are historically determined and cannot be questioned.

Complaining at Western reactions to various Soviet aggressions, Mikhail Gorbachev denounced them in 1985 as diversions "in order to avoid the demands of Time."[3] The ideology teaches that Soviet communism is destined to triumph everywhere and destroy Western democracy, referred to in the dogma as imperialism or capitalism. Since the legitimacy and morale of the ruling party depend on history being proven correct, however, that party must ensure that communism is indeed seen to expand at the West's expense.

Lenin has been called the first statesman to accomplish the "militarization of politics." From Marx he took the themes of conflict and class struggle and resolved them into a single policy of perpetual struggle to exterminate the "class enemy." From the military philosopher von Clausewitz, Lenin acquired the dictum that war was the continuation of politics by other means. The ideology provided the means and justification for seizing and consolidating absolute power. The concept of a perpetual class enemy rationalized constant military effort and domestic repression.[4]

Since the time of Stalin the CPSU has proclaimed the theory of the "just" and "unjust" war, the former earning its title by being fought in the interests of the party and by being "defensive." For in Leninist theory, stated in 1917, the "character of the war" is decided not by who is the aggressor, but by "the class that is waging the war," a formula that makes all Communist wars "defensive."[5] Lest it be thought that glasnost and perestroika have modified these views, they were reiterated thus in 1986: "To determine the character of a war, the questions of who has begun it, or who is the aggressor, are irrelevant."[6]

In 1980 a professor of philosophy at Toronto's York University, K. T. Fann, argued that

> It cannot, therefore, be said that with the emergence of nuclear weapons Lenin's thesis on war and peace has become outmoded. There is soil for wars as long as imperialism and the system of exploitation of man by man exist. The destruction of capitalism and imperialism is the precondition for achieving world peace . . . No matter how paradoxical this may sound, it reflects the only realistic program: world peace can be achieved only through world revolution.[7]

Boris Ponomarev was head of the International Department of the Central Committee of the Communist Party of the Soviet Union when in 1979 he explained: "There is nothing wrong about strength. What matters is who has it and for what purpose it is used. Strength in imperialist hands is a source of war danger. Strength in the hands of Socialism has become an instrument for ensuring peace and lessening the war danger."[8] That this peaceful Soviet policy embraced the possible use of nuclear weapons was made abundantly clear in 1980 by Maj. Gen. A. S. Milovidov and Dr. Ye A. Zhdanov when they wrote that "Marxist-Leninists decisively reject the assertions of certain bourgeois theoreticians who consider nuclear missile war unjust from any point of view."[9]

The nuclear weapons the Soviets do object to are those in non-Communist hands. Stalin knew in advance that the West was developing the atom bomb: he had spies in every Western country. As early as 1942 he ordered the development of a Soviet bomb.[10] When President Truman informed Stalin officially at the 1945 Potsdam conference that "we had a new weapon of unusual destructive force," Stalin replied that he hoped that the United States would make "good use of it against the Japanese." After two bombs had been used against Japan, ending the war, the British ambassador to Moscow reported that "Russia was balked by the west when everything [all of Europe] seemed to be within her grasp. The three hundred [Soviet] divisions were shorn of much of their value."[11]

The nuclear weapon certainly reduced the offensive and intimidating potential of Soviet conventional military strength. Consequently it represented and still represents an obstacle to the USSR's "historic mission" of carrying communism to the far ends of the earth. The history of Soviet diplomacy, arms control negotiations, military strategy, propaganda and deception in the years since 1945 is largely a record of its leadership's endeavors to escape the restraints imposed by nuclear weapons in non-Communist hands.

In the early days, under Stalin, Soviet propaganda downplayed the importance of the bomb while the military-industrial complex worked flat out to produce the Russian version. Success came in 1949, ending the US nuclear monopoly. Thereafter, the race to catch and overtake the West continued, with the Soviet hydrogen bomb in 1953, operational intercontinental missiles in the 1960s, and "rough parity" in strategic nuclear forces by the early or mid-1970s.[12] Parity with the United States in nuclear weapons meant superiority overall, since the USSR had long been dominant in conventional forces. Between the two alliances, NATO and the Warsaw Pact, however, the balance remained less unfavorable for the West—unless the East should succeed in concentrating for a surprise attack.

Had the Kremlin shared the West's interest in the concept of mutual assured destruction, the USSR could have ended the nuclear arms race and, come to that, the arms race in its entirety, as soon as nuclear parity was achieved. But MAD is the last concept Communists would ever accept, because it reinforces the status quo imposed in 1945; it ignores the "demands of Time."

Instead, the Soviets have accepted a kind of de facto or tactical MAD; they share the West's desire not to destroy the world in a full-scale holocaust and therefore respect a temporary need for caution so long as there is a high risk of any East–West conflict escalating to the nuclear level. At the same time they have striven to minimize the likely penalties by deploying extremely accurate land-based missiles, each carrying multiple, independently targeted warheads, aimed at the US land-based missile force plus fixed assets (airfields, ports) of the bomber and submarine components. The strategy contradicts MAD because it requires a Soviet first strike to be effective. It is a "war fighting" doctrine, rather than a war-prevention policy.

The evident purpose is to be in a position to inflict such damage on the US land-based missiles—the only part of their deterrent with the accuracy to hit Soviet missile silos—that the US president would be deprived of the option of striking back at Soviet missile sites. Instead, he would have to hit back at Soviet cities, or surrender. If he decided to target cities, he would have to recognize that the Soviet strategic forces were still intact and capable of delivering a greater destruction on Western cities.[13]

This is not to suggest that the Soviets have ever intended to initiate a full-scale nuclear war. They are aware that risks cannot be calculated. As one Russian military analyst put it in 1986, "Once it becomes nuclear, war ceases to be a factor of social changes and a way to solve the domestic and international contradictions."[14] This observation implies that the Leninist belief in non-nuclear war as a factor of social changes and a way to solve domestic and international contradictions persisted into Gorbachev's second year. Also, that the unacceptable nuclear war is the one where the opposition possesses the weapons. Nuclear weapons that bring down nuclear retribution on the motherland belong to the category of unusable military force, which cannot serve the demands of Time. Where retribution is impossible, because the opposition has no nuclear arms or dare not use them, Ponomarev's dictum applies: "There is nothing wrong about strength. What matters is who has it and for what purpose it is used." As recently as 1987, another team of USSR Defence Ministry analysts wrote that "a change in the political position of some states during the [next] war can be induced by nuclear strikes."[15] In such a setting, nuclear war becomes "just," because instead of hindering the advance of communism, it accelerates it.

The ruling party that poses this "Soviet threat" to the non-Communist world is in the broadest sense the Communist Party of the Soviet Union, composed of some 18 million members. However, only the top echelon benefits from the system they are controlling, and this élite is what really threatens us. This is the *nomenklatura*, the "privileged political-scientific class" that actually runs the state. Estimated at 750,000 individuals, including the Central Committee of the party and its departments, top echelons of the military and administrative apparatus, all KGB officials, diplomats, and top propagandists, the *nomenklatura* receive high salaries, enjoy special shops, hospitals, schools, and every kind of privilege. Their living standards are comparable with those of their Western counterparts; set against the national averages, however, the differential in the USSR is many times greater than in the West. The *nomenklatura* and their families total some three million—less than 1.5 percent of the Soviet population.[16]

Michael Voslensky, a former Soviet diplomat and nomenklaturist who defected to the West, observes how the theory of historical determinism has been distorted by modern Soviet leaders from a confident, radiant view of the future to a frantic, dangerous strategy of survival. The myth is valued as propaganda to demoralize the West and to persuade the Soviet people that hope of change is illusory. In Voslensky's opinion, this part of the ideology is no longer cherished as a guarantee of victory. The *nomenklatura* knows that the West's living standards and freedoms far exceed those of ordinary Soviet citizens; it also knows that Soviet citizens share this knowledge, that they can be contained only by perpetual intimidation, and the day may come when the dispossessed masses tire of living in fear. The *nomenklatura* lives in perpetual fear of that day, and it blames the affluent West for this. For without the contrast, the Soviet people would have no hope, no aspirations; the *nomenklatura* could then breathe more easily.

Historical determinism has accordingly become a poetic cloak to cover a ruthlessly practical intention by Soviet leaders to destroy the "threat"—a visibly successful and free Western system. Voslensky warns:

> Thus we see that the idea of defence is actually an inherent part of the *nomenklatura*'s aggressiveness and is, in fact, the most dangerous element in its ruthless policy of expansion. There is nothing paradoxical about that statement. If expansionism were merely an idea, a whim of the *nomenklatura*, it could be dropped like any other, but since its power and privileges, and hence its existence as a class, are at stake, it cannot drop it.[17]

The West is threatened not because it is armed or poses any military danger to Soviet Russia, but because it is relatively successful, affluent, and free—in short, because it exists. The *nomenklatura* always attributes intentions identical to its own to its adversaries, blaming the danger of war, Third World disorder, terrorism, and the cold war on the United States and the West. This propaganda is intended for soft-headed Westerners; no one in authority in Moscow is so stupid as to actually believe it. Consequently, efforts by the West to persuade the *nomenklatura* that we have no hostile intentions are useless—the Soviet ruling class already knows this perfectly well. Indeed, the relatively pacific nature of Western society is another reason why it is envied by the Soviet proletariat and hated by the *nomenklatura*.[18]

Some sovietologists may regard Voslensky's opinions as idiosyncratic and even unbalanced. The West has a long record of disregarding the warnings of Soviet emigrés only to discover in due course they were true. But even if the *nomenklatura* were less paranoid than Voslensky claims, and therefore less fearful, it would still be committed to aggression of one sort or another by the need to fulfil the party's "historical mission." This mission is constantly restated as an integral part of intimidation.

We have seen that severe asymmetries exist between Western and Eastern views of war, politics, and peace. Yet these differences are apt to be overlooked, perhaps because it is much less difficult to treat the USSR as though it were similar to other great powers. In practice, however, it is the asymmetries that govern the real nature of the East–West relationship; to ignore them is to fumble in the dark. They may be stated as follows:

• In the USSR, foreign and defence policies are decided in absolute secrecy by the top party leaders; even quite senior officials are kept in the dark. The outside world, including the West, has rarely had the slightest inkling of the Politburo's plans and intentions.

In the democracies, such policies are openly debated. Actual operational plans are graded secret, but security is often so sloppy that even these find their way into the media. Because of the open nature of Western societies, agent penetration has also been relatively simple.

The asymmetry here brings obvious results: the West is always guessing at Moscow's real intentions; the East knows with fair certainty what we have in mind. Thus Soviet planning is soundly based, while ours has to rest on hypotheses. In addition, Eastern secrecy provides the Kremlin with a firm base for deception, consisting of dissimulation, or hiding the real, plus simulation, creating a false picture of reality. Having the first as a given, the Soviets enjoy great powers to deceive.

• In the East, publics have no influence whatsoever over foreign and defence policies. Glasnost has not altered this, as the party, the KGB, defence and foreign affairs are all off limits for debate. In any case, there is no possible way for public opinion to make any impact, as there are no real elections, and party leaders have no need to please their constituents. Moreover, glasnost notwithstanding, Western statesmen, spokesmen, and the like have very limited and tightly controlled access to Soviet publics; they cannot hope to influence them to any great extent. So it is that the Politburo can pursue its aims free of domestic considerations.

In the West, our publics are open targets for Soviet influence, both overt and covert, factual and deceptive. Suitably primed, these publics can influence and ultimately decide their countries' foreign and defence policies. Thus, through propaganda and deception, Moscow could come to control the West's agenda.

• Communist ideology provides the East with a clearly stated mission—to convert the world to Marxism-Leninism. Thus the Kremlin has only to address one question—how? The single-minded pursuit of power, coupled with the dogma that history is on the side of the revolution, making eventual victory inevitable, results in an open-ended commitment that is impervious to argument, amendment, or compromise. Perestroika carefully preserves the historical imperative (indeed it is stressed) while providing to the West the illusion of fundamental change.

Democracy is an idea that can succeed only by community endorsement; consequently it cannot be an ideology, nor can it express itself through propaganda.[19] A flourishing democracy is bound, by its very nature, to attend primarily to domestic needs, looking to its defences only to the extent of minimum safety and not always that.

The East can accordingly devote to its armed forces, secret police, propaganda apparatus, and other instruments of foreign policy as many resources as the leadership considers necessary; the West typically devotes only what is left over when all competing claims on the budget have been met. While there are exceptions in time of war and mortal danger, over the long haul defence is difficult for democracies to maintain. As for a god-given mission in the world, each and every one of us in the West is free to find his or her own.

• Lenin's legacy absolves Communists from any moral constraint in the history-given cause; the good end justifies all means.[20] Tactical alliances can be made with *any* nation or group, such as Idi Amin's Uganda, provided this helps the cause. Stalin has been criticized by his successors not for killing millions of non-Communists, but for turning his terror inward on the party. Restraints developed over the centuries that separate mankind from a brutal past were dismissed by Lenin as "bourgeois morality."

The West, conversely, subscribes to these moral codes and is constrained by them—even to the point of finding it objectionable to question the good faith of Communists. Nevertheless, the codes do inhibit cooperation with authoritarian regimes resisting communism. When individuals or groups in the West act in disregard of the norms, retribution is severe. Moreover, the guilt generated by these transgressions tends to paralyze national wills and to stimulate self-hatred. Because they have become subliminally accustomed to the idea that the Soviets are exempt from moral restraint, Western publics tend to adopt a double standard, judging the West against its best traditions and absolving the East because it does not share this heritage.

• The commitment to world revolution led, immediately after October 1917, to the creation of the Communist International, comprising Communist parties with overt and covert members throughout the Western world. Although the name has changed, this huge apparatus of treason and subversion—the greatest Trojan horse the world has ever known—is now stronger and more tightly controlled from Moscow than ever before.[21] The asymmetry is total; the West has no equivalent organization in Eastern countries.

• The USSR and clone nations possess dual power structures—the party, which rules, and the State, which executes party orders. Moscow operates on two fronts: the party–secret police–clandestine front, which uses the international traitor network as its web; and the state-to-state relations of the civilized world.

Democracies have only the second apparatus, although from time to time private enterprise, secret services, and maverick individuals or groups within the public service have created frail and short-lived mirror images of the Soviet party front.[22] This asymmetry provides the Soviets with additional flexibility.

• Truth, for Communists, must submit to the same test that judges other behavior—if it advances the cause, it is good; if not, it is bad. Good truth is called objective truth, or in these days of glasnost, constructive truth. Bad truth cannot be truth at all and is suppressed.[23] Under glasnost, the categories of truth that are deemed to serve the cause have been substantially widened, and a great deal of ideological confusion has resulted. The basic rule, however, has not changed. The fact that the Soviets were researching a system equivalent to the US Strategic Defense Initiative was bad truth for many years, and denied by Gorbachev.[24] When in December 1987 the Soviet leader decided that the cause would be better served by admitting the research, the same fact became objectively good for communism, thus earning the title of truth.[25]

• Lenin's precondition for "real peace" is the victory of communism; peace in a world divided into socialist and capitalist camps can only be a truce or interlude.[26] There is no evidence that Gorbachev has tampered with this golden rule, which underpins the whole structure of party legitimacy. A book published in 1986 by the USSR Ministry of Defence stated that "Communists never have been pacifists and they cannot be pacifists . . . Socialism and peace are indivisible."[27] It follows that in the current period of undeclared war, no peacetime restrictions limit Soviet behavior, and for all practical purposes, the words *peace* and *victory* are synonymous for Moscow.

The West views war and peace as distinct conditions and feels constrained in its activities unless there is a state of war. If constraints are kicked aside, as in the US action in Grenada, France's in Chad, or Britain's in the Falklands, there is heart-searching and domestic political opposition. The usual outcome is that while the democracies seek peace through negotiation and compromise, the Soviets see no contradiction in the phrase *fighting for peace*. All Soviet treaties are therefore necessarily tactical in purpose and deceptive in character. For the Soviets, the treaty banning medium-range missiles is a step toward victory; for the West, a step toward a more peaceful world. Only in the Communist lexicon are the two ambitions the same.

Soviet foreign policy exploits these asymmetries, and through the international application of Leninist principles conducts revolutionary warfare against its opponents. Indeed, it would seem that the Soviets intend to expand the areas of one-sided advantage.

When in June 1988 the espionage and subversive activities of Soviet intelligence agents in Canada exceeded what the host government could any longer tolerate, the offending "diplomats" were ordered home. But Mikhail Gorbachev had already begun to establish a new asymmetry in East-West relations under which the USSR attempts to use diplomatic blackmail to obtain the *de facto* right to suborn the loyalty of citizens in the democracies and to steal the West's secrets *without Western protest or penalty.*

CHAPTER III

REVOLUTIONARY WAR AND PROPAGANDA

Revolutionary war differs fundamentally from inter-state war of the sort the West is accustomed to dealing with. In traditional wars between states, attrition is the overriding factor. Each side hammers away at the other from the *outside*, destroying assets—whether these be people, weapons, or production facilities—and occupying land. The side that can stand the pace longest, wins.

In revolutionary war, the battle is fought from the *inside*, for the allegiance of the people. Clearly, any East–West conflict would combine features of both types of warfare, as Lenin predicted.[1] The Soviets, however, would likely prefer that revolutionary activities such as propaganda, intimidation, deception, terrorism, and subversion weaken their opponents prior to the outbreak of actual hostilities to such an extent that the regular forces would meet little if any opposition. Soviet leaders do not underestimate the difficulties of creating what they call the objective conditions for revolutionary war; they would think twice before trying it out on a healthy society. Nevertheless, they will not have forgotten the combined impact of Communist and Nazi subversion on France's morale in 1940 and the military collapse that followed.

Nations and groups fight because they regard their cause as just and the conflict as necessary or unavoidable. They also fight because the hostile force that has provoked the war is perceived as evil—either for what it has done or for what it might do. Finally, they fight because, rationally or irrationally, each side thinks it is going to win. This trinity of beliefs provides the mobilizing crystal for taking up arms. Clearly, one side's trinity is almost the complete opposite of the other's: the white hats versus the black.

In traditional wars between nations, it has been rare for the perceptions of good and evil to change greatly during a conflict. If anything, the brutality of war reinforces them. The element that can change is the belief in inevitable victory. This was the Germans' Achilles heel in 1918, and it enabled the British and Americans to mount a highly successful propaganda offensive against them. Similar doubts of being able to win prompted the generals' revolt against Hitler in 1944 and the intellectual (as opposed to radical) opposition to the Vietnam War in the United States.

That radical opposition of the 1960s represented something different, for Vietnam was part of the international civil war Lenin had talked about. Western radicals exchanged their original views of the good cause and the evil enemy for those of the opposition. After their conversion, a considerable constituency in the West saw the North Vietnamese as the good guys and the Americans as the bad. The propaganda and deception that wrought this change demonstrated how effectively the Soviets and their clones had manipulated the East–West asymmetries to their advantage. Ideological warfare was fought and won by the Communists on Western soil only; the East was not part of the battlefield, and its peoples' perceptions were never at risk: another benefit of asymmetry.

The revolutionary form of warfare does use attrition to some extent—to destroy impediments such as vital targets and leading personalities or classes deemed incapable of reform—but its real motive force is conversion. It is, quite literally, armed politics, and what *every* politician wants is your allegiance. To the Communists, it matters very little if allegiance is obtained voluntarily or, as the Russians have it, at the point of a bayonet. What matters is that you do exactly what you are told and eventually that you think as you are told. Lenin boasted that the "dictatorship of the proletariat had been successful because it has been able to combine compulsion with persuasion." He went on to assure his audience that the party did not fear "any resort to compulsion and to the most severe, decisive and ruthless forms of coercion by the state."[2]

Conversion changes the mathematics of war. If ten rebels face ninety government troops and, by some miracle of manoeuvre, manage to kill ten soldiers without loss, they will have improved the odds from 9-to-1 to 8-to-1. If, instead of killing them, they convert the same number, they will have improved the odds to 4-to-1.

Conversion presents other advantages. Some of the new adherents can conceal their changed allegiance, remaining in their positions as, for instance, policemen, soldiers, news reporters, or deputy ministers of the regime they are working to destroy. They can supply the rebels with intelligence, disinform the public, influence the government, recruit more converts, and be ready to play a vital role in the final showdown. This is evidently what the Soviets expect of their Western quislings, as this quote from a 1987 USSR Ministry of Defence publication confirms: "Inside the capitalist and the developing countries there will be forces which will fight against their own government, and according to their means they will help the socialist coalition during the [next] war."[3]

Revolutionary mathematics can also be used to help the rebels overtake the opposition's initial advantage in military hardware. If a target regime can manufacture rifles at the rate of ten thousand a year, and the rebels can obtain theirs from suppliers and backers at half that rate, the task of catching up and overtaking is severe. In inter-state conflict, the methods adopted would involve a redoubled effort to procure and attacks from the air on the opponent's production facilities. In revolutionary war these methods would be used, with sabotage replacing air attack. Additionally, the rebels would steal weapons from the soldiers, or urge converts to bring weapons with them, and they would do whatever was possible to slow down production by the regime.

This might be accomplished by persuading the regime that the rebel threat was far smaller than supposed and that rebel supplies of rifles were minuscule; the smaller the threat, the less the regime's need for rifles. Or the idea might be floated by sympathetic opinion-formers that rifles were inappropriate, immoral, or counterproductive, using whatever arguments suited the climate of opinion—such as a fear of "militarizing" the nation, or of accidents, or the like. If the rebels doubled their supplies and at the same time induced the regime to halve its production, the balance of rifle power would tip very quickly in their favor.

In its international revolutionary activities, the Soviet Union has always used all of these methods. The size of its military inventories is kept secret, and aspects are variously magnified or diminished in Western perceptions by deception operations, which form a part of *every* Soviet military endeavor.[4]

In areas of intended or existing Soviet superiority, the usual technique is to understate the size of the USSR's arsenal, thus removing Western incentive to keep pace. Or sympathizers in the West may be ordered to create opposition to new weapon systems on moral or other grounds, the campaign in the late 1970s against the neutron bomb and the 1980s assault on nuclear deterrence being cases in point. Sabotage by pro-Soviet terrorists in the West seems not to have been neglected either, with the Strategic Defense Initiative as a major target.[5]

Theft of weapon technology is conducted on a huge scale by Soviet military intelligence (the GRU), its network of foreign agents and greedy middlemen. The recent Soviet acquisition from the West of sophisticated milling equipment used to manufacture quieter submarine propellers received publicity, but thefts are numerous and frequent, covering a vast scientific spectrum.[6]

Once the nature of the revolutionary struggle is understood, Communist tactics over the last seventy years can be seen as perfectly logical. In the West, the Communist parties and their supporters have busied themselves trying to change perceptions. From time to time they have done this openly, offering Marxism-Leninism as a preferable alternative to democracy. In the Great Depression of the 1930s, this approach had some appeal. The apparent failure of capitalism led many in Europe and some in North America to believe that there must be something better and that the Russian experiment was it. Later in the same decade, after communism's glitter had faded, the appeal came wrapped as an anti-fascist crusade, or postured in the clothes of "peace."[7]

Indirect means of altering perceptions have included "social criticism," a constant duty for Communists, designed to gradually erode faith in Western institutions, traditions, history, religion, and democracy itself by dishonest and one-sided presentation of events; industrial unrest, which lowers workers' incomes and robs them of jobs, thus creating alienation; and the aggravation of social and racial tensions in the name of class warfare, to divide communities. These and similar activities erode the "good cause" part of a nation's trinity of beliefs. If successful, they convince many that there is nothing worth defending.

The alienated frequently look far afield for inspiration, providing potential converts to exotic religions, drug addiction, and political utopianism. As the Soviet Union has failed so miserably to live up to its utopian pretension, each new Marxist country has tended to attract pilgrims from the West seeking a new vision of "the good cause." Mao's China, Cuba, North Vietnam, and now Nicaragua have all represented this image for a time, only to have it dissipate in the cold light of day and be replaced by the next mirage on the horizon.[8]

In revolutionary situations, the rebel always enjoys a propaganda advantage. This is because the benefits he can offer lie in the future, unsullied by contact with reality, while the regime's "good cause" invariably suffers from the failures, errors, and injustices that every country exhibits to some extent. Insofar as the revolutionary challenge forces the regime to tighten its controls, its good cause can be further tarnished. The Communist challenge has made much use of this advantage, as brilliantly described in 1960 by the French writer Susan Labin.[9]

According to Labin's analysis, Communist propaganda subtly changes the frame of reference and lighting when passing from the Soviet Union to the free world. Thus, in discussing the USSR, the terms of reference are "the future," "the historical process," and "ends." In respect of the democracies, however, the terms are "the past," "the blemishes of the present," and "means." Similar tricks are applied to other areas: while the West is judged by its own notion of ethics, the East is discussed dialectically; we are measured by achievements, the East by promises.[10] This has never been more vividly demonstrated than by perestroika, which seeks to obliterate the appalling record of seventy years of communism and so permit the USSR once again to posture as the fresh-faced revolutionary.

While any revolutionary, as an armed critic, enjoys a propaganda advantage, the ideological revolutionary has a secondary commitment to propaganda inseparable from his very being. The sovietologist Peter Kenez, who has specialized in the study of propaganda, describes the USSR as "the propaganda state."[11] He explains how Communists believe that Marx developed the *only* scientific analysis of society and that this analysis is a necessary part of changing reality. Seeing themselves as the possessors of the one and only true theory, their chief task is not to search for truth, but to take the fruits of their knowledge to the people, especially the proletariat.

This enterprise is fundamentally different from the wartime propaganda effort of the democracies, which is mainly concerned to mislead on concrete issues. The Communist undertaking is far more comprehensive and ambitious—as it must be. Any regime that bases its legitimacy and hence its power on an unfounded nineteenth-century superstition could not hope to survive for long without a highly functional propaganda machine.

Until quite recently, the dogmatic, ideological foundation of Communist propaganda tended to make it dull. Yet even then it was quite successful. Stefan Possany, a leading authority, speculated in 1960 that, instead of aiming to "persuade" people through their minds, Communists seemed content to "orient the souls of their audience." His views are summarized below.[12]

Communists hold that behavior, especially that of groups, can be manipulated through the conditioning of reflexes. In this, they acknowledge their debt to psychologist Ivan Pavlov, whose experiments with dogs involving the denial of food and the ringing of bells led to his discovery of the conditioned reflex. Soviet propaganda, with its monotonous repetition and its concentration on all the symbolic words that, so to speak, ring a bell, applies Pavlov's discovery to mankind. By the manipulation of stimuli, the desire for independent action—the "freedom urge"—can be weakened or extinguished and neurotic behavior induced. Unpredictable behavior on the part of the sponsor, acceleration then calming of crises, alternation between growls and smiles, and the unceasing maintenance of tension may induce such neurosis.

Most schools of psychology agree that fear and anxiety are among the main hindrances to the proper functioning of the mind. Communists have always laid stress on terror, violence, and purges; today they use the threat of nuclear war for a similar purpose. Within society, the individual needs emotional security and close human relations. The overall structure must be intelligible, so that the individual can orient himself and achieve satisfactions such as loyalty, pride of membership, and conviction.

Communists and their allies aim to overturn such stability by all means at their disposal—especially fear. This may create neurotic behavior characterized by hopelessness, obsessions, compulsions, and fears, which in turn undermine motivation, dedication, loyalty, and all attitudes that support a stable society. The final result is listlessness and defeatism. Much that follows in this book will confirm Possany's thesis.

In theory, propaganda can serve any purpose, good or bad. It may consist of empirical fact or outrageous lies. More often than not, it contains a mixture. Often, the *facts* presented are verifiably accurate, but the *interpretation* of those facts is false. The Communist commitment to "objective truth," being the truth that supports the historical process (in other words, the party), has the effect of making all Soviet propaganda deceptive in character. Alex de Jonge observes that, in place of evidence, the young Communist idealist feels that "if the party decrees it, it must be necessary, if it is necessary, it is correct and, since it is correct, it must be true." As example he provides the story put about by the party that Trotsky was an agent of the Gestapo. It was widely understood that, subjectively speaking, Trotsky was innocent of the charge but that the party required him to be an agent for reasons of historical necessity; so he could at one time be both subjectively innocent and objectively guilty.[13] Thus the line between propaganda and deception operations is blurred. In one sense, communism is simply armed propaganda; in another, it is government by deception.

Within the sphere of deception, the Soviets talk of a particular technique they call reflexive control. This is defined by one of their military writers as "influencing an opponent's will and mind when that opponent is making decisions."[14] Two civilian analysts have expanded on this notion, saying that control of an opponent's decision is not achieved directly, not by blatant force, but by "providing him with the grounds by which he is able to logically derive his own decision, but one that is predetermined by the other side."[15]

When the direct appeal of an ideology is weak, as is the case with Marxism-Leninism, converts may be won through substitute appeals. The 1930s anti-fascist crusade was one example; peace is another. Communists view pacifism in the reverse manner to nuclear weapons. Whereas the bombs should all be in the Communist camp, pacifism must be confined to the opposition. In 1922 Lenin explained that it was the party's duty to support "pacifists in the other, i.e., bourgeois, camp . . . This will both have bite and be 'polite' and will help to demoralize the enemy."[16]

The 1928 World Congress of the Communist International resolved that the "peace" policy of the USSR was "merely another—under present conditions—more advantageous form of fighting capitalism."[17] And so it has continued. In 1961 the Czechoslovak president explained that "the struggle for peace is quite a concrete form of class war."[18] In 1972 two Soviet philosophers insisted that "with all the inconsistency of the pacifists, their campaign against nuclear war constitutes an important social factor which cannot be discounted."[19] In effect they were saying, "Don't knock it; however ideologically unsound, Western pacifism works for us."

Apparently not all Soviet intellectuals had got their minds around "objective factors" in the way they should have, because in 1983 a *Kommunist* editorial writer found it necessary to explain:

> It is no secret that at first certain comrades were unable to grasp the nature of the [Western] antiwar movements . . . were not always able to overcome their prejudices against pacifist and ecological organizations with their inconsistent and contradictory arguments, and did not perceive the members of these movements as their objective allies in the struggle for [Soviet] peace.[20]

By the time of the 1980s peace offensive, Soviet techniques in this field were well developed, and they possessed an extensive international infrastructure for manipulating anti-war sentiment in the West to Communist advantage. In line with well-established revolutionary practice, the offensive aimed to:

• Improve the correlation of forces by preventing the development, production, and deployment of certain categories of weapons by NATO, so that Soviet military expansion would go unchallenged.

• Improve the correlation of forces by persuading segments of Western publics that the prevention of nuclear war was more important than anything, including the defence of political freedom. Such converts might gradually be turned into subversive contingents who would "fight against their own government" in any future conflict. At least, they would create domestic political opposition to all forms of defence and resistance, become a "surrender lobby," and help to break up NATO.

• Overturn and possibly reverse the trinity of concepts that, in a crisis or a war, would be necessary for Western psychological mobilization. The attack on Western values would be intensified; fear of communism or Soviet imperialism would be replaced by fear of nuclear war, or removed by sophisticated deception; confidence in an ability to resist Communist expansion would be eroded by knowledge that the correlation of forces had slipped so far in the USSR's favor that nothing could be done to recover.

• Reinforce the ongoing policy of "arms control" by increasing Western public demand for more and more treaties, regardless of their impact on Western security.

• Create irresistible domestic demand for renewed détente, this time under conditions of Western military inferiority and political subordination.

• Isolate and discredit proponents of defence in the West by psychological and physical intimidation and, by the same process, isolate and discredit the United States because that country possesses the main strategic nuclear deterrent and is the leader of democracy's resistance to communism.

In Soviet endeavors to achieve these objectives, we hear the echo of words uttered sixty-five years ago by Lenin. When Felix Dzerzhinskiy, creator of the Soviet secret police, was planning the first strategic deception operation of post-revolutionary Russia, he reportedly asked Lenin's advice on the tone of communication to his "target audience." Lenin's reply could serve as a motto for all dissemblers. "Tell them," he answered, "what they want to hear."[21]

CHAPTER IV

THE CHURCHES AND THE MAINSTREAM PEACE MOVEMENT IN CANADA

The Canadian peace movement is composed of myriad groups and associations. People who belong to organizations nominally dedicated to strengthening peace generally regard themselves as being part of a wider movement, even though principles and agendas may differ among groups. Although there is no ideological entry test, it is perhaps fair to assume that members of all groups that make up the Canadian peace movement are in favor of peace, are opposed to war, and believe that collective actions of one sort or another can and will advance the good cause. There is, therefore, a commitment, and this witness or dedication is what sets the movement and its members apart from the rest of Canadian society.

In very general terms, and for purposes of analysis here, the movement consists of three main components: the churches; the broad mainstream, including various radical groups that are not directly or indirectly allied to Moscow; and the Communists and close allies who are. Of course, it is attractive to separate mainstream from radicals. However, both within groups and within coalitions, the mixing of mainstreamers with radicals is so great that drawing the line is virtually impossible. Additionally, the distinction between churches and others is somewhat artificial, especially where liberation theology has exposed Christianity to Marxist ideology. Nevertheless, it remains just possible to look at this component apart from others. This is where we will begin.

In his valuable mimeographed *History of the Peace Movement in Canada*, Gary Moffatt notes that in 1936 the United Church of Canada stated in General Council: "As Christians we positively reject war because war rejects love, defies the will of Christ, and denies the worth of man."[1] Moffatt points out that the New Testament is often contradictory or ambiguous on the matter of peace, a condition that has been reflected in Christian churches' attitudes to war. In 1939, for instance, the United Church along with Catholics and Anglicans endorsed the war against Hitler. Considering how the Nazis rejected love, defied the will of Christ, and denied the worth of man, the switch was understandable; indeed, the contradiction between pacifist principle and political reality remains with us.

In the view of the Quakers, Mennonites, Doukhobors, and other pacifist sects, however, the evil in man is never to be resisted by force. These sects have been influential far beyond their numerical size in mobilizing the church component of the modern Canadian peace movement. They have found a powerful ally in the United Church, which has set the pace within the major denominations.

Mobilization began in the early 1960s, over the possible fitting of nuclear warheads to US-made anti-aircraft missiles that were installed in Canada as part of the North American air defence system. The United Church's Committee on Evangelism and Social Service in 1960 advocated to the annual conference in Toronto a policy of Canadian neutrality and rejection of nuclear arms. This went too far for the General Council at that time—they came out instead against nuclear testing. Mobilization continued in the late 1960s in opposition to the war in Vietnam, seeking an end to Canada's lukewarm support for the United States' role.

The Vietnam War, it need hardly be said, overturned the US defence and foreign policy consensus and seriously damaged her international image as the champion of freedom. When, in the 1930s, the economic depression in the West undermined confidence in the capitalist system, intellectuals and others flocked to the USSR eager to be convinced that the socialist alternative offered a solution to the world's problems. It was as though a loss of faith in one economic system automatically promoted belief in the other, because of a need for certainty. Likewise, in the 1960s and 1970s, some Westerners whose faith in the United States had waned travelled to Hanoi. The perceived moral weakness of the West had to be balanced by a myth of Communist benevolence.

Many Jews and Christians, for whom the duty to love thy neighbor had coexisted uneasily with an awareness of the evil inherent in communism, now felt able to resolve the apparent contradiction by overlooking or denying the evil. For others, liberation theology provided a bridge between Christ and Marx, albeit one that could be crossed only by denying the reality of Lenin. Aside from these ideological trends, the liberal myth of the perfectibility of man seemed to be influential in many churches, particularly the United Church. The utopianism that this myth inspires has proven to be a powerful factor in contemporary Canadian theology, philosophy, and politics. It is strongly represented in the Canadian Movement for Peace, an ecumenical organization whose Canadian branch came into being in 1968, the Canadian Catholic Organization for Development and Peace, and the Quakers' Canadian Friends Service Committee.

The convergence of some church opinion with the radical left enabled the Canadian churches to stay in the peace business after the end of the Vietnam War and before the West began to update its arms in the 1980s. This was the period of détente, of Western relaxation of its psychological and military defences, and of a massive Soviet build-up.

Mobilization for Survival began as a far-left US group headed by Michael Klare, Sidney Peck, Sidney Lens, and Terry Provance. The Canadian branch was created by the Canadian Friends Service Committee, the Grindstone Co-operative (an island retreat devoted to utopian seminars), the Christian Movement for Peace, and the so-called People's Assembly on Canadian Foreign Policy—an amalgam of "socialists" and Christians formed in 1974 by Unitarian Eryl Court and United Church minister Robert Wright. Canadian Mobilization for Survival sent a delegation to Parliament Hill in 1977 to urge the government to pull Canada out of NATO, disavow the strategy of nuclear deterrence, and end its support for nuclear power generation. The movement in the United States meanwhile concerned itself with devising tactics of mass confrontation similar to those used during the Vietnam War, but this time aimed at the "military-industrial complex." Meanwhile, Canada's Inter-Church Committee on Corporate Responsibility began a major push on disarmament.

The Canadian University Service Overseas (CUSO) had earlier discussed with the Friends Committee and Mennonites the need for a peace and development research and publicity organization. Next, the United Church and some Toronto congregations came on board. The outcome was Project Ploughshares, based during the 1970s at Conrad Grebel College, a Mennonite affiliate of the University of Waterloo, and since adopted by the Canadian Council of Churches as its peace research and policy centre. Ploughshares subsequently opened an Ottawa office as well, for political lobbying. Journalist Ernie Regehr headed research while Murray Thomson, formerly executive peace education secretary of the Friends, moved to Ottawa.

Virtually the entire Canadian Christian hierarchy had delegated its thinking on the matter of peace to two individuals schooled in minority pacifist sects. Regehr had already written a book, published in 1975 in co-operation with the Mennonites, *Making a Killing: Canada's Arms Industry*, in which he concluded:

> Disarmament and non-violence represent a measure of political and diplomatic maturity devoutly to be wished, but first we will have to grow out of the political adolescence that places such a narrow interpretation on self-interest as to permit us, while speaking piously of favouring non-violent solutions, to run guns for profit.[2]

The sincerity of Regehr's position is not to be doubted, informed though it seems to be by a socialist perception of the world. In 1978 Regehr and Thomson were co-authors of the pamphlet *A Time to Disarm*,[3] which offered advice on the line Canada should take at the forthcoming First Special UN Session on Disarmament. The pamphlet did not advance from a true pacifist position; instead, Project Ploughshares rushed headlong into the nitty-gritty of politics and strategy, throw-weights, and multiple re-entry vehicles, offering advice that was neither a forthright appeal to the spirit nor a rational recipe for survival in an age of nuclear-armed totalitarianism. Indeed, in this and all its subsequent pronouncements, Ploughshares tended to offer advice broadly in line with the policies advocated by Canada's social democrats, the New Democratic Party.

As a political lobby, Ploughshares has been remarkably successful. When the Canadian Council of Churches submitted a brief, "Concern for Peace Expressed by Canadian Churches," to the Standing Committee on External Affairs and National Defence in Ottawa on February 16, 1982, Thomson and Regehr provided the key components. The brief was designed to influence Canadian policy at the Second Special UN Session. Canadian church leaders were evidently glad to be relieved of the agony of trying to reach decisions for themselves in an area where high technology and Christian ethics overlapped: Ploughshares, it seems, told them what they wanted to hear, and they embraced the material gratefully.

What the hierarchs, the committee, and the Canadian public were told by Thomson can be summarized as follows: deterrence strategy is unsound and is almost certain to lead to war; in any case Europe's long peace has been at the expense of the Third World, to which we have exported our wars; arms procurement has beggared Third World development; Canada is wicked to subscribe to NATO, because the alliance's doctrine is un-Christian; it is evil for Litton Systems to build cruise missile components in Canada; similar villainy attends other military production; the Soviet military expansion is to be played down, or at least excused as a "catch-up" process ("It seems to us that if an overall advantage exists . . . it tilts towards the West").[4] These conclusions were offered at a time when:

• Seventy-five percent of US nuclear missile launchers were more than fifteen years old, while the same proportion of Soviet launchers were five years old or less.

• Between 1966 and 1981, the Soviet Union had built sixty new ballistic missile–launching submarines, while the United States had built none.

• As a percentage of gross national product, the USSR was spending three times as much as the United States on military build-up.

• The Soviets were energetically deploying their SS-20 missiles and launchers in Europe, while NATO had no remotely equivalent weapon system.

• During the 1970s the Soviets introduced ten variants of three new types of intercontinental ballistic missile, while the Americans effectively froze their nuclear force levels.[5]

Regehr went much further than Thomson, constructing what can only be described as a fantastic strategic scenario of "militarization of the international economic order," a US shift from nuclear deterrence toward "nuclear intimidation"—nuclear forces being committed not only to deter but to "coerce" and to "posture," an alleged US willingness to fight limited nuclear wars, and an apology for Moscow's deployment of SS-20s. Regehr's recommendations were that Canada should support a missile flight-test ban, stop producing components for nuclear weapons, cease its participation "in the operation of strategic and intermediate-range nuclear weapons systems," declare Canada a nuclear weapons-free zone, propose an international arms trade register, and provide public funding for "peace education and research."[6]

In December the same year the presidents of the Canadian Conference of Catholic Bishops, Canadian Council of Churches, Lutheran Church of Canada, the primate of the Anglican Church of Canada, and the moderators of the United and Presbyterian churches of Canada delivered a statement to

Prime Minister Trudeau.[7] This digested and updated the Ploughshares agenda, going this time three steps farther by urging that
Canada insist on a "no-first-use policy within NATO," should
support "a mutual freeze on the production, testing and deployment of new nuclear weapons systems" (the hierarchs omitted
the word *verifiable* that usually accompanies this scheme), and
should refuse permission for cruise missile flight tests. The
nuclear-free zone idea was reiterated.

Five years later the council published a critique of the Defence
White Paper, "Challenge and Commitment: A Defence Policy
for Canada." The bishops objected to the identification of the
USSR as a potential aggressor and went on to criticize the
government's decision to equip the navy with nuclear-powered
submarines.[8]

What Ploughshares had created, and the hierarchs had endorsed and recommended, was a blueprint for Canadian defencelessness and neutrality. Neither Ploughshares nor the
church leaders were courageous or forthright enough to say in so
many words that Canada ought, in their view, to abandon her
alliances, allies, and defences and seek salvation through God.
Instead, they connived in a deceptive agenda in which Canadians could continue to rely on some kind of defence but would
enjoy the moral approval of their churches only if they did so
without allies and with inadequate means of their own.

Writing of the inter-war period, Hans Kohn described a
similar condition:

Pacifism—entirely legitimate as a religious pattern of life, as a
witness through sacrifice and martyrdom, and, as such, a salt
of the earth and a reminder of the verities—underwent a
strange corruption. It began to cater to the egotism and understandable longing for peace of the people, promising them
peace and happiness only if they would not declare their
readiness for timely action.[9]

Such a corruption of the pacifist ideal seems to have affected the
Canadian churches in the 1980s. Nothing describes this situ-

ation better than Kohn's subsequent words: "The principle of nonresistance to evil degenerated into a denial that evil exists, into an appeal to accept the evil and to condone the injustice. Thus pacifism, instead of bearing witness to the verities, became in the universal crisis one of the elements which could be used and abused by the aggressor nations for the destruction of the verities."

The English Christian writer C.S. Lewis once produced a series of articles, *The Screwtape Letters*, in which a senior devil offered encouragement to a junior tempter. One of these ended with this devilish advice:

> Then quietly and gradually nurse him [the Christian] on to the stage at which the religion becomes merely part of the "cause", in which Christianity is valued chiefly because of the excellent arguments it can produce . . . Once you have made the world an end, and faith a means, you have almost won your man [for the devil], and it makes very little difference what kind of worldly end he is pursuing. Provided that meetings, causes, and crusades, matter more to him than prayers and sacraments and charity, he is ours—and the more "religious" (on those terms) the more securely ours. I could show you a pretty cageful down here.[10]

The mainstream peace movement draws upon several strands of Canadian political and social life, as well as its own history and traditions. Easily the most pervasive political strand is the liberal tradition—shared to some extent with liberals elsewhere in the West—which sees violence in the hands of enemies as too dangerous to oppose and violence in the hands of friends as immoral and doomed to failure, and when confronted by the alarming implications of this philosophy denies that evil exists.

This last trend has been much strengthened by a secular utopianism, which insists that warfare, and therefore defence, are outmoded—that the human race is turning the corner into a new and peaceful world, but that this advance is threatened by doubts and questions. Blind faith is not only desirable but essential, and old-fashioned rationality is a menace: history should therefore be banished from school curricula and de-emphasized in universities. In its political manifestation, utopianism depicts Canada as morally superior, pointing as proof to our decision in the 1940s not to make our own nuclear weapons. Lester Pearson's Nobel Peace Prize–winning diplomacy in the 1950s seemed to endorse this moral mythology, and Canadians have traded on it ever since.

One result of this mindset has been the diversion of morality from its proper course, as an end, into a means of public manipulation and personal advancement. The outcome? Almost nothing can be discussed in Canadian politics without claim that one's position is endowed with high moral sentiments.

Canadian nationalism had combined with liberalism in the 1970s to expand the power of what US writer Irving Kristol has called the New Class. In Ottawa, utopianism created a secular rationalism within the civil service that pandered to politicians' hypocrisy. This spread to the universities, the arts, the media, and other institutions that depended on patronage for their existence. These in turn succeeded in monopolizing public attitudes that were attractive to the élite. Canadian history and values that had been part of our tradition were no longer fashionable. For the successor generation, all this has led to some woefully unstringent thinking—ideal ground for social action groups promising utopia.

At the same time the political convictions of a single-minded prime minister, Pierre Trudeau, lent the power of that office to the democratic left, his position as leader of the Liberal party notwithstanding. One result was the conversion of that party from classical to reform liberalism; another was the general strengthening of socialist ideas in Canada.

Writing in *Saturday Night* in 1978, Sandra Gwyn discussed Canada's international role and perception of that role. "A myth that once helped define us as a people, helped us reach beyond ourselves," she wrote, "no longer exists. When you shatter a nation's myths, something Trudeau should have realized, you weaken its will to endure."[11] It is doubtful if Trudeau intended to shatter Canada's liberal myths; what he may have done was to stretch them to breaking point. Canada may have entered the 1980s in something of a cultural-spiritual vacuum. Nature abhors a vacuum; a nation spiritually empty would be easy prey for ready-made creeds.

With its internationalist tradition and yearnings, the democratic socialist left has always tended toward some kind of political pacifism. Nevertheless, the experience of 1939–45 and of the early years of the cold war convinced the European social democrats of that era that appeasement did not provide an effective answer to armed totalitarianism. As a result, democracy's resistance to Soviet expansionism of the 1940s and 1950s was often led by democratic socialists.

Canada's New Democratic Party did not share this experience. Separated by geography and time from the hot breath of Hitler and Stalin, the party gradually distanced itself from international realities, denied the need for effective Canadian defence, and incorporated Canadian neutralism into its platform. The Canadian labor movement, influenced by Marx, allied to the New Democrats, and penetrated by Communists, is apt to take a similar or farther-left view. Federal New Democratic delegates to their 1983 convention answered a survey questionnaire in a tone that indicated the strength of anti-Americanism in the party. Asked "Which of the two superpowers is the greater threat to world peace?," 65 percent suggested that the United States and the Soviet Union were about equal in blame. Among the remaining 35 percent, nearly five out of every six delegates regarded the US threat as greater.[12] The party's intention to pull Canada out of NATO was "postponed indefinitely" in April 1988 in an effort to improve election prospects, but it is doubtful if underlying anti-defence convictions have evaporated.

Canada's geography inevitably inspires a sense of hopelessness so far as defence is concerned. The land area is so vast, and our population so small, that the task of defending it is easy to dismiss as impossible. But geography also provides a solution. Being far removed from the centres of major conflict, Canada "the country-that-threatens-no one" is safe. Hence, the feeling that nothing need be done about defence, that nothing effective *can* be done. These irreversible geographical factors have helped to shape both Canadian policy and the peace movement's tactics.

The advent of intercontinental ballistic missiles and the realization that Soviet Russia would be their likely source caused Canadians to consult a polar projection. As neighbors of the USSR and the United States, we lie beneath the flight paths of missiles aimed either way. Yet again, the defensive task seemed impossible. Politicians and officials argued, however, that the task could be made *unnecessary* provided means were found to ensure that the missiles were never fired. The means selected was the NATO policy called deterrence. It is around this policy that the peace debate has raged.

Canadian nationalism charts the struggle to be free of Britain's imperial control and influence, the subsequent resistance to US economic and cultural domination, a desire not to spend money on defence but at the same time maintain sovereignty over defence activities, and the ongoing search for national identity in a country divided regionally and ethnically. Present-day Canadian nationalism is also overlaid with anti-Americanism, or, alternatively, its nationalism is manifested as anti-Americanism.

Membership in two alliances was one way that Canada in the late 1940s sought to overcome the otherwise insurmountable difficulties of national defence and to enable herself to play her part in defending Western Europe—deemed, incidentally, to be a better place to halt the Russians than Baffin Island. These alliances were NATO and NORAD. As the United States was and is the senior partner in both, the same fears of eroded sovereignty arise within the context of peace and war.

Another strand of Canadian political thought, one deeply imbued with utopianism, is what might be termed transnationalism or globalism. The World Federalists and Humanists are exponents, as are socialists who preach global socialism. They believe that the world has outgrown nationalism and the nation state and its people must, for their very survival, develop global methods of control.

The United Nations concept of eventual world government, which has always been well supported in Canada, represents another version of this strand. There is a contradictory overlap between xenophobic nationalism of the "I hate the States" sort and utopian internationalism of the "I love the United Nations and Third World" school. We also see a massive mutation of the yearning for world authority in a rejection of *all* authority. Adherents of this view accept that national governments are incapable of reform or of meeting mankind's needs. But instead of constructing the Brave New World, they would tear down existing institutions in order to rebuild society from the bottom up. Both the old globalism and the new anti-nationalism are visible within the peace movement.

Pacifism in Canada has a long history. In his carefully researched volume, *Witness Against War*, Thomas Socknat describes the movement between 1900 and 1945, covering conscientious objection in the two World Wars, the conscription crises, and alternative pacifist service in time of war.[13] It is not intended to deal with this period here: instead, we will begin where today's peace movement found its feet.

A quarter of a century ago, at the dawn of the 1960s, two books appeared in Canada that are milestones to the New Jerusalem. James M. Minifie's *Peacemaker or Powder Monkey* was a clarion call for Canadian neutrality. Norman Z. Alcock's *The Bridge of Reason* called for a worldwide network of peace institutes, independent of their national governments but interconnected in their endeavors. Alcock hoped that such research would clear the way for world government. Both books were written early in the Khrushchev era and reflect the optimism of their day. The Russian leader had denounced Stalin, declared that full-scale war between East and West was no longer to be seen as "fatalistically inevitable," and implied that future competition between blocs would be economic. The realities lying behind these words, and Khrushchev's future "adventurism," were still hidden.

Minifie's case rested on fears that "close military integration with the United States means acceptance of the military doctrine of the United States for the defence of North America, or more properly for the defence of the United States. And that military doctrine is a calculated preparation for the annihilation of mankind." As for NATO, "there is no military advantage for Canada in serving as a convenient glacis for the dumping of nuclear bombs out of fallout-range of American soil."[14]

Minifie, who was the CBC's senior reporter in Washington, DC, did not disguise his agenda. He acknowledged the hostility and power of the Soviet Union. His objection to Canada's alliances sprang from his rejection of deterrence doctrine, with its explicit commitment to initiate nuclear warfare if a Soviet offensive against NATO could not be halted by lesser means. He could not accept that Canada should play any part in deterrence strategy, in either NATO or NORAD. He did not address the wider question of how the West might reform its strategy so as to remove the need for nuclear weapons. He seemed content that Canada should continue to live with and benefit from the doctrine of deterrence, provided she did not soil her own hands. Although these contradictions have not been answered in the ensuing twenty-five years, Minifie's wishful agenda remains central to the thinking of the modern Canadian peace movement.

Alcock's thesis acknowledged the work already begun at the Pugwash Conference of scientists, which had met for the first time in the Nova Scotian town of that name in 1957.[15] The thesis represents another persistent element within the movement—the desire of scientists of various disciplines to save mankind from politicians—and it illustrates the globalist strand of thinking. But the belief that international peace research might play a crucial role in solving problems of peace and war overlooked the ideological element in man, which is unresponsive to logic outside the ideology, and it failed to anticipate the possibility that a certain type of "peace research" could be a form of conflict in its own right rather than a means of resolving conflict.

Although Minifie played no active role in the peace movement, his book inspired the author Farley Mowat to collect a "Palgreave Committee" to promote Canadian neutralism. This committee was swallowed up in Dr. Hugh Keenleyside's moderate Canadian Committee for the Control of Radiation Hazards. As nuclear anxieties grew, moderation surrendered to activism and, in February 1962, the committee changed its name to the Canadian Campaign for Nuclear Disarmament—a clone of the British CND. CND had always been, and remains, the champion of unilateral nuclear disarmament, believing—or hoping—that if one country disarms, others on both sides of the East–West divide will follow. CCND adopted the CND's symbol, the semaphore letters N and D, black on white.

The CCND had a short and troubled history. The Quebec equivalent, Le Mouvement pour le désarmement nucléaire et la paix, headed by Jacques Larne-Langlois and supported by such powerful radicals as Dimitrios Roussopolous, wanted to operate outside the system, while the anglophones wished to work within it. CCND limited its agenda to disarmament, while the French Canadians called for "a total disengagement on the part of Canada in the cold war conflict and a role of leadership for our country, at the head of a third group of nations." CCND helped to fund a Montreal-based journal, *Our Generation*. Roussopolous was the editor: contributors included Bertrand Russell, Norman Alcock, Farley Mowat, and Minifie. The campaign also set up the Ottawa Peace Information Bureau to lobby MPs. But the failure of the movement to prevent the Liberal government accepting US nuclear warheads demoralized CCND followers. The organization fell apart in the latter half of the 1960s.[16]

Before the creation of CCND in 1962, Toronto had formed its own Campaign for Disarmament, composed initially of 657 of the 1200 professors at the University of Toronto, including Claude Bissell, then president. The leader was Abraham Feinberg, rabbi of Holy Blossom Temple and civil rights activist. The campaign became the local branch of CCND in 1962 and was instrumental in sustaining the national CCND against the anti-NATO leanings of Roussopolous and the Quebecers. Before the Toronto group folded in 1965, Feinberg addressed a public meeting and told them of his recent trip to Hanoi with the American writer and peace activist A.J. Muste. The political pilgrimages to North Vietnam had begun.

Opposition to the war in Vietnam came from many sources. However, it was the Communist-dominated Vietnam Committees that co-ordinated and set the agenda. The labor movement, university faculty and students, Voice of Women, numerous small peace groups, and the churches played parts. "Moscow Communists" were gradually ousted by more violent extremists. The movement's historian, Moffatt, records that by 1968, anti-war demonstrations were "more and more reflecting positions and tactics of the Trotskyists with moderate peace supporters withdrawing in dismay." By 1970, the willingness of peace activists to take part in demonstrations where they risked being caught in armed clashes between Maoists and police was "visibly declining."[17] A frustrated Communist intellectual, Alfred Dewhurst, wrote that "the full effectiveness of the anti-war movement has been seriously undermined by the disruptive activity of the Trotskyists as they seek to utilize the mass peace sentiment, particularly of young people, to advance their own narrow sectarian aims."[18] As good an example of the pot calling the kettle black as one is likely to find. However, in Canada the significant impact of the Vietnam War was on our perceptions of US values and US government credibility. Both suffered harm that has influenced an entire generation.

Norman Alcock had meanwhile been putting his theory into practice. Having advocated peace research in his book, he set to work in 1962 to form a peace research institute in southern Ontario. After raising $300,000, he formed a board of directors with himself as president and with Kenneth Boulding, Brock Chisholm, Hugh Keenleyside, former United Church moderator James S. Thomson, Voice of Women president Helen Tucker, and Pierre Trudeau as members. Alcock is reported as saying that Trudeau proved to be the most radical member of the board.[19]

The work of the Canada Peace Research Institute consisted of peace research, public attitude testing, and publishing. Research covered alternative approaches to world government, sociological theories of political violence, peace-keeping operations, theories of conflict management, and reform of the UN Security Council. In 1967 research moved into the theoretical field, using mathematical, computer-assisted techniques. Hanna and Alan Newcombe were leaders in much of the institute's research and formed an associated institute of their own. All this was serious, academically responsible work. The institute avoided ideology. All the sadder that in October 1981, just when the present-day Canadian peace movement was gathering momentum, Alcock's institute closed for want of public support. Nevertheless, the Newcombes continued their work at their "Peace Research Institute—Dundas," Ontario.

By 1980, a new and dangerous condition had gripped the Western democracies, Canada included: fear. For reasons to be discussed later, Western publics suddenly accepted the notion that nuclear war between East and West was imminent. This danger was attributed to the "arms race," said to be out of control, and amidst so much uncertainty only one thing was certain: the imminent war would kill us all and end civilization. For many in the democracies, this supposed crisis called for urgent action. For the fearful, governments and alliances had clearly failed their publics; otherwise, how could the present danger be so severe? As Australian commentator Harry Gelber has put it, "these people therefore assemble in peace marches not to support the Soviet Union, or to display anti-Americanism, or to make a revolution. They are rather saying to politicians and governments 'look, we don't understand the details. But we do know that the present situation is dangerous. We are frightened. So do something.' "[20] This was, in a nutshell, the psychological mobilizing crystal that created the mass movements of the 1980s; in Europe, in the United States, in Australasia, and in Canada. Gelber's analysis is in some respects overgenerous, as we will see later. However, it describes well the appearance and the spirit of the movements in the early 1980s—an appearance that concealed as much as it revealed, and a spirit that was soon to change.

Whether mainstream or radical mainstream, the new waves of peace groups were more activist in character than their 1960s forebears. Perhaps they had acquired confidence and techniques from the series of single-issue campaigns that had influenced public policy in the previous two decades—campaigns about the environment, animal protection, consumerism, feminism, and energy and resource conservation. All these movements used similar techniques: they worked through the courts, particularly by injunctions; they demanded rigid application of existing rules, laws, and regulations, where these hampered the opponent's operations; they persuaded elected representatives to change the law, or government policy, so that the campaign's objective was met.

These mass movements involve relentless public pressure on the legislators. Thus the organizers must seek to dominate public opinion by setting the agenda and the parameters of debate. By seizing the moral high ground and keeping the initiative, they create a climate of opinion in which it is more than any commentator's reputation or politician's future is worth to utter contradictory remarks. Indeed, in a really successful campaign, the climate may require public figures to utter confirmatory remarks, regardless of their personal opinions, so strong is the combination of ideology and propaganda.

Obviously, the news media are one key to the movement's success, since they more than any other institution can create climates of opinion. However, one should not underestimate the importance of élite opinion—people directly or indirectly involved in shaping policy. Here lobbying in its many forms is fundamental. Overcoming apathy is the major challenge to campaign organizers, and the course normally selected is to personalize the emotional core of the issue. Campaigners follow the advice of the celebrated activist Saul Alinsky to "do what you can with what you have and clothe it with moral garments."[21] The emotional and moral aspects are always superior to rational argument as mobilizing forces. Arguments have two sides, whereas emotion and morality, skilfully presented, are beyond challenge. The emotional response that is stimulated may be compassion, or indignation, or anger, or hate. But more often than not it is mankind's most intimate emotion: fear. For the peace movement in the 1980s, fear has been the primary mobilizing force. The moral high ground is "peace." Fear that peace is about to give way to war links the emotional element to the moral.

By 1982 James Stark, a prominent Canadian peace activist, was exploiting a newly acquired climate of opinion through a disarmament referendum that his peace organization, Operation Dismantle, staged in communities across the country. The question asked of Canadians was unlikely to stimulate a negative reply: "Do you support the goal of general disarmament and mandate your government to negotiate and implement, with other governments, the balanced steps that would lead to the earliest possible achievement of this goal? Yes . . . No . . . The results of the vote will be sent to the Prime Minister, the Parliament of Canada, and the United Nations."[22]

Stark's technique was to persuade city fathers to tack this question onto municipal election forms, and he was remarkably successful. The question added an estimated $10,000 to the cost of the Toronto City Council election, and its inclusion was, in many opinions, illegal. Nevertheless, Toronto went along with the charade, as did Ottawa and some 120 other cities. Since there could be no logical reason for councils with no responsibility or power over external affairs to sponsor a referendum whose outcome was as ineffectual as it was obvious, it is reasonable to conclude that—in the span of some eighteen months—the peace movement had succeeded in creating a climate of opinion in which it was dangerous for elected officials to question or oppose any resolution or harebrained scheme that included in its title the word *peace*.

Operation Dismantle's original goal was to persuade the United Nations to sponsor a similar referendum on a global scale. Stark's rationale exactly illustrates the peace movement's mistrust of governments. One of his pamphlets stated: "People have lost confidence that governments can or will stop the arms race and proceed to disarmament on their own."[23] However, the international aspiration seemed to fade as domestic issues consumed Dismantle's energy.

These issues included the "freeze" proposal, opposition to flight-testing of the US cruise missile over Canada's North and

NATO air force flight training over Labrador, rejection of President Reagan's Strategic Defense Initiative or "Star Wars," and support for various manifestations of Canadian neutrality —"nuclear weapons-free zones" and opposition to deterrence, NATO, and NORAD. A similar progression from the general anti-nuclear position through the various "Canadian" issues to a highly political advocacy of anti-defence, anti-American policies has been the norm for Canada's mainstream peace movement. The way these issues were linked together is discussed later.

The mainstream consists of Canadian affiliates or branches of international organizations, national groups that may or may not have regional offshoots, and purely regional organizations or coalitions. Excluded from this summary are the arms control lobbies such as John Lamb's Canadian Centre for Arms Control and Disarmament, William Epstein's Canadian Pugwash, and Professor Naidu's Canadian Peace Research and Education Association. Some mention will be made of such organizations in a later chapter, but they are certainly not in the peace movement's mainstream.

The Women's International League for Peace and Freedom has a head office in Geneva, and its Canadian branch was established in 1921. It works with UN agencies and Amnesty International as well as promoting its own agenda, which often tackles peace on a regional basis. From the early 1960s onward, the league has moved away from its socialist-pacifist origins into alignment with organizations such as the World Peace Council and Mobilization for Survival. In 1983 the league's secretary-general co-chaired with Romesh Chandra the World Peace Assembly in Prague, a Soviet-controlled front.[24]

Physicians for Social Responsibility, now called Canadian Physicians for the Prevention of Nuclear War, and Science for Peace, groups formed around professions, are also linked to international umbrella groups, which are described in a later section. The World Federalists of Canada and the Greenpeace Foundation are also international, although Greenpeace originated in Canada. An important indigenous group is the Voice of

Women. This group was founded in 1960 to unite women in their concern for the world's future, to protest war, the arms race, nuclear technology, and environment pollution, and to promote human rights. According to reports in the Toronto *Telegram* in 1968, Mrs. Jo Davis, who had helped start Voice of Women because she felt strongly about peace, quit the organization in 1962 "because she felt extremist and unwholesome forces were seizing control." In her opinion a "machine-like juggernaut moved in and the Voice of Women was taken over by really hard-liners. It was rather horrifying to see and frightening to experience." At the same time, and for the same reasons, Norman Alcock's institute reportedly severed relations with Voice of Women.[25]

Operation Dismantle and the Peace Research Institute—Dundas (which, although committed to research, has nevertheless remained in the mainstream and sends delegates to World Peace Council meetings) remain active. Other national organizations are Lawyers for Social Responsibility and a similar group of engineers, the University Nuclear Disarmament Organization, and Performing Artists for Nuclear Disarmament. The Halifax-based Veterans Against Nuclear Arms, formerly Veterans for Multi-lateral Disarmament, also belong in this category.

There are some fifteen hundred local peace groups and women outnumber men at least sixty to forty. Some groups that have attracted national attention include the Toronto-based Cruise Missile Conversion Project, which focussed indignation against the Litton Systems plant; Conscience Canada, in Victoria, British Columbia, which seeks to persuade Canadians to divert their tax dollars to "peace"; the Nanoose Conversion Campaign, another west coast initiative, this time opposing U.S. testing of maritime equipment at the Canadian Forces Experimental and Test Range off Gabriola Island; the North Atlantic Peace Organization, a Labrador group opposing NATO flight training; and, in Quebec, Dimitrios Roussopoulos' Coalition Québécoise pour le désarmement et la paix and the Union des pacifistes du Québec.

The mainstream and the churches are served by the Canadian

Disarmament Information Service (CANDIS), which publishes a journal, *Peace Magazine*. The editor, Metta Spencer, maintains an even-handed policy, opening the journal's pages to many currents of peace movement thought.

Whereas radicals, including neo-Marxists and the New Left, are in the mainstream, there are some extremists who belong neither here nor in the Communist camp. This small nucleus includes anarchists, represented in a rather dangerous form in Canada by the loosely knit brotherhood called Direct Action. One cell of this hazy network turned violent in 1982, bombing an electricity transformer in British Columbia before turning its attention to the Litton plant near Toronto. At their trial it emerged that this group—the Stewart Cell—had plans to bomb air force jets at the Cold Lake base in Alberta, a Gulf Corporation ice-breaker, two Atomic Energy of Canada buildings in Ontario, and National Defence headquarters in Ottawa.[26]

The term *direct action* was used as a euphemism for terrorism before World War I by syndicalist revolutionaries. After 1917, most syndicalists became Communists: those who did not have been perpetual misfits in the political and social spectra.

CHAPTER V

THE COMMUNIST DIMENSION IN CANADA

The Communist element in the Canadian peace movement differs fundamentally from church and mainstream. Whereas the latter are essentially indigenous groups seeking peace within the democratic process, the Communists are agents of a foreign power waging revolutionary warfare, so to speak, behind "enemy"—that is Canadian—lines. Although the term *Communist* includes Trotskyists and splinter Marxist-Leninists—these being Communists who have adopted different tactics from the orthodox parties and who reject close direction by Moscow—we are concerned here mainly with the orthodox, Moscow-line party and its close allies.

What we are looking at is Canada's oldest and largest Communist party—the Communist Party of Canada and its offshoot, the Parti communiste du Québec. With some three thousand overt members, plus its Young Communist League, the party combines rigid ideological conformity within the membership with tactical flexibility and an emphasis on popular local issues in its public dealings. It has sometimes used aliases, such as the Committee of Progressive Electors in Toronto and Vancouver and the Labour Election Committee in Winnipeg, to deceive voters. In the 1984 federal election, the combined vote for all communistic parties was about one tenth of one percent of the whole. No candidate was returned. However, at the municipal level, and as a power within the New Democratic Party, the Canadian Labour Congress, individual unions, and the peace movement, Canadian Communists are influential far beyond their numbers. Toronto, Vancouver, and Winnipeg city councils have all had Communist members.

The Communist Party of Canada publishes *Canadian Tribune; Pacific Tribune; Combat; Communist Viewpoint; Le Communiste; Rebel Youth* and *Jeunesse militant.*[1] It is inconceivable that so small a party could fund all these publications, and there is as well ample evidence that the Soviet Union pours millions into such endeavors on an international basis.[2]

Although ideologically at loggerheads with the Communist Party of Canada and with each other, the unorthodox communistic parties are in broad agreement over many essentials: the evil of democracy and the glory of "socialism"; the West's monopoly of guilt in respect of "war," and communism's glorious commitment to "peace." The Communist Party of Canada (Marxist-Leninist), with between five hundred and a thousand members, was originally Maoist but now sees Albania, the last outpost of Stalinism, as a model to be copied by the world. Trotskyists belong either to the Revolutionary Workers League, the Trotskyist League, or the Forward Readers Group. Combined membership is probably in the hundreds.

The militancy of these groups is undiminished, but their power has been reduced since they lost their influence over the New Left. It seems highly unlikely that they could wrest control of the mainstream movement out of the Communist Party's hands in the late 1980s, as they did in the 1960s. Passing mention should also be made of the International Socialists, another Leninist party with no important following.

As well as its Quebec and youth wings, the Communist Party of Canada has control over several auxiliary organizations—the Association of United Ukrainian Canadians, Congress of Canadian Women, Workers Benevolent Association of Canada, and the Canada-USSR Association. In the realm of peace the party co-operates with a front organization, the Canadian Peace Congress and its Quebec sidekick, Conseil Québécois de la paix. These last are the national affiliates of the Moscow-controlled World Peace Council.[3] The Communist Party also exploits the fact that the New Democratic Party's foreign and defence policies correspond in many respects with their own. Their program requires members to work for a united front with the social democrats and to push that party farther left toward Leninism:

> The more effectively the Communist Party works for the united front and strengthens its independent political activity, propagating its Marxist-Leninist program and policies, the more it will encourage and strengthen the left wing in the New Democratic Party and the struggle for genuine socialist policies.[4]

During the 1930s, Canadian Communists responded to the Communist International's call for a popular front against fascism by forming the League Against War and Fascism, which in 1936 changed its name to the League for Peace and Democracy. This was Canada's first exposure to the broad front technique by which Communists, following Lenin's dictum of tactical flexibility to secure inflexible strategic ends, mobilized widespread support by single-issue campaigns. In common with later campaigns of this sort the organizers tried to confront the public with a black and white either/or choice, no third option being permitted. In the 1930s the choices were either to support the popular front, supposedly favoring "peace and democracy," or accept a fascist victory. The Communist role of absolute control was always concealed, with prominent "innocents" persuaded to fill nominal positions of authority. In Toronto, for instance, the Rev. Spence of the democratic socialist Co-operative Commonwealth Federation was regularly elected chairman of the popular front's annual United Labour May Day parade, while the Communist Norman Freed occupied the post of secretary. P. M. Draper, president of the Trades and Labour Congress of Canada, was another of the innocents who worked on united front activities.[5]

The abject subordination of Communists and their fronts to Moscow's commands was illustrated in August 1939. As soon as the USSR signed the Nazi-Soviet Non-Aggression Pact that secured Germany's eastern frontier and permitted Hitler to launch World War II, Soviet propaganda praised Hitler and described the British Commonwealth, French, and Allied war efforts as "imperialist." Soon, the Communist Party of Canada fell into line and campaigned under the slogan "Withdraw Canada from the Imperialist War." The party explained that "for us in Canada the danger of fascism comes not from Nazi Germany but from the war policies of the King Government."[6] Communists led the Canadian Seamen's Union into a strike that paralyzed shipping on the Great Lakes for six days just as Nazi troops were conquering Norway. Only after Nazi Germany invaded the USSR did Canadian Communists support the war effort, which, at that point, had become for them part of the global Communist revolution.

After World War II the Soviet Union decided to institutionalize "peace" as a weapon against the non-Communist world by establishing an international front organization, the World Peace Council, in a major West European capital—Paris. This bold move was thwarted by the French government when in 1951 the council was expelled for fifth-column activities. It moved to Prague and then to Vienna, where it remained until banned in 1957 by the Austrian interior minister for "activities directed against the Austrian state." The council disguised itself for the next eleven years as the International Institute for Peace, a stratagem that enabled it to remain in Vienna. In 1968, however, the organization under its original name opened an office in Helsinki and has operated from Finland ever since. The council has succeeded in creating cells, or affiliates, in about 140 countries.[7]

Political direction of "peace" activities comes from the International Department of the Central Committee of the Communist Party of the Soviet Union, passes through Helsinki, and thence to affiliates. Separate communications link the department with all Moscow-line Communist parties in the non-Communist world. The International Department supervises all Soviet foreign policy as well as directing subversion and international terrorism. Under the Politburo, it is the most powerful instrument of international policy, and the fact that "peace" features so prominently on its agenda, alongside deception and terrorism, is instructive.

Both the World Peace Council and the Canadian Peace Congress came into existence in 1949. The congress was established under the energetic leadership of United Church missionary James G. Endicott, who for more than a year had been promoting "peace" with the help of various utopian and Communist activists. In 1948, accompanied by Canterbury's Hewlett Johnson, the "Red Dean," Endicott had toured the country preaching his new gospel. Later the congress issued a letter calling for the abolition of nuclear weapons. This blended nicely with the World Peace Council's first major operation, the 1950 Stockholm Appeal—a classic popular front deception.[8]

The Stockholm Appeal was directed specifically against the weapon that offset the Soviet preponderance in conventional arms: the atom bomb. Its organizers claimed that 500 million signatures were collected. On August 29, 1949, the Soviet Union exploded its first atom bomb. Moscow said nothing, but the United States detected the test and made it public. We do not know whether there was co-ordination in Moscow between the propaganda departments and the Scientific-Technical Council responsible for the test, whether Soviet psychological specialists appreciated in advance the importance of fear in the "peace" offensive, or whether it evolved from the Stockholm exercise. Whatever the planning or lack of it, it is reasonable to assume that the success of the Stockholm Appeal owed much to the Western public's knowledge that the US nuclear monopoly had been broken and that the West as well as the East was now threatened by this terrifying new weapon. The appeal was thus an exploitation of fear. It began the syndrome of guilt, doubt, and fearfulness that has ever since made the West vulnerable to Soviet "peace" propaganda.

Herbert Romerstein quotes the American Trotskyist James P. Cannon, who had attended the World Peace Council conference that launched the appeal, as referring to "the recent Warsaw peace conference of professional fellow travellers, congenital stooges and moon-struck clergymen steered, like all such gatherings, by hard-faced jockeys from the Stalinist riding stables."[9] In Britain, Communists promoted the appeal through a front, the British Peace Committee. The seeds then sown sprouted in 1957, when J. B. Priestley wrote in the *New States-man* calling for a mass movement against nuclear weapons themselves. Within months, the Campaign for Nuclear Disarmament, CND, had been born. The connection was psychological, rather than political or organizational. Nevertheless, Communists quickly infiltrated CND to occupy key positions, ensuring that the campaign focussed its attention exclusively on Western nuclear weapons.

Endicott's political ideal was Mao's Communist China, where appalling experiments in social engineering were killing millions and making the survivors' lives miserable. During the Korean War Endicott supported the Communist side and assisted the Chinese over their germ warfare hoax, which tried to persuade world opinion that the United States had descended to this form of warfare. In 1952 he accepted a Stalin Peace Prize. His Canadian Peace Congress went on to oppose West German rearmament, to support the Soviet invasions of Hungary and Czechoslovakia, and, in conjunction with the Canadian Friends Service Committee, to marshal the anti–Vietnam War campaign. The Sino-Soviet split, caused in part by China's refusal to accept Khrushchev's "revisionist" views on the inevitability of war, left Endicott on the wrong side of the fence so far as his Moscow-line comrades in the Canadian Peace Congress and the World Peace Council were concerned. He quit the congress in 1971.

In 1946 the United Church of Canada had called upon Endicott to resign from the ministry, Christ in those days being seen as incompatible with the Antichrist of scientific atheism. By 1982, however, a combination of the Vietnam syndrome, liberation theology, the secularization of the churches, and the dominant Canadian mindset of utopian liberalism had evidently dissolved that incompatibility. In a Canada exposed to extreme relativism in schools, universities, politics, and religion, there was no longer a right or a wrong, a good or an evil, only the comforting Muzak of "relating" and "relevance." On August 12, 1982, the General Council of the United Church of Canada passed a resolution expressing regret that the church had caused Endicott "much personal hurt and anxiety" in 1946, adding that "events of the past 30 years have borne out many of his predictions and prophetic actions on the issue of world peace."[10]

If the United Church was willing to forgive, and even to humble itself before this apostle of Stalinist peace, the Soviet Union and its congenital stooges certainly were not. In 1982 the Communist *Tribune* launched a vitriolic attack on Endicott.[11] In March 1984 the Canadian Peace Congress met to celebrate its own thirty-fifth anniversary and its parents', that is, the World Peace Council. Eric "we stand perhaps on the brink of nuclear war" Blair, the Ontario president, introduced his national president, John "the threat of war comes exclusively from the USA" Morgan. In his remarks, Morgan—clergyman, Lenin Peace Prize–holder, vice-president of the World Peace Council, and sometime Unitarian minister—succeeded in celebrating the congress's thirty-five years, twenty-two of them under Endicott's leadership, without once mentioning his name. Nor was any mention made of Endicott in the lengthy speech by council president Romesh "the world is nearer a nuclear war than ever before" Chandra. Endicott had been well and truly consigned to the totalitarians' memory hole. For a true believer who is loyal to the wrong master—Mao in this case—there is, apparently, no forgiveness.[12]

The strategic objectives of the 1980s peace offensive were discussed at the end of chapter 3. Within each Western country the Communist Party and its peace congress use three main methods to help advance the cause:

• Providing a psychological channel for ideas that form the key themes of peace propaganda, and also a physical conduit for massive quantities of Soviet-produced or inspired propaganda.

• Organization of overt and covert groups to set the pace and the tone for others to follow, and the provision of organizational support to groups in need.

• Penetration of existing non-Communist groups to covertly influence or control their agendas and, in key situations, the imposition of a Soviet agenda on the majority from a minority position.

We will now examine how these methods have been applied in Canada and elsewhere.

CHAPTER VI

"PEACE" WITHOUT FREEDOM

Any serious attempt to identify the causes of war would have to examine contending political doctrines. On the one hand such a review would find the doctrine that cherishes military strength for the power it gives a state or party to impose its will on others; on the other, the doctrine that relies on military strength to defend the state against incursions. Such an assessment in today's world would disclose that Soviet ideology, doctrine, and practice all stress that military superiority is one of the keys that unlock the door to world power. It would show that Western political and military policies have attempted to prevent Soviet power from becoming overwhelming, to deter Soviet leaders from trying to benefit by using their power, and to contain incursions—whether political, military, or psychological. No doubt a review would uncover numerous misperceptions and errors of judgement and of execution—such as Vietnam—in the Western response. No doubt present Western policy would benefit from constructive criticism. But so long as it remained honest, the assessment could not fail to note that the totalitarian political system threatens world peace in a way that the democratic system does not. Fundamental, yes. But the Canadian peace movement has consistently failed to address this.

If the church and the mainstream Canadian peace movement had defined their core beliefs in a pacifist manner, "peace" would have come within the United Nations or Christian meaning of the word, which most certainly links it to human rights and freedoms. "War," in such a context, would have been *all* war and *all* political violence, from no matter what source. Hope of success would have rested on faith in the Almighty or confidence in the beauty of human nature and its capacity to overcome evil. The challenge to the conventional wisdom would have been based on the rationality of nonviolence. Behind this rationality would lie the spiritual force of adherents willing to lay down their lives for the cause.

Such sacrifice might be necessary, because the logic of a movement so inspired would require members to press their beliefs by nonviolent means toward all those conducting or advocating violence for political ends. To be sure, the Canadian, United States, and West European governments and peoples would suffer the rebukes of such a movement. But the main thrust would inevitably be against totalitarian regimes, particularly those whose ideology glorifies revolution and war as the engine of change, and most particularly the Soviet Union, whose sole claim to superpower status rests on her military might. This was the spirit of the Peace Army, a British Christian pacifist movement whose members in 1931 proposed putting their bodies unarmed between the contending forces in a Chinese–Japanese clash.[1]

It may be objected that pacifism of this sort is unworldly and incapable of providing answers to today's pressing problems. It remains the pacifist case: that evil is not overcome by force but rather by sacrifice and love. By their failure to endorse this, Canadian churches and the mainstream banished morality from the debate. On the contrary, their apparent concern is for personal survival regardless of cost.

Having dodged the central political issue, and having failed to define its core beliefs in pacifist terms, the Canadian peace movement has left these beliefs vague. No doubt this allows the movement to be all things to all people, while permitting organizers with narrow political agendas to operate freely. In this way the rank and file can be recruited on the basis of motherhood appeals and then gradually led into support of hidden causes. Thus, "peace" can mean anything from its UN definition, linking it to human rights and freedom, to the Communist concept of victory. Although the human rights ingredient is staunchly defended by a handful of courageous peace activists—particularly Metta Spencer, Derek Paul, Frank Sommers, and some radicals—the majority consistently ignores or denies it. For example:

• "Some organizations, like Amnesty International, have argued that we must link the campaign for disarmament with the campaign for 'human rights.' We disagree." Editorial, "Open letter to the Peace Movement," *Canadian Dimension*, November 1983.

• In April 1984 Dr. Roman Fin, a cancer researcher who once underwent two years' "re-education" in a Soviet labor camp, approached Canadian peace demonstrators in Toronto with a petition calling for humane treatment for Soviet physicist Dr. Andrei Sakharov, then in exile. Most refused to sign. *Globe and Mail*, July 23, 1984.

• At the sixth annual conference of the International Physicians for the Prevention of Nuclear War in Cologne, West Germany, in June 1986, the majority of the Canadian physicians' group voted against a proposal that they write an appeal on behalf of Dr. Vladimir Brodsky, then confined to Siberia for his disarmament activism. Their reason? An appeal "might antagonise [our] Russian counterparts and impair their effectiveness in working for disarmament." *Peace Magazine*, August/September 1986.

• "In my experience in the peace movement, the support for human rights in the Soviet Union hasn't been a big issue." Bob Penner, co-ordinator, Canadian Peace Alliance, *Peace Magazine*, February/March, 1987.

Perhaps it should not be surprising that human rights count for so little. Today's peace movement is the direct descendant of the Vietnam anti-war movement, which failed so dismally to address the subject as it affected—and still affects—the peoples of Indo-China. It is, moreover, the movement that emerged at the precise time Soviet troops began their rape of Afghanistan; yet it failed to protest this real and terrible war. In September 1985 *Peace Magazine* reported:

> Grace Hartman sees CUPE [the Canadian Union of Public Employees] and the United Auto Workers as exceptionally concerned about peace issues. During the Vietnam days, she and UAW president Dennis McDermott seemed always on the same platform speaking at rallies opposing the war. The same holds true today.

The road to hell is paved with good intentions.

The United States deserves at least some of the criticism that came out of the war in Vietnam. That war could not have been won under the conditions and by the methods with which it was fought. Since the resulting destruction and deaths were to no good purpose, Americans and others who argued for an end to the fighting were right, while Canada and other Western countries that kept out of the conflict were proven wise. These were rational conclusions. Equally rational was the need for the war to be ended in a manner that secured peace as defined in the United Nations Charter.

How remarkable, then, that the Canadian peace movement learned so little from the experience of the post-Vietnam war period. Even more remarkable was the continued, concentrated indignation against the United States and the apparent conniving by some members of the international peace movement with the atrocities committed by the victorious Communists. For the sad fact is that, in "giving peace a chance" in Vietnam, that movement also *left* to chance the fate of millions. From this recklessness, a terrible evil emerged.

In Cambodia the victorious Communist Pol Pot regime proceeded to carry out massacre on a scale to rival and even to exceed the slaughters perpetrated in the names of Lenin, Stalin, and Mao. The Pol Pot exterminated all members of the previous, pro-Western government, all Communists sympathetic to Hanoi, and virtually the entire middle and professional classes. There are no absolutely reliable figures, but it is generally assumed that at least one third of the population of seven million was murdered. As Arthur Koestler wrote, statistics do not bleed; it is the detail that counts. "We are unable to embrace the total process with our awareness; we can only focus on little lumps of reality."[2]

Here is a detail that counts, a report in l'Humanité of how Lola Sivath, cousin of Prince Sihanouk, lost her family:

> Seeing her father standing beneath the mango tree, my daughter began running. One of the Pol Pot soldiers fired from his rifle and shot her in the head. She fell to the ground. Then they shot my husband before my eyes . . . Earlier, when I saw films about the Nazi concentration camps, they had seemed incredible to me.[3]

Koestler, writing in the early 1940s, had been warning us about the Nazi death camps.

The Cambodian genocide worried Moscow not in the least, so long as a hope remained that the Pol Pot regime might be wooed away from its loyalty to China. In 1976 President Kosygin sent a congratulatory telegram; in 1977 New Times (Novaya Vremya) lauded Pol Pot's "progressive social and economic reforms"; in 1978 the Central Committee of the Communist Party of the Soviet Union (CPSU) welcomed the reorganization of the Khmer Rouge along orthodox Communist lines.[4] Only when hopes of a political reorientation were dashed did the Soviets, for pragmatic purposes, condemn conduct that so closely resembled their own.

Early in 1979 Vietnam's powerful army crushed the Khmer Rouge and set up a puppet government in Cambodia. Thereafter, Moscow-line Communists tried with some success to blame the mass murders either on the United States—for having tried and failed to defend the country against Pol Pot—or on "Peking hegemonists." The plain fact remains, however, that the killing fields represented "peace" by Communist definition. William Kashtan, then general secretary of the Communist Party of Canada, endorsed this interpretation in March 1985 when he wrote that socialism (by which he meant Marxism-Leninism) "must triumph world-wide in order to eliminate the threat of war once and for all."[5]

In Vietnam, Communist victory brought a peace of similar quality. In the South, the nationalists who had fought for their country's independence from foreign domination, and had accepted Communist leadership in this struggle, were rudely disabused of their hopes that North Vietnam would honor its promises, formally confirmed in the 1973 Paris Agreement. All the founders of the National Liberation Front—many of them non-Communists who had been so useful to Hanoi in deceiving the West about the nature of the war—were dismissed. Trung Nhu Tang, one of these leaders, wrote sadly: "With other liberals I shared a romantic notion that those [the Communists] who had fought so persistently against oppression would not themselves become oppressors."[6] But he concluded that the Communists had imposed a system of oppression "unparalleled in Vietnam's history."

The flight of the boat people was one symptom of this oppression. Less publicized, but more deadly, was the process called re-education, a version of which the Nazis had copied from the Soviets in the 1930s. Anyone suspected of opposing the Communist regime, including priests, monks, critics, small-property holders, and elements considered "harmful to society" were bundled off to concentration camps. Finally, Vietnam emerged as both an imperial power, by taking control of Laos, invading Cambodia, and threatening Thailand, and as the pawn of a greater imperialism—by granting military bases and sending labor brigades to work in the Soviet Union in return for foreign aid. Now, with the fourth-largest armed force in the world, this small, bankrupt nation has earned the title, the "Prussians of Asia."[7]

The response of those Westerners who had given peace in Vietnam a chance was mixed. Jean Lacouture, a French journalist famed for reporting US sins during the war, wrote in 1976: "Never before have we had such proof of so many detained after a war. Not in Moscow in 1917, not in Madrid in 1939, not in

Paris and Rome in 1944, nor in Havana in 1959."[8] Peter Collier and David Horowitz, key anti-war radicals in the 1960s, were so disgusted by their formers associates' "self-aggrandizing romance with corrupt Third Worldism, . . . casual indulgence of Soviet totalitarianism . . . [and] hypocritical and self-dramatizing anti-Americanism" that they denounced them in a 1985 *Washington Post Magazine* article.[9] Among those who recognized the bitter consequences of peace as defined by Communists were singer Joan Baez, who spoke out on behalf of the boat people, and other former anti-war activists who in 1977 signed and published an Appeal to the Conscience of Vietnam because of the 200,000 plus prisoners in re-education camps.

In contrast to these honest statements, the hardline radicals of the anti-war movement refused to see, hear, or speak of the evil their good intentions had wrought. Lacouture was dismissed as a "sellout"; Baez was attacked for breaking ranks with Hanoi; the authors of the Appeal were chastised by "activist David Dellinger, Institute for Policy Studies fellow Richard Barnet and other keepers of the flame in a *New York Times* advertisement."[10]

The British Arabist and writer Freya Stark once wrote that she found Canadian audiences "full of rock-like integrity, impervious to sense."[11] Because one party to a dispute had captured the moral high ground, her audiences would not listen to the rival argument. While this is not a peculiarly Canadian reaction, the observation would seem to hold true today. Canadians who opposed the Vietnam War seemed unable to comprehend that their good intentions could be blemished in practical impact. They believed all the positive stories about the Communist North because it suited their agenda to do so; they accepted the Communist promise of peace but did not wish to enquire too deeply what this meant. Insofar as they acted in good faith—and the great majority did so—no one can reasonably blame them. Two questions arise, however, which cannot easily be brushed aside: one asks, Do you care about the consequences of your actions? The other assumes a positive answer to the first and enquires: In that case, will you not learn from experience?

For to repeat the same mistakes—accepting Communist

assurances of goodwill at face value and glossing over the difference between the Communist and non-Communist meanings of "peace"—after the lessons of Vietnam, would surely be folly. And it would be a betrayal of justice, not to mention an end to all hope of peace with freedom.

With the onset of détente in 1972, the Soviet leaders publicly declared that the danger of war had declined. They could see that US military spending, in real terms, had already started to go down; SALT I, signed in 1972, recognized Soviet strategic parity with the United States. Soviet optimism should also have been reinforced by the 1975 Helsinki Agreement, which virtually ratified Soviet hegemony over central Europe, and by the final US withdrawal from Vietnam that same year. Canada's contribution to this process had come early.

In 1971 she had signed a USSR-Canada Protocol of Consultations, which bound both nations to make contact and exchange views in the event of a threat to peace. The accurate Soviet perception of a reduced war danger could have led to a corresponding cut in Soviet military spending, moderation of Soviet bloc interventions in the Third World, and a lessening of hostile propaganda against the West. Considering the decline in Soviet economic growth and prospects, a consolidation of the peaceful trend would surely have served domestic as well as international interests. It is inconceivable that the West would not have continued to respond in kind.

Unhappily, Soviet leaders decided instead to increase the arms burden, a decision that was certainly not forced on them by heightened fears of war. Military interventions in Angola and Ethiopia demonstrated an invigorated commitment to an old revolutionary tradition or a new form of imperialism. Propaganda to domestic and foreign audiences remained bellicose and bitterly anti-Western. Promises to respect human rights that had been incorporated into the Helsinki Agreement were betrayed by Moscow. The military build-up threatened the SALT process by deployment of super-accurate land-based intercontinental ballistic missiles; it upset the European balance by a dramatic improvement in Warsaw Pact conventional offensive capability and by the introduction of a completely new class of "regional" nuclear weapons, the SS-20.

Unfortunately, neither Project Ploughshares nor the secular organizations moved a finger to oppose these developments. By the end of the decade the Soviets were evidently convinced that the West now accepted "peace" on their terms. Thus encouraged, they despatched 120,000 troops to conquer Afghanistan.

Claude Malhuret, executive director of the Paris-based Médecins sans frontières, which has operated in Afghanistan since May 1980, notes that one difference between the Russians in Afghanistan and the French in Algeria or the Americans in Vietnam was the politico-military objective. In the Algerian and Vietnamese wars, the French and Americans tried vainly to fight their enemies while simultaneously seeking the support of the rest of the population. The Soviets, he says, are not so naive. "They understand that a guerrilla war will be won by the side that succeeds in making terror reign."[12] The Soviet decision to withdraw troops from Afghanistan is a monument to Afghan courage: but it is yet to be seen whether communist terror will be eradicated.

Out of a pre-Communist population estimated at 15 million, approximately one million Afghans have been killed or have died from war-related injury or disease. This includes an estimated 200,000 to 500,000 outright executions by the Communist regime or Soviet troops. Nearly six million Afghans—close to half the population—are refugees: three million in Pakistan, a reported 1.5 million in Iran, and another million or more inside their own country. Soviet troops in Afghanistan were supposedly fighting for peace. In the period of Gorbachev's "new political thinking," the Soviet embassy in Ottawa put out propaganda claiming that "the Soviet troops in Afghanistan are defending peace, justice, freedom, and a life worthy of human beings."[13] Not one demonstration against these barbarities has been mounted by the Canadian churches or the peace movement, in remarkable contrast to their reactions to the Vietnamese war.

Reviewing a book by the Czechoslovak Charta 77 spokesman Vaclav Havel in 1986, *Peace Magazine's* Peter Wade reported that Havel "criticizes Western peace groups for two major failures: failure to realize and incorporate into their activities the inseparability of peace and human rights and failure to oppose loudly (if at all) the only war in which a European state is currently engaged."[14]

The inseparability referred to by Havel is another way of distinguishing between the non-Communist notion of peace, which incorporates human rights, and the Communist definition, which ignores everything but party power. Many Canadian peace activists respect United Nations principles. These principles endorse human rights unequivocally. Chapter 1 of the UN Charter, Article 1, paragraph 3, declares that a purpose of the UN is "to achieve international cooperation in solving international problems of an economic, social, cultural, or humanitarian character in promoting and encouraging respect for human rights and fundamental freedoms for all." Actions giving effect to this commitment are specifically authorized in Articles 13, 55, 56, and 62 of the Charter.

There is no acceptable reason for any Canadian to try to separate the concepts of peace and human rights. Nevertheless, those who are Communist will deny the linkage for Leninist reasons of power. They then observe another Leninist principle—"to use every trick, cunning, illegal means, concealment of the truth or prevarication"—while pretending to share the Western world's definition of peace.[15]

If the lessons of Vietnam and Afghanistan are too fresh to be digested, earlier examples of promises broken by the Soviets are legion. Sufficient to mention only one here: the Yalta Agreement of 1945, to which they were signatories, promised "free elections of governments responsible to the will of the people" *throughout occupied Europe.*

None of this is the least surprising, considering the deceptive nature of communism as such. Aleksandr Solzhenitsyn pointed out in his Nobel Lecture that anyone who has once proclaimed violence as his method "must inexorably choose the lie as his principle." No Communist party has ever won a majority in a free election. Whatever electoral success such parties have achieved has been in direct proportion to their capacity to deceive. After all, which pacifist would vote for permanent conflict, which peasant for collectivization, and which worker for state monopoly? What appeal would rigid ideological conformity have for intellectuals, or censorship for journalists, or employer control of working conditions for trade unionists? How many religious people would welcome scientific atheism, and how would social action groups and rival political parties enjoy the psychiatric gulag?

And which Canadian, accustomed to so much freedom that the whole wonderful experience is taken for granted and regarded as the global norm, would voluntarily abandon this entirely? As Jeane Kirkpatrick explained a quarter of a century ago, the "Communist movement is a Trojan horse because it systematically conceals its identity—in its propaganda and organizational tactics."[16] Events in the past twenty-five years have proven nothing new in this regard. During the 1980s, Western peace movements have been systematically deceived into supporting Soviet objectives; the abandonment of human rights is the first step along the road to all manner of compromises.

CHAPTER VII

USING FEAR TO REDEFINE THE ENEMY

No one has written about propaganda with more clarity than the French philosopher Jacques Ellul.[1] In his book *Propaganda: The Formation of Men's Attitudes*, he explains the special form of communication that he calls pre-propaganda. By conditioning reflexes and creating myths, it forces its audience to live in a certain psychological climate, ready to respond in a predetermined manner to the right stimulus. It is as if pre-propaganda created the necessary conditions for a huge avalanche, conditions that appear stable but require only one falling stone or a gust of wind to set hundreds of tons of rock hurtling down the mountainside. Creating the conditions may take years, as one example of this long-term investment shows. It is the "imminent nuclear war" deception: the pre-propaganda theme of fear.

According to documentation provided by Bundestag member Count Hans Huyn, Vadim Zagladin—in 1970 the Soviet International Department's first deputy—issued propaganda instructions that year for fear of nuclear war in general and of alleged US plans for limited nuclear war in particular to be aroused in Western Europe.[2] These instructions to nonruling Communist parties were subsequently translated into the various European languages and made the subject of internal party indoctrination in Western Europe and North America. In Canada, E. F. Crist wrote in a 1971 issue of *Communist Viewpoint*: "But imperialism is now threatening to carry out its greatest of all crimes. By using the unravelled secrets of nature to sow fire, disease, poison and death, Mankind will experience a catastrophe such as history has never known before."[3]

At the same time, the World Peace Council through its national affiliates made the theme of fear an important priority. Nevertheless, at this stage of detente, it was not easy to spread fear while encouraging unquestioning trust at the same time; an issue was needed. For this groundwork took place while the United States, still traumatized by Vietnam, was observing a self-imposed unilateral freeze, and when Ronald Reagan was still governor of California.

As often happens in propaganda battles, the break was provided by the Western media and was then taken up and made into an effective campaign by Communist propaganda and organization.

On June 6, 1977, the *Washington Post* published an article by Walter Pincus entitled "Neutron Killer Warhead Buried in ERDA Budget." The neutron weapon was designed to destroy enemy tanks. Pincus, however, saw the neutron bomb issue as an opportunity to grind his political anti-nuclear axe. He used phrases uttered by officials at earlier Atomic Energy Commission hearings, such as the bomb that "destroys people and leaves buildings intact." Then Herbert Scoville, a former defence official who has been on the board of the anti-defence lobby, the Center for Defense Information, wrote in the *New York Times* that "neutron bombs have been proclaimed the 'supercapitalist weapon,' preserving property while killing and sickening people."[4] The *Times* ran the quote in bold type across the middle of the page.

Immediately, the World Peace Council's affiliates in Western Europe set up Stop the Neutron Bomb fronts to focus on this single issue, inspire fear, and attract new supporters. Nico Schouten, the Dutch Communist who led the Netherlands attack, abridged Scoville's irresponsible comment and created the slogan, "The perfect capitalist weapon: kills people but saves property." He went on to allege that the neutron warhead was part of a US strategy to initiate limited nuclear war in Europe. In this period the Soviets devoted 13 percent of all broadcast items to the neutron issue, while *Pravda* carried a regular feature on the subject.[5]

President Carter first persuaded his West German ally to accept the new weapon—at some political risk to the chancellor, Helmut Schmidt—and then changed his own mind, dropping Schmidt in the mire and presenting Moscow with a propaganda triumph that was both a coup in itself and a massive incentive to turn up the heat in the peace offensive. For if the Americans could be deceived into abandoning a defensive weapon designed to offset the Warsaw Pact's massive preponderance in tanks—a weapon that would kill tank crews with the minimum collateral damage to the NATO territory over which any war in Europe would doubtless be fought—the West might surely be persuaded to forgo other new weapons. In the process, fear could become the dominant emotion governing Western public perceptions of all defence issues.

Between their victory over Carter and the launching of the main peace offensive in the early 1980s, the Soviets conducted a series of preliminary operations. Throughout 1979 they used mainly diplomatic channels to try to persuade the West, and particularly West Germany, not to agree to any updating of NATO's arms in response to the Soviet deployment of SS-20s. Brezhnev threatened that countries that accepted new weapons would "suffer dire consequences" in any conflict. US advocates of arms-control-at-any-price Herbert Scoville, Arthur Cox, and Richard Barnet flew to Copenhagen to urge Danes to oppose any NATO plan for new weapons. But these efforts by Moscow and presumably well-intentioned Westerners failed. On December 12, 1979, the North Atlantic Council endorsed the theatre nuclear force modernization program, which contained the "dual track" provision that, if the Soviets agreed to dismantle their SS-20s, NATO would rid itself of the cruise and Pershing II missiles.[6]

The Soviets apparently decided to go public by lifting the issue over the heads of Western governments and creating extra-parliamentary opposition in the streets. Before battle was joined, there were important briefings to be given.

The first, held in Paris in April 1980, was for European Communist Party officials. The keynote speech was given by Boris Ponomarev, then head of the International Department; it

called for a full-scale peace offensive against the new NATO policy. Beginning with a warning about the "grave danger of war,"
Ponomarev called on Communists to organize a popular front:

> The Communists have a full moral right—moreover, it is
> their duty!—to appeal to the working class, the peasantry and
> the intelligentsia, to the trade unions, to religious circles,
> women's, young people's and other organizations, to people in
> the sciences and the arts, parliamentarians and businessmen
> to exert every effort. . . .[7]

And there he listed the inevitable objectives for frustrating
Western defence initiatives. Apart from difficulties in many
European NATO countries of identifying "peasantry," there is no
doubt that Europe's Communists broadcast the message to considerable effect.

An equal measure of success seems to have attended Ponomarev's call for disinformation networks. Communists were instructed to "work towards getting the mass news media to serve
. . . the cause of [Soviet] peace."[8] Nor could he have been disappointed at the return on investment in calling for tactical
alliances with social democrats.

The second conference was more ambitious. It was the so-
called World Peoples' Parliament for Peace held in Sofia,
Bulgaria, in September 1980. The World Peace Council supplied the organization; the International Department controlled
the propaganda. Ponomarev's speech once again set the agenda
and provided the 2260 delegates from eighty-three countries
with marching orders. He reminded delegates that "the war danger originates with US imperialism and its allies, with their reck-
less policy, and their main tool—the aggressive NATO bloc."
Soviet propaganda objectives, when stripped of their verbiage,
were listed as follows:

• Opposition to Western defence (the "arms race"), especially
cruise and Pershing II missiles; support for SALT II and for
"negotiations"; enforcement in the West of existing arms control
agreements.

• Western public opinion to accept the rape of Afghanistan.

• The Helsinki Agreement to be observed by the West but not by the East.

• The West to accept "political detente" on Soviet terms, world-wide—a steady, unopposed surrender.

• Western economies to be crippled by Third World policies of "complete equality and mutual benefit."

• An end to all Western resistance to Soviet ideological warfare and propaganda.

Ponomarev went on to praise the "highly diverse and multifarious movement against war," specifically mentioning Pugwash, the World Council of Churches, and the Conference of European Churches, the last being a front of his making. Then, warning that "the hour for action has come," the head of the International Department issued battle orders. Delegates were to "get the majority of people behind the drive for ending the arms race" so as to "compel governments that are sabotaging or holding back solutions of vital problems to take action and to help curb the arms race, to consent to negotiations." Negotiations, in the Soviet lexicon, are not for the purpose of reaching compromise; they are an alternative means of class warfare. The faithful were also instructed to get their local news media onside and to promote the vanguard role of the working class in the war called peace.[9]

According to the World Peace Council's "Preliminary List of Participants," Canadian representation at the Sofia conference included officials of the Communist Party of Canada; the Canadian Peace Congress with its Quebec opposite number and several local branches; and the Association of United Ukrainian Canadians. Surprisingly, the Canadian delegation also included Lorne Elliott, representing the Voice of Women and Operation Dismantle; Eyrl Court of the People's Assembly and of Operation Dismantle; Ontario New Democratic Party MLA Mac Makarchuk; British Columbia member Alan Passarell; and Quebec member Guy Bisaillon. There were also ten labor union representatives, four of them schoolteachers from Quebec; Dr. James Steele and Prof. André Jacob, from Carleton and Quebec universities respectively; and Rodrigue Dubé, president of the professors' alliance in Montreal. Edith Ballantyne was there as secretary general of the Women's International League for Peace and Freedom, and Ray Stevenson as a member of the World Peace Council Secretariat.

A fellow delegate was Charlie Biton of the Black Panthers.

The World Peace Council followed up these conferences by issuing written orders. In its "Programme of Action, 1981," the council required activists to infiltrate and manipulate all relevant UN committees and agencies, especially those dealing with disarmament, peace institutes, nongovernmental organizations, religious groups—including the Holy See and the World Council of Churches—women's organizations, international trade unions, youth and students' groups, and, for good measure, all mass movements working for peace. Those in politics were to form parliamentary peace groups; the "popular front" technique was to be used, to disguise Communist leadership behind "common united mass action."[10]

The instruction went on to stress the value of local issues. Neighborhoods close to proposed cruise or Pershing II sites were to be mobilized. But such "direct action" was to be concentrated exclusively against Western weapons; once again, no criticism of Soviet power was to be tolerated. The peace offensive was to be linked in people's minds to "development," wars of "national liberation" against "fascist" and "racist" regimes, and the struggles for a "new international economic order" and a "new world information order." In short, not a single liberal guilt was to be left untouched. The program listed the main propaganda themes to be used: fear; relating fear to Western weapons; plans for limited nuclear war; advocacy of nuclear weapon-free zones; economic costs of defence; advantages of a no-first-use treaty.[11]

Like many Communist publications aimed at the West, the World Peace Council's program used what John Clews in his classic work on Communist propaganda termed the imperative indicative formulation. To the outsider, the writing seems to be descriptive: "people are striving . . . " But to the initiated, the words are taken as orders: "people are to strive . . . "[12] So that when, early in the Introduction, we read, "The peoples of the world are alarmed. Never before has there been so great a danger of a world holocaust,"[13] we should be aware that this is not an observation; it is an order to Communists and their allies to get out there and make people feel afraid.

As Soviet peace propaganda shifted in 1980 to counter the proposed deployment in Western Europe of cruise and Pershing II missiles, fear of imminent war was manipulated so successfully that something close to a controlled panic swept the continent. Communist-controlled or -inspired peace activists were seen everywhere in black and white death masks. "Angst" or dread seemed everybody's declared condition. Fear was redirected into hatred of the new US administration and of President Reagan personally.

Now it was time to plant the emotional stimulus for the spread of terror in North America. On November 15, 1981, the Reverend William Sloane Coffin of the Riverside Church in New York and his disarmament director, Cora Weiss, hosted a conference, "The Arms Race and Us." Among the five hundred delegates were a KGB agent called Kapralov and the Australian-born pediatrician and peace activist, Helen Caldicott. The latter had just toured Europe, and the news she offered was, by her beliefs, joyful: "It was a wonderful feeling to be over there; the fear was palpable but realistic." But she complained, "The Americans seem to have no panic. Why?"[14]

One has only to read the North American peace literature of the following weeks and months to see how seriously the rebuke was taken. As for Canada, our National Film Board was particularly anxious to do its bit. It featured Caldicott in a blatantly propagandistic film, *If You Love This Planet*, which seemed to have but one intention: to leave its audiences in a state of shock, unable to make rational decisions, and vulnerable to further propaganda. In a clumsy effort to keep the film out of the United States, officials there formally labelled the film propaganda. However, in an open society, such accurate but gratuitous description merely served to heighten public interest.

For Canada's peace movement, the theme of imminent holocaust, the apocalyptic premise, has dominated all others. Examples:

- "Mankind must choose. Halt the arms race or face annihilation." Heading in *Ploughshares Monitor*, December 1981.

- "We are driven to despair by increasing threats of war. Is there to be any future for our children?" *Women's Petition for Peace*, sponsored by Voice of Women, 1981.

- "The world's atomic clock is ticking on towards midnight . . . You have every reason to be frightened. This is the nuclear arms race." Opening words in NDP fund-raising appeal, signed by party leader Edward Broadbent, June 1984.

- "Every week, every month, it's worse. You can't escape the helpless knowledge that the arms race is constantly escalating and the possibility of nuclear war is growing." Opening words in fund-raising letter by James Stark, Operation Dismantle, March 1984.

- "Fear of annihilation lurks in the minds of everyone." Editorial, *TDN Networker*, June/July 1986.

The theme was reinforced by the theory that a nuclear war would be followed by a nuclear winter, during which survivors of the bombing would freeze to death, and by doomsday movies such as ABC TV's *The Day After*. Although the terrible consequences of nuclear war need no exaggeration, in their haste to propagate the nuclear winter theme, "committed" scientists and anti-nuclear activists went far beyond the evidence and distorted science into political propaganda. An unproven thesis was used to reinforce the theme of terror.[15]

Evidence that the theme was having some effect was provided by a 1982 Gallup poll that showed that one in three Metro Toronto residents under the age of thirty-five believed there would be a nuclear war in their lifetime, and 74 percent of those polled believed they would not survive such a war.[16] In June 1984 the *Globe and Mail* reported that "the threat of nuclear war is the greatest source of fear and anxiety among most Metro Toronto teenagers and it is affecting their plans for the future."[17] In December that year MP Douglas Roche told the same paper that the threat was "having a harmful psychological effect on children."[18] Writing in the same month in *Saturday Night*, David Macfarlane recalled that "sometime in the autumn of 1983 it came to be generally understood that the earth was about to be blown up."[19]

Considering the mechanical way that peace activists and organizations have used this theme of nuclear terror year after year, it is difficult to accept that much sincere belief lies behind it. Compared to crises in the 1960s, such as the Cuban missile deployment, East–West relations in the early 1980s were remarkably stable. To be sure, the Soviets were frustrated that the West seemed no longer to accept the inevitability of world Communist victory, that the American people had emerged from the Vietnam trauma determined to resist Soviet ambitions, and that Soviet deployment of SS-20 missiles in Europe had not gone unanswered. However, Moscow moderated her Third World interventionism in the face of opposition; there was no special threat of aggression in Europe; and by the mid-1980s Soviet leaders seemed anxious to mend fences with the West, diplomatically and in arms control. Almost the only destabilizing factors were the continuing Soviet arms build-up—conventional as well as nuclear, qualitative as well as quantitative—and the continued Soviet aggression in Afghanistan.

Yet people far beyond the peace movements *were* afraid that war was imminent, believing that harsh words and an absence of new treaties and summit meetings would somehow plunge the world into disaster. The media, responding to peace movement themes, and in many cases bitterly anti-Reagan, contributed to this irrationality.

It was pointed out in *Newsweek* in 1984 that the US nuclear inventory had been sharply reduced, containing eight thousand fewer warheads and 25 percent less megatonnage than in the 1960s.[20] No one, it seems, paid heed.

The US activist Michael Klare confessed in *The Nation*, June 29, 1985, that the peace movement in the United States had "relied too much on stimulating what has been called 'nukophobia,' fear of nuclear war." This statement confirmed the calculated nature of the theme of nuclear terror.

The intended "benefits" of deliberately stimulated terror, from the movement's point of view, are not difficult to identify. A public that really believed that the end was nigh would presumably respond to an invitation to help postpone the disaster and find ways of removing the dire threat. That task, logically, would take precedence over all else, justifying the abandonment of principle, friend, and allies. There would be no time to question or think. Indeed, logical thoughts might lead audiences to rational conclusions, such as support for deterrence, defence, and negotitions. That is why fear could never be allowed to degenerate into mere concern. It had to be intensified to the point of panic.

Such orchestrations of fear go back to the 1930s. In February 1933 Cyril Joad wrote in the *Oxford Mail* that the next war would see "men poisoning women with bacteria, choking men with gas; it will see children retching out their insides in the convulsion produced by the inhalation of mustard and chlorine . . . A thousand aeroplanes would bomb London to pieces in a few hours and plague and famine would complete the work done by bacteria and explosives."[21] In the late 1940s the atomic scientists depicted atomic war in equally chilling and doubtless more accurate terms. As already stated, there has never been the need to exaggerate the horror of nuclear war—nor does deceit enter into statements explaining such horrors.

Deception *does* become a factor if the imminence of war is deliberately exaggerated in order to generate fear that is then exploited for political reasons. The fraud impacts cruelly upon its victims, particularly the old, the gentle, and the young. A generation of Canadians has been burdened by anxiety to satisfy the needs of a manipulative minority.

The Canadian peace movement and its counterparts in the United States and Western Europe have tended to blame the war threat on the West—particularly on the United States. As Pierre Trudeau remarked of this phenomenon in an open letter dated May 10, 1983: "It somehow becomes possible to portray the Soviet Union not as the aggressor, but as the innocent target. This represents a curious amnesia and reversal of roles which the Soviet leaders are quick to exploit for their own purposes."[22] It is safe to assume that the mindset described by Trudeau owed more to fear and utopian liberalism—the vain hope that a bully will spare a victim if no resistance is offered—than to Communist sympathy. It is also safe to assume that, once placed in circulation, Communist propaganda made sure that the error was made myth.

A variation of this myth depicts the United States and the Soviet Union as two morally equivalent superpowers. Particularly popular in Western Europe, this formula enables fear of Russia to be redirected into anti-Americanism. It frees its adherents from having to take a stand between Western democracy and Eastern totalitarianism and permits a form of intellectual neutrality. Since the Soviets regard any form of neutrality as being merely a stepping stone between one camp and another—between capitalism and what they are pleased to call socialism—the moral equivalence notion is welcome. Nevertheless, because it offends Communist ideology, equivalence must always be attacked in their public statements.

While these delusions enabled the movement to place most of the blame for the risk of war onto the West and the United States, it was impossible to totally deny the fact that the nuclear warheads that might strike Canada in time of war would be Russian and not American. Too much deliberation along these lines could lead to undesirable consequences, however. Consequences such as straight thinking and a reassessment of the myths. The movement accordingly made nuclear weapons *themselves* into the enemy and the cause of war, excluding discussion of their source so far as possible. Here are some illustrations:

• "Our greatest enemy is not Russia. Our greatest enemy is nuclear war." Rev. Clarke MacDonald, United Church, on the occasion of the walk to Litton Industries, Good Friday, 1981 (quoting William Coffin).

• "Far from contributing to international security, the arms race has itself become a cause of global tension. The immediate cause of World War III may be the preparations for it." The Very Reverend Lois M. Wilson, in Ploughshares fund-raising letter, June 1984.

• "Public opinion in both East and West seems to be moving towards a common vision of the 'enemy' as nuclear war itself." Geoffrey Pearson, executive director, Canadian Institute for International Peace and Security, writing in the Summer 1986 issue of *Peace and Security*.

Provided it was understood that the danger to mankind came from nuclear weapons themselves, and not from the nation that aimed the weapons, it would follow that the removal of the threat and the removal of the weapons were synonymous. If it was additionally understood that the West and especially the United States bore prime responsibility for the threat of war, it would follow that the urgent need was for Western nuclear disarmament. Acceptance of this conclusion would clear the way for action by the peace movement against its own and its allies' governments.

Given the recent history of Western protest movements, a desire on the part of the peace movements to operate along the lines that have proved successful in respect of unsafe automobiles, outdated university administration, dangerous drugs and pesticides—not to mention the Vietnam War—would be very natural. A strategy that permitted the movement to turn inward against its own government might be more readily acceptable than one achieved through more rigorous mental effort.

Successful mobilization requires a vision of victory. And the

Canadian domestic political scene was a battleground on which a victory might indeed be won. Lingering doubts about Soviet disarmament could be dealt with by further bouts of wishful thinking. An article in the journal *Canadian Dimension* recommended that "we must nevertheless fight for policies and practices that will, here and now, enhance the possibility of peace. We cannot do that for Russia; the Russians must and will do that for themselves."[23]

The mindset that depicts the weapons as the enemy ignores completely the words of Salvador de Madariaga, in the 1930s chairman of the ill-fated League of Nations Disarmament Commission. In 1973 he wrote:

> The trouble with disarmament was (and still is) that the problem of war is tackled upside down and at the wrong end . . . Nations don't distrust each other because they are armed; they are armed because they distrust each other. And therefore to want disarmament before a minimum of common agreement on fundamentals is as absurd as to want people to go undressed in winter.[24]

It would seem that the Canadian peace movement, in common with its look-alikes in the West, relied on fear to overcome the logic of de Madariaga's remarks; people in a state of terror do not think clearly, and they reach out to any ray of hope. In addition, the movement developed another theme, one that attempted to deny the factor of mistrust.

The US journalist Midge Decter has written that understanding in general has become a kind of magical talisman in our society. "The thought that I might understand you perfectly and dislike you all the more for it is a shocking and alien one in a culture positively besotted with the idea that most human behaviour is either unintentional or uncontrollable." Such a liberal retreat from the recognition of evil, Kohn's "denial that the evil exists" degenerating into "an appeal to accept the evil and to condone the injustice," provides the Soviets with a ready audience for the propaganda theme we may call "See no evil, hear no evil, speak no evil," which denies the true nature of Soviet communism and sometimes constructs a false moral equivalence between the two superpowers.

Writing in *World Marxist Review* in July 1977, Ponomarev stated: "Our Party considers it important, therefore, to coordinate its work still more closely with the work of other fraternal parties in the ideological offensive against imperialism, in . . . revealing the advantages of the socialist system."[25] This was nothing new. The USSR, like most countries, had always tried to project a flattering self-portrait. It differed from the norm only in the lengths it was prepared to go in calculated deception. Fraternal parties had been doing their bit for years. For instance, in the May/June 1974 issue of *Communist Viewpoint*, Alfred Dewhurst had devoted a whole section to "The myth of Soviet aggression."

Once the strategy of the 1980s peace offensive had been drawn up, however, the key role of the "no evil" theme became apparent to Soviet psychological planners. At the 1980 Paris conference, it was accorded pride of place. Ponomarev:

> Anti-Sovietism and anti-communism have been turned into an instrument for whipping up the arms race, an instrument for putting pressure on public opinion in the West . . . For this reason, comrades, the vigorous exposure of the slander and misinformation spread by bourgeois propagandists and politicians is a serious political and ideological problem.[26]

And he added an important caveat, which may have sounded innocent enough to untrained ears, but which the Communists who composed his audience would have understood instinctively. "If it is not solved, we cannot count on success in the struggle to achieve lasting peace and curb the arms race." In other words, we cannot disarm the West and destroy democracy unless this deception succeeds.

When in 1983 Operation Dismantle's James Stark visited the USSR, he was quoted in the *Ottawa Citizen* as telling a Moscow news interviewer: "I do not consider myself one of those who say, 'But why don't the Russian peace supporters criticize their own government?' This is not necessary, because the Soviet government takes a stand for peace."[27] In the same year, in England, one of the Campaign for Nuclear Disarmament's vice-presidents, John Cox, wrote in *Communist Focus*: "I believe that our work in destroying the 'big lie' about the Soviet threat is one of the most important things we do."[28]

In propagating this theme, the Soviets have needed to conceal, deny, or justify the true facts about *nomenklatura* rule at home and in the overseas empire. Afghanistan has been a constant embarrassment, in spite of weak coverage in Western media. The shooting down of a Korean airliner in September 1983 threatened to let the cat out of the bag, so massive disinformation efforts were made to confuse world publics. Generally speaking, however, committed peace activists simply closed their minds to facts that threatened to upset their preconceptions, even to the point of militancy. Writing in *Saturday Night* thirteen months after the shootdown, Judith Timson described a scene in Toronto's Queen's Park during a peace rally. A mourner for one of the Canadian victims of the attack carried her picture "like a leper ringing his bell . . . through the masses of anti-nuke demonstrators until he was stopped by a young man who yelled, 'Why don't you go back across the street with the rest of the assholes?' "[29]

Both Stark and the foul-mouthed demonstrators were simply echoing the "no evil" theme that had been adopted uncritically by all segments of the peace movement. It grew out of some sloppy thinking that may or may not have been kept sloppy deliberately.

This theme varies in intensity between presenting the United States and the Soviet Union as two morally equivalent superpowers and depicting the former as the source of all evil with the latter as the benign, peace-loving world savior. At this outer limit, the theme spins off a reverse image—"Hate thy neighbor"—which focusses hatred against the United States and against all in Canada and the West who support NATO and defensive policies.

At one level, the "no evil" theme downgrades Soviet power, explaining and excusing every new development as being in reaction to some Western move, or being purely defensive. Soviet weapon systems are portrayed as few in number, lacking in capability, and inadequate for offensive purposes. Anyway, it is said that Russian soldiers are always drunk.

At a deeper, more political level, the theme tries to re-educate Western publics by depicting the USSR as being quasi-democratic, seeking to live peacefully with neighbors, anxious to lessen international tensions, and concerned to promote "socialist justice" in the Third World. The two strands are pulled together by fables about World War II. These allege that the USSR lost 20 million in that conflict and is therefore not only determined to avoid another world war but also entitled to a measure of national security far in excess of other states. Deterrent policy, so dangerous in the West, is apparently to be thoroughly approved of in the East. Nothing is said about the collapse of the Red Army under the Nazi onslaught and the frightful vengeance of the party against those Russians who did not wish to fight for their Communist oppressors. Stalin counted the war dead at seven million, so the remaining 13 million must presumably have been murdered or invented by the party.[30]

A 1982 Friends Service Committee report on a visit to England by the official Soviet Peace Committee, composed of senior party officials and propagandists, described the responsibility laid on this Quaker group: "We are called upon to initiate radical change in the minds of ordinary people as regards their attitudes to the Soviet Union and the stereo-typing of its leaders as aggressors, ruthless cruel and cunning, seeking world domination at all times."[31]

The Ploughshares Monitor of December 1981 advised that "survival of the human race depends on a total shift in thinking about nations as friends or enemies . . . Time is running out. New creative concepts of international understanding must replace outmoded, inflexible perceptions." In short, empirical enquiry must be abandoned in favor of ideological conformity. New Democratic parliamentarian Andrew Brewin wrote in the *Globe and Mail* in 1982:

> Although fear and suspicion of the Soviet Union was justified in the past, there is evidence that recent attitudes in the Soviet Union are more conducive to the development of peace and disarmament . . . Many students of the Soviet attitude are increasingly discounting exaggerated fears of Soviet aggression outside the Soviet sphere of interest.[32]

Brewin's closing qualifying phrase was presumably intended to excuse the Afghan atrocities. By the same technique, Soviet genocide in, say, Newfoundland, could be justified, since once the bear has a new victim in its hug, it too is within "the Soviet sphere of interest."

Leonard Johnson asserted:

> Yes, I think you can trust the Russians, but what you have to do is to look for their interests . . . [Soviet generals are] not concerned about fighting an offensive campaign that will carry them to the English Channel; what they're concerned about is fighting a defensive campaign against us.[33]

Remarkably, considering his former position as commandant of the National Defence College, Johnson had failed to appreciate that the Soviet notion of a defensive strategy in Europe does indeed carry their tanks to the English Channel. The maps used in their senior staff exercises show their divisions advancing westward across the Weser toward the Rhine, and their concept of a "defensive" battle is one started by them and fought entirely on NATO territory.

Mr. Geoffrey Pearson, executive director of the Canadian Institute for International Peace and Security, had previously been our ambassador in Moscow. In March 1986 he lent his considerable authority to the "no evil" theme. Writing the first of his new institute's *Points of View* papers, Pearson argued that "the revolution of 1917 did not, as we often assume, imprison the Russian people in a system of values repugnant to them." He went on to question whether the USSR was still totalitarian and complained that "the overwhelming Western media and political attention to 'dissent' in the USSR and to tales of life in the camps recounted by emigré writers, obscures, if it does not stifle, investigation, for example, of popular attitudes to the regime, of elite satisfactions, and the role of competing interest groups."[34]

One wonders how Canadian audiences might have reacted to papers by former ambassadors to Chile, South Africa, and South Korea that argued that local populations, having experienced nothing better, did not find their regimes repugnant, and that urged our media to focus on "elite satisfactions."

To audiences persuaded that weapons represent a mortal threat to mankind, the provision of arms at the expense of development aid is an obvious affront. Originated in the churches and the United Nations disarmament agencies, this theme was quickly adopted by the World Peace Council's "Programme of Action" and has spread throughout the movement. UNICEF's 1981 report claimed that, every minute of every day, $1,500,000 was spent worldwide on military forces and equipment, and in the same minute, twenty-seven children died for lack of food and vaccines. In Canada, Ernie Regehr and Mel Watkins joined forces to write a chapter on the theme, stressing both the waste and the additional social, economic, and moral costs.[35] In his book *Misguided Missiles*, Canadian writer Simon Rosenblum repeated the statistics and added the opinion that "military spending by northern countries obviously contributes to global insecurity. But the diversion of resources from human needs to the instruments of war is in itself a cause of conflict."[36]

On the face of it, military spending is indeed an appalling waste. However, taken out of context by a lobby convinced that crime did not exist, the costs of maintaining police forces throughout the world could also be made to appear obscene.

One must count the likely cost of abandoning law and order before condemning the price of its maintenance, both in the domestic and international arenas. Rosenblum was honest enough to admit that, of the world's 1985 military spending of $1 trillion, only one-fifth (a hefty $200 billion) was spent on nuclear arms and delivery systems. All analysts agree that nuclear arms are relatively cheap; that any serious attempt by NATO to match the Soviet challenge at the conventional level would multiply costs many times. Moreover, whatever the facts within the Third World, there is no special linkage between Western military spending and Third World hardship. Development assistance can be provided if the political will to do so exists. If savings are required, these could equally well come from tobacco, alcohol, cosmetics, drugs, and rock music. Moreover, the theme neglects altogether the Soviet role in the arms trade.

Soviet arms are used throughout the Third World by Marxist revolutionaries and throughout the First World by terrorists, and the West's exports of arms to governments are now outstripped by the East's. Half the tanks in Africa and Asia and nearly half the tanks in Latin America and the Middle East have been supplied by the USSR. Nearly 60 percent of the world's supersonic combat aircraft come from the same source.[37]

The "hate thy neighbor" theme is muted in Canada, compared to its blatant expression in Western Europe. It nonetheless finds sponsors in the "new nationalism" as well as communism. Besides its base in the far left, the theme is propagated by Canadian residents who were once US citizens but who came north to avoid the Vietnam War. The left hates the United States and the Canadian defence establishment for ideological reasons. Fugitives must invariably live out their exiles justifying their flight. For war-avoiders (whether draft-dodgers or not), justification takes the form of demonology. For if the United States is less than totally evil, their own past act is open to question.

Nevertheless, at a low-key level, parts of the Canadian media maintain constant carping criticism of all things defensive and of US policies in particular. Anyone depending on these sources for information might easily conclude that US defence preparedness, often referred to as preparations for nuclear war, and the United States' refusal to surrender—described as political intransigence—were the major causes of world tensions. From time to time the theme overflows into Canada. A union-sponsored Quebec booklet, One F-18 for Peace, attacks provincial arms producers. Another Quebec book, Notre Défense et nous, holds the Canadian military up to ridicule as a menace to peace. Although softly stated in the documents quoted, the message nevertheless undermines national cohesion and defence.

A more radical proposal, published in 1986, suggested that:

> The actions of the movement must also be destabilizing. In practice this implies that state and corporate business cannot be carried out as usual. The movement must introduce an element of non-violent uncertainty into daily life. This not only includes the limited and largely symbolic forms of civil disobedience, such as occurred at Litton Industries, but also extends to wider measures, including boycotts, strikes, and tax resistance, which disrupts the normal functioning of corporations and the state.[38]

A much more extreme message had been used by the Direct Action terrorists to justify their bombing of Litton Industries. The group's communiqué explained: "There is every reason imaginable to tear down the systems and the makers of nuclear war for the survival of all life on earth, for all peoples' hopes and visions."[39]

The "hate thy neighbor" theme had been given a spectacular launching by the indefatigable Ponomarev at the Sofia gathering of professional fellow travellers and congenital stooges. His dual role as co-ordinator of international revolution and terrorism —the "just wars" of Marx and Lenin—and high priest of "peace" would have led him quite naturally to the position he adopted. Lenin had said that "we can't expect to get anywhere unless we resort to terrorism."[40] Ponomarev wrote an article in *Kommunist* in 1971 in which he expressed fairly open sympathy for "radical" left-wing terrorist groups. He placed organizations like the IRA in the "national liberation movement" category and, as such, absolved them from being "terrorist" at all.[41] At Sofia, he blended the themes of terror and peace thus: "It is now more than ever essential to foster among the mass of the people a sense of irreconcilable opposition, a sense of anger and wrath if you like, to the preparations for nuclear war."[42] He then defined the enemy —"professional militarists," "monopolists," and of course the "military-industrial complex," the Pentagon, CIA, bankers, transnational corporations, all working like mad to start a nuclear war—and reminded his audience of the fate of war criminals after World War II. Then he issued orders, in their usual disguised form:

> It would be a good thing to remind the militarists and the tycoons of the war-industrial complex about this, and to tell them in their face: you bear the responsibility before humankind . . . The wrath of the peoples should already now be turned against those who are cashing in on the arms race. They should be continuously reminded of the fate that befell the nazi war criminals who had started World War II.[43]

When President Reagan described the Soviet Union as the "evil empire," the wails of protest could be heard from Rosedale to Ulan Bator. When Ponomarev used the indicative imperative formulation to advocate terrorism within Western societies, it went unprotested by his audience, unreported by our media, and unremarked by Western governments.

Whether or not Canada's Direct Action terrorists committed their crime at the Litton plant in compliance with Ponomarev's command, we do not know. We do know, however, that in spite of the essentially nonviolent character of most of Canada's and some of Western Europe's peace movements, Ponomarev's message has taken hold. *Die Tageszeitung*, a left-wing West Berlin paper, reported in July 1982 that Colonel Khadafy, the Libyan leader, had offered to help the Green Party close US military bases in Western Europe by "military effort." "Fedayeen groups will be founded again in order to reach this goal." Also present at the meeting with Khadafy were "peace" representatives from Austria, Italy, and Britain.[44] In Britain the "Greenham Common women" obeyed the World Peace Council's order for direct action against US missile bases. It has been alleged in British newspapers that the women harbored Soviet agents. Whatever the truth of this, the protesters undoubtedly provided the Soviets with an advance base in close proximity to an important NATO asset.

The Soviets had to wait until the end of 1984 before seeing real results from the terror instructions issued on their behalf by Ponomarev in Sofia. Terrorism, even more than propaganda, requires organization, and organizing new, efficient secret cells in the Western European terror network took time. What emerged was Euro-terrorism, an alliance of far-left radical groups dedicated to attacking NATO targets exactly as described by Ponomarev. Three groups—France's Direct Action, West Germany's Red Army Faction, and Belgium's Fighting Communist Cells—have set the pace with assassinations of officers, industrialists, and US servicemen, and bomb attacks on any targets which are remotely connected to Western defence. Although small in numbers and of limited potential, they do represent the vanguard of the Soviet army. Also engaged in the "peace" crusade are Holland's Action Group Against Nuclear War, Italy's Red Brigades, Portugal's FP-25, and smaller groups in Greece and Spain.[45]

In an article in *Conflict Quarterly* in the fall of 1985, Abraham Miller wrote:

By attacking NATO, this new generation . . . has found a symbolic issue that has the potential to attract a number of sympathizers among the current generation of alienated youth in Europe. In one tactical leap terrorism in Western Europe has gone from the periphery of the youth movement to merge ideologically with a radical politics which perceives NATO and the basing of nuclear weapons on the soil of Western Europe as the most pressing issues of the day.[46]

The links between Euro-terrorism and international terrorists generally ensure support for Arab and Iranian groups, and vice versa. Armed by the Soviets, trained by the Iranians or Syrians, and in many cases indirectly controlled by the KGB, Middle Eastern terrorists spread the anti-NATO campaign across a wider battlefield.

Considering what had happened in Europe, it was disturbing to read in the *Bulletin of the Atomic Scientists* that in the opinion of two peace activists, Peter M. Sandman and JoAnn M. Valenti, anger "at those responsible for the arms race" frees energy for action that is otherwise bound up in fear, guilt, and depression. "Those who threaten the world's survival must be identified, and one must be willing to feel the surge of anger their behaviour merits." The writers quote Joel Kovel, who believes that "working against one's own terror, against nuclear war, and against the state are ultimately the same work." Sandman and Valenti consider that nothing can better symbolize anger than the powerful bolt-cutters with which the Greenham Common women routinely destroy the fence surrounding the cruise missile site.[47]

Obviously, Sandman and Valenti were not advocating murder. Nevertheless, in July 1986 Prof. Karl-Heinz Beckurts and his driver died when a powerful remotely controlled bomb exploded beneath his car near Munich. In 1985 the German Communist youth newspaper, *Spartacus*, had named Beckurts as a member of a Siemens SDI research group. Later the same month bombs were exploded at the Fraunhofer Institute and the Dornier Company, also engaged in defence research. Responsibility for all three attacks was claimed by the Red Army Faction in a communiqué that urged radicals to "organize the revolutionary front in Western Europe! Attack the present projects of the political, economic and military formation of the imperialist system." Between Beckurts's death and April 1987, eleven more Western European scientists and officials engaged in defence

research were murdered, or died or disappeared in mysterious circumstances.[48] Small wonder that in that same year Soviet social
scientists should be predicting that, in a future war, "inside the
capitalist and developing countries there will be forces which
will fight against their own government."[49]

The concept of "militarism" is applied by Moscow and Western
peace activists only to the West, in keeping with the theory that
the West bears sole responsibility for the arms race and for
beggaring the developing nations. A document issued by the
United Church of Canada in 1982 argued that "militarism in our
world takes many forms, but some are particularly important to
Canadians, in view of the role Canada plays in relation to the
superpowers. The militarism of the 1980s involves not just an
arms race but a race for 'better' weapons that . . . enhance a nation's ability to out-perform any enemy." The Canadian Catholic
Organization for Development and Peace issued a special eight-
page *Position Paper on Militarization*, which described a "poverty-
militarization-repression-poverty" cycle.

The Peace Research Institute—Dundas' 458-page handbook,
How We Work for Peace, might better have been called *One
Thousand and One Ways to Disarm Canada*. It contains a section
on "Actively opposing militarism," which advocates forty methods of opposing defence, including spying on universities, with-
holding taxes, civil disobedience, and the denigration of
Canada's armed forces.[50] The book was partly funded by the
Canadian Institute for International Peace and Security, out of
tax dollars.

The militarism concept goes back to 1907, when Karl Liebknecht published his *Militarism and Anti-Militarism* in
Germany.[51] The author's father had been a friend of Marx and
Engels, and he followed in his father's footsteps as a social
revolutionary.

In his book, Liebknecht describes the Germany of Wilhelm
II, the post-Bismarck era, the epoch of German imperialism,
and preparations for the Great War. It was the view of some

political thinkers of the time that Germany's only means of securing a position as a great world power was by force. Efforts were made to popularize such views by means of such organizations as the Pan German League, the Colonial Society, the Military League, and the Navy League. Propaganda for war, or at least for policies that accepted war as a necessary or even desirable corollary, was as widespread in the Germany of 1907 as propaganda for peace-at-any-price in West Germany today. Militarism was apparent in the creed of violence, the organizations that spread the creed, the German officer corps, the nobility, and the reverence in which the army and navy were held by a disciplined society.

Liebknecht saw militarism as "the strongest, most concentrated and exclusive expression of the national, cultural and class instinct for self-preservation, the most elementary of all instincts." By drawing on the Marxist notions of class warfare and imperialism, the author had no difficulty identifying "capitalist militarism" as the tool of the ruling class for external aggression and internal repression. The evil consequences included military influence or control over politics, enormous costs and the impoverishment of social programs, obligatory military service, rigidity in modes of thought—even to the detriment of military efficiency—and an autonomous threat to world peace. In contrast, Liebknecht foresaw a Communist world free of class antagonisms from which militarism would be banished.

Poor Liebknecht! Had he lived to see "socialism" in action he would have observed in Russia under the *nomenklatura* precisely what he had abhorred in imperial Germany: the strongest, most concentrated and exclusive expression of the national, cultural, and class instinct for self-preservation. To be sure, he would have found lingering traces of militarism in the Western democracies of the 1980s and some gross expressions in the Third World. As it was, he was spared this disillusionment. By 1918, along with Rosa Luxemburg, Clara Zetkin, and Franz Mehring, he had formed the Spartacus League, which became the core of the German Communist Party. In January 1919, Liebknecht and Luxemburg were killed by the police.

The peace movement's application of the term *militarism* to Canadian and other Western efforts at self-defence is a remarkable exercise in semantic deception. Third World militarism is also blamed on the West, although the Marxist Third World sets the pace in this respect. Speaking in Helsinki in 1978, Boris Ponomarev advised: "Combatting militarism is one of the finest traditions of the international labour movement,"[52] and hardly a speech or article emanating from the International Department fails to use the word.

These themes of "peace" propaganda provided the mobilizing impetus of fear and then used that emotion to accomplish a brilliant redefinition of the enemy. At least for those who accepted the peace movement's line, the threat to Canada and the West was no longer a political one, of armed totalitarianism. The threat now was nuclear war. Partly because the human mind cannot accommodate two overwhelming fears at the same time, and partly through the skilful denial of the Soviet threat, this audience came to see nuclear weapons as the enemy. And in the absence of a credible Soviet threat, obviously it was in the West's nuclear weapons, the West's deterrent strategy, the West's militarism, and the West's crazy determination to defend itself that the enemy was to be found.

CHAPTER VIII

OPTING OUT

The redefinition of the enemy permits the development of subsidiary themes, such as the arms race, a term used to describe any Western efforts to keep pace with Soviet weapon development and production, and the notion that these same efforts are part of a suicidal and in any case doomed US plan to regain strategic superiority. More importantly, the generation of fearful uncertainty undermines confidence in existing and successful security arrangements and legitimizes otherwise unconvincing arguments against deterrence policy and Canada's alliances.

Within a movement that sees the West as its own worst enemy, the strategy of deterrence obviously has no merit. In December 1980, James Stark was quoted in *Maclean's* magazine as saying that "the moment deterrence fails, we are left with global assured destruction."[1] Clarke MacDonald, at the Litton plant, asked: "Why do we pursue this race to the brink? Why are we obsessed with this suicidal tendency? It is because of the seduction of the military industrial complex."[2] In one of his films the distinguished print journalist Gwynne Dyer ridiculed nuclear deterrence in a labored story about elephants.

But none of the critics of deterrence offers alternative policies. So far as they are concerned, the West has no right to defend itself, because the risks are too great. Therefore, even a policy that has kept the world free of nuclear war for forty years should be abolished. Obsessed with self-inflicted horrors, they behave like some shipwreck survivor who, overwhelmed by the terror of his experience, jumps overboard rather than face the possibility that the lifeboat, too, will sink.

By the same distorted logic, the peace lobby embraced the theory that Canada's membership in military alliances—NATO and NORAD—was also a potential cause of war. The Canadian government's decision to permit the flight-testing of unarmed US cruise missiles over Canadian territory stimulated this no-tion, and opposition to the tests was for several years a major theme of peace propaganda.

The theme was not finely focussed, however, until the Na-tional Film Board made certain propaganda films. These were the work of Gwynne Dyer and film board producer Tina Viljoen, who had earlier co-operated in the making of the seven-part series, "War." The first piece was a three-part television "documentary," "Defence of Canada," which favored Canadian neutrality along Finnish lines. The second was a one-shot called "Harder Than It Looks."

Dyer's "argument" was effective only to audiences devoid of knowledge and understanding of twentieth-century history. Since educational authorities and professionals have succeeded in helping several generations of Canadians achieve this vul-nerable condition, Dyer's misleading messages may well have been accepted. For anyone with minimal knowledge of the facts, however, his argument was similar in intellectual quality to the notion that spare tires cause flats. Interviewed by Shirley Far-linger for the June/July 1986 edition of *Peace Magazine*, Dyer asserted: "If we just walked out of NATO and NORAD this could be a catalyst for dissolving the alliances; other nations might follow [they might indeed]. Nobody has a stronger reason than Canada for doing this." Farlinger reviewed the last of these films thus: "In just 28 minutes this National Film Board documentary wraps up the argument that alliances are dangerous and Canada might better look at ways of keeping the superpower blocs apart."[3]

In his interview, Dyer was echoing the words of NDP parlia-mentarian Andrew Brewin, who had written in his 1982 article that "we [Canada] are no longer served by military alliances . . . We cannot afford to rely on nuclear weapons to prevent aggres-sion."[4] Retired major-general Leonard Johnson shares these views. Having joined Generals for Peace and Disarmament on leaving the armed forces in 1984, Johnson has campaigned for Canadian neutrality, going so far as to recommend a constitutional amendment that would "prohibit Canadian forces from fighting in foreign wars."[5] By "foreign wars" Johnson presumably means fighting Canada's wars on foreign soil; his recipe encourages a "fortress Canada" form of isolationism. Thus Canada would be back to attempting the impossible: the unilateral defence of an enormous land mass with a relatively tiny population. However, this does not seem to concern the proponents of neutrality. Ours is not to be the fully armed go-it-alone resistance of a Switzerland or a Sweden, but rather the virtually defenceless "neutrality" of a Mongolia, a Lithuania, or a Tibet. Canadians are promised peace and happiness only if they do not declare their readiness for timely action.

Gwynne Dyer continues his anti-defence propaganda through his column as a print journalist. In all his films he consistently refuses to acknowledge the significance of ideology and psychological warfare in Soviet strategy, and he fails to address the revolutionary nature of that strategy.

Another campaign designed to make Canada a neutral country and to promote a defeatist mindset involves the creation of symbolic nuclear weapons-free zones. Although there is some pressure at the federal level—for zones in the Arctic, and the like—the main thrust of this campaign has targeted municipalities and provinces. Project Ploughshares has been a moving force at the local level, the Canadian Council of Churches has given its blessing, and the theme has been picked up by the entire movement. No less a figure than Iona Campagnolo, signing as "Former President of the Liberal Party of Canada," endorsed a nationwide campaign to make the whole country a nuclear-free zone.[6]

Canada's decision in the aftermath of World War II not to produce her own nuclear weapons was militarily sensible, in that the economics of scale favored concentration of such effort in the major industrialized nations of the West. It was also moral, because it discouraged proliferation—the acquisition of such weapons by more and more countries. Canada's later decision to support the policy of nuclear deterrence by joining NATO and NORAD was also moral because this policy offered the best chance of preserving peace with freedom. There was no contradiction between these two moral decisions.

As a non-nuclear nation in nuclear alliances, Canada was free to choose whether or not to permit US nuclear weapons on her soil. Neither the 1963 decision to allow such deployment nor the later decision not to host the weapons had any moral quality. These were instrumental decisions by which Canada, in her own way, continued to support the policy of nuclear deterrence. But few Canadian politicians have resisted the temptation to bestow a false morality on their refusal. In this way they opened a door through which peace activists have driven a horse and cart.

The August/September 1986 edition of *Peace Magazine* republished a map and listing provided by Ploughshares supposedly depicting nuclear support facilities in Canada. Much of this was extravagant demonology, reinforcing the "hate thy neighbor" theme. However, the underlying "logic" was that Canada's supposed moral decision not to accept US nuclear weapons on her soil radiates a moral rainbow across the country. The spectrum extends from pea-shooters to brass bands, which might be used, respectively, to protect or to entertain the crews of some US nuclear launcher at some undisclosed place and time.

Because the idea has been put about that banning nuclear weapons from Canadian soil—all the while supporting and benefitting from nuclear deterrence—was somehow moral, the peace movement has been able to argue that the same morality requires that every conceivable airfield, barrack building, radio station, and port, any of which might be used in support of nuclear deterrence, be declared "immoral" and abolished. Journalist Gordon Barthos converted the Ploughshares chart to pop art and published a full-page article about it in the *Toronto Star*. "Canadians who thought our nuclear role evaporated in July 1984 when the Trudeau government shipped our last Genie nuclear-tipped missiles back to the United States," he wrote, "may be surprised to see how much nuclear-related military activity goes on here."[7]

The nuclear-free zone concept is simply an appeal for Canadian neutrality deceptively wrapped. It is a useful staging post for public opinion. On superficial inspection, the proposal seems to offer improved security without added cost. In reality, the small print suggested by Project Ploughshares, for instance, stipulates that a nuclear-free Canada would bar allied airplanes and ships from territorial airspace and waters respectively, even in times of crisis, and eject all "support systems for nuclear weapons" from Canadian soil—which would mean all military communications and early-warning devices connected to allied networks. Neither condition would likely be considered compatible with continued membership of NATO and NORAD. An editorial endorsement of the idea in *The Canadian Forum*, August/September 1985, implied that the authors of the scheme were under no illusions: "The concept of a nuclear-free country . . . would mean an end to the defence-sharing agreement with the US; it would mean an end to participation in NORAD."

There is in fact no historical evidence that alliances cause wars and a great deal of evidence that NATO and NORAD—each with Canada as a member—have helped to keep the peace. For the church and mainstream parts of the peace movement, the appeal for neutrality is presumably attractive because defence of any sort is considered dangerous and wrong. Free zones and neutrality are seen as convenient ways of opting out. For the Communist element, however, these themes have operational value.

Strictly speaking, Marxist-Leninist ideology has no time for neutrality. In the class struggle one has either to be for the party or against it. However, as a tactical means of shifting the correlation of forces in communism's favor, the removal of any member nation from the bloc opposing Soviet expansionism into a non-aligned or other neutral position is clearly advantageous. Once opposing forces have been destroyed altogether, the so-called neutrals can all be scooped into the Communist bucket.[8]

The nuclear weapons-free zone concept provides Moscow

with one means of neutralizing nations, zones, or areas that are or might become parts of the opposing forces. Generally speaking, all Soviet proposals for such zones, from their beginning in 1956, are aimed at neutralizing non-Communist countries or territory, although sometimes a strip of Warsaw Pact real estate that is not crucial to the bloc will be offered to match demands for the removal of Western weapons from territory vital to NATO, such as in central Europe. But Soviet demands for a Nordic zone have included no concessions. Finland and Sweden, already neutral, and Norway and Denmark, already non-nuclear countries where governments have forbidden the peace-time positioning of nuclear weapons, and the seas around them would constitute the zone. The most concentrated forward military deployment area in the world, bristling with every sort of nuclear weapon—the Soviet base on the Nordic Kola Peninsula—would be excluded from the zone. Mikhail Gorbachev's more recent proposal for a "zone of peace" in the Arctic is similarly one-sided.[9]

Writing in *Communist Viewpoint* in October 1982, Nicholas Prychodko claimed that the demand that Canada be declared a nuclear weapons-free zone was first expressed by the Communist Party of Canada in its 1971 program. The nuclear free zone or "zone of peace" is therefore a fraud and another Trojan horse; the only beneficiary would be Moscow. In his 1974 article in *Communist Viewpoint*, Alfred Dewhurst asserted that the "decisive element for an independent foreign policy is for Canada to withdraw from NATO and NORAD." As a Communist, Dewhurst presumably knew that Canadian "independence" was not an acceptable condition for his Moscow thought-conditioners. In due course our country would be required to share the fate of Poland and Latvia, Afghanistan and Cambodia. For the time being, however, the immediate task was to turn Canada neutral and weaken the West.

With hindsight, it is reasonable to guess that Soviet planners calculated that, however effective the campaign against the deployment of cruise and Pershing II missiles might be in Europe, it would not sell in North America. A parallel issue was needed that might galvanize North Americans into anti-defence action. Moreover, it may have been evident to the International Department that North Americans were not so far down the defeatist road that appeals for blatantly one-sided disarmament could succeed.

"The freeze" provided another halfway house. It was a campaign designed to appear multilateral in its impact, although the situation it sought to make permanent was one of Soviet advantage. Additionally, talk of the freeze being verifiable was deceptive in the extreme. Had such an agreement ever been struck, the Western peace movement would doubtless have dutifully monitored Western compliance, as ordered by Ponomarev, while the Soviets would have frustrated verification on their side. Win or lose, a freeze campaign was greatly to Soviet advantage, since it stimulated fear and focussed North American public attention on the weapons as the threat. Questions of political system and trust were effectively outlawed from the debate.

In Canada the freeze was advocated by the Canadian church leaders in their December 1982 statement to Prime Minister Trudeau. The Toronto Association for Peace pressed the idea on Prime Minister Brian Mulroney in a letter dated October 4, 1984. The Canadian Union of Public Employees endorsed it in their journal, *The Facts*, in May 1984. Operation Dismantle embraced the freeze. While lying in second place to the neutralizing of Canada through such stages as the nuclear free zones and "doing a Finland," the freeze provided a useful tool for drawing into the peace movement individuals interested in arms control but opposed to surrender. It is listed as one of the basic objectives of the Canadian Peace Alliance.

Rael Jean and Erich Isaac analyzed the origins of the freeze movement in *The American Spectator*, June 1982. Quoting mainly peace movement sources, they established that the proposal first surfaced in the United States at the American Friends Service Committee, summer 1979. Sidney Lens is quoted as naming Terry Province and Randall Forsberg as key initiators. Province was a sponsor of the US Peace Council, the World Peace Council affiliate. He was also disarmament director for the Friends and head of the Movement for Survival International Task Force.[10]

The Soviets made small effort to conceal their sponsorship. In August 1981 the Friends organized a march by some four hundred people from Washington, DC, to Moscow, Vermont, to hear a special guest speaker, agent Kapralov. The KGB officer stayed close to the freeze movement throughout its development. Encouragement was also given by Georgi Arbatov, head of the International Department's Institute for the US and Canada, a deception and intelligence-gathering establishment jointly staffed by the International Department, the KGB, and military intelligence—the GRU. The World Peace Council and the Moscow front, the Christian Peace Conference, pushed the proposal hard. Michael Myerson, of the US Peace Council, made the freeze into the centrepiece of his propaganda, presumably because it sounded so apolitical and harmless.[11]

The International Department's ability to influence the agenda in the US Congress was established beyond reasonable doubt in spring 1982. It was then that senators Edward Kennedy and Mark Hatfield sponsored a joint resolution calling for a nuclear freeze. Congressional attention to the issue had been preceded by intense grassroots politicking. For example, in March of 1982, 177 towns in New England voted in favor of a nuclear freeze resolution. The Soviets and their Western allies had discovered the advantages of misusing lower levels of government and community groups to popularize anti-defence issues, making the issues into tempting balls that ambitious politicians at the federal level might pick up and run with. At the same time, such community action had its effect on the general climate of opinion; it dictated what could and could not be said publicly without risk of social isolation.

Soviet reports of the freeze movement indicated approval of the way things were going. On March 10, 1982, *Pravda* quoted one of Kapralov's assistants, A. Tolkunov, to the effect that he had manipulated the movement and stage-managed the adoption of freeze resolutions by the state legislature in New York, Massachusetts, Connecticut, and Wisconsin. The October issue of the Moscow journal *International Life* claimed that the short-term goal of the movement was to topple the Reagan Administration and to have Walter Mondale, Alan Cranston, Gary Hart, or some other freeze supporter elected president. *Pravda* for November 11 expressed satisfaction with the results of the 1982 congressional elections. The paper noted that some additional Democrats with anti-defence credentials had been elected, and in Washington, DC, Minnesota, Michigan, and elsewhere Communists had gathered more than their traditional meagre votes by using the freeze issue. Earlier, on August 14, *Pravda* had quoted a leading US freeze advocate, Ms. D. Cooper, national co-ordinator for Mobilization for Survival, as saying, "We are thankful to the Soviet Union for its continuing persistent efforts to stop the mad nuclear arms race."

The World Peace Council listed the freeze as an important objective in its 1983 "Programme of Action" and went on to popularize the idea internationally. One of its many lavishly funded publications, *Disarmament Forum*, reported in June 1984 that five heads of state, Indira Gandhi, Miguel de la Madrid, Julius Nyerere, Olof Palme, and Raul Alfonsin, had issued a joint statement promoting the plan.

While these neutrality ploys may be perceived by most peace movement activists as a means of opting Canada out of the arms race, it is possible to see that for some, and increasingly for the movement's leadership, the Soviet idea that neutrality is merely a stepping stone between one camp and the other is being proven correct. The final theme of the movement to be considered here is the justification of war, which on the face of it is inconsistent. For the Communist element this theme merges the "peace is victory" formula with the worldwide revolution. Obviously, all who are fighting for "peace" deserve to be supported, and all the World Peace Council's publications indicate which violent movements are to be assisted in the name of "peace."

The Canadian mainstream is confused and divided on this issue, but to a remarkable extent groups go along with the Communist line while finding non-Communist rationalizations. The latter are sometimes provided by the churches, in the form of liberation theology, which has simply absorbed Communist dogma and served it up in clerical grey garb. The churches have even adopted the 1930s notion of socialist justice, disguising it ever so slightly in the form "social justice." Has a part of Christianity learned in this way to serve the cause of scientific atheism?[12]

CHAPTER IX

AN IDEOLOGY OF PEACE

Until 1987, there had been no Canadian white paper on defence since 1971. Because Canadian governments had failed to explain and justify their defence policies for so many years, it was hardly surprising that the general public questioned these policies when confronted with the spectre of nuclear war in the early 1980s. Regardless of whether the spectre was real or imagined, a free-ranging debate was overdue. Peace activists might have made a valuable contribution to that debate, had they retained their independence of thought and their commitment to rationality. Instead, it seems they fell victim to their own mobilization propaganda, which developed into a fully fledged "ideology of peace." Trapped within this culture, the peace movement's arguments reflected predetermined conclusions rather than rational consideration. The movement's political potential was enhanced; its contribution to the debate was made worthless.

The US scholar David Easton has written that ideologies are:

articulated sets of ideals, ends, and purposes, which help members of the system to interpret the past, explain the present, and offer a vision of the future. Thereby they describe the aims for which some members believe political power ought to be used and its limits. They may be deceptive myths about political life; they may be realistic appraisals and sincere aspirations. But they have the potential because they are articulated as a set of ethically infused ideals, to capture the imagination. From a manipulative or instrumental point of view they may be interpreted as categories of thought to corral the energies of men; from an expressive point of view we may see them as ideals capable of rousing and inspiring men to action.[1]

If it is reasonable to suppose that the many diverse elements composing the Canadian peace movement share three rather hazy beliefs, these then must inevitably form the core of any peace ideology. These beliefs are: a desire to promote "peace," being the good cause; opposition to "war," seen as the evil enemy; and some measure of confidence that collective actions by the movement can lead to the triumph of good over evil —belief in victory. As noted previously, all ideologies are founded upon similar trinities, which set the goal, define the enemy, help create a sense of identity, and establish confidence.

The peace ideology that emerged in the early 1980s catered to two needs. For the movement, it provided moral certainty and a sense of righteous mission. It created a "peace culture" that fitted Jacques Ellul's description: "deadly serious, heavy, grim, accusatory, aggressive, armor-clad in a 'good conscience' . . . The disguise guarantees the legitimacy of the judgement these people pass on others."[2]

For the wider Canadian audience the ideology and its propaganda would outflank rationality, forcing emotional responses to issues and situations presented out of context. Cumulatively, shocks to the emotions would disorient, opening the way to acceptance of the "peace culture." By a combination of propaganda and lobbying, a climate of opinion could be created in which it would be impossible for any public figure to withstand the culture. In a country such as Canada where serious foreign affairs and defence issues rate very low against domestic items in any election, politicians might feel obliged to subscribe to the peace ideology—which in spite of its international implications has an essentially domestic texture—to gain votes from a confused electorate and to curry favor with a movement that possessed the power to damage any candidate daring to oppose its views.

Thus the core of a peace ideology came into existence. An ill-defined "peace" unlinked in most minds to human rights would prevail over a rather narrowly defined "war," meaning nuclear weapons in the hands of the West. "Good" would prevail over "evil" because the domestic battleground was familiar and the battle-drills well tested.

Out of a series of interlocking themes, a disoriented and frightened Canadian public is evidently supposed to arrive at a sequence of conclusions. Reduced to bare essentials these are:

• Nuclear war is imminent and will inevitably lead to the end of civilization and possibly the obliteration of the human race.

• The threat does not originate in the Soviet Union, but in our measures to protect ourselves against an imagined threat.

• Therefore, regardless of other considerations, the West must get rid of all nuclear weapons, because these are the real danger.

• Any failure on the part of the West to heed this advice makes our governments culpable for the war danger.

• All defensive measures by the West, including alliances and deterrent policy, collectively known as the arms race, are therefore illegitimate, provocative, destabilizing, and, indeed, merely "preparations for nuclear war."

• Canada should opt out of such alliances, the arms race, and any defence or resistance to the imagined Soviet threat by seeking "neutrality" and by abandoning the concept of peace with freedom as altogether too dangerous.

For the most part, these ideas have been displayed quite openly by the movement, although wrapped in glittering packages. The exception has been the last conclusion—that peace with freedom is too dangerous and must be abandoned. This is the downside of the glitter, that Canadians should be prepared to lose their sovereignty and freedom to save their skins. The movement tends to evade or deny this issue, although in internal debates some members apparently recognize it as their Achilles' heel.[3]

The ideology and its supporting propaganda have created myths that recruit, unite, direct, and confine the Canadian peace movement. No one has described the mental processes of myth addicts so concisely as Arthur Koestler:

> The inner defences are unconscious. They consist of a kind of magic aura which the mind builds around its cherished belief. Arguments which penetrate into the magic aura are not dealt with rationally but by a specific type of pseudo-reasoning. Absurdities and contradictions which outside the magic aura would be rejected at once are made acceptable by specious rationalizations. The higher developed the mental facilities of the person, the subtler the patterns of pseudo-reasoning which he develops . . . Under the circumstances, almost every discussion with myth-addicts, whether public or private, is doomed to failure. The debate is from the beginning removed from the level of objectivity; arguments are not considered on their merit, but by whether they fit the system, and if not, how they can be made to fit.[4]

Within a movement so conditioned, discussion of the various issues is potentially a waste of time. Every national peace movement naturally focusses public attention on local issues. In those Western European countries that were to receive cruise or Pershing II missiles, these weapons became the key issues. In Norway and Denmark, which have no nuclear weapons on their soil, the issue was a nuclear free zone in the Scandinavian region. Similar appeals were heard in Greece. New Zealand protesters found an issue in visits to New Zealand ports by nuclear-armed US warships. Within the United States, the issues have been the "freeze" and opposition to all new US weapons projects: the neutron warhead; the B1 bomber; the MX missile; the Strategic Defense Initiative.

Although often argued by specious reasoning, peace movement attitudes to the issues themselves are predetermined by the ideology and the propaganda of the movements. Defence and deterrence are dangerous and must be opposed. Period. If NATO and the United States decided to rest their defences on pea-shooters, opposition to pea-shooters would overnight become the new issue for the movements. The only Western equipment acceptable to the peace movements is a white flag.

This may seem a drastic oversimplification, but it is only by pursuing the internal logic of the movement to its end that its absurdity or its real operational intent can be understood. Certainly it is not understood by many rank-and-file peace activists. Applied to Canada, the movement has focussed on the flight-testing of unarmed cruise missiles, US or NATO naval or military testing or training, declaring Canada a nuclear free zone, leaving NORAD, leaving NATO, "doing a Finland," generally opting out. Pseudo-reasoning is developed to explain the movement's attitude over an issue, but in reality its attitude was never in doubt. The peace ideology supplies answers to all questions, and it gives them within a framework devoid of visible foreign influence. It is, apparently, a homespun, good, clean Canadian concoction.

And that perception, more than any other feature, distinguishes the ideology of the Canadian peace movement as a masterpiece of Soviet propaganda and deception. Backed by the power of the Soviet propaganda apparatus, but nevertheless operating inside Canada from a minority position, the Communist element has succeeded in shaping an ideology that has no apparent connection with communism or the USSR, but which actually serves Soviet policy in every respect.

In the June 1984 edition of *This Magazine*, Alison Acker recalled a protest in Ottawa at which

> we set down the coffins in front of the police outside the Department of External Affairs, poured blood over the dolls to symbolize Canadian guilt and the slaughter of the innocents, and sat down on the road. (The blood was donated by supporters in Ottawa, and taken just like Red Cross donations. It felt marvellously sticky and mysteriously powerful, so that pouring it was almost like a mass.)[5]

In an earlier chapter we discussed Pavlov and the power of Soviet propaganda to orient the souls of audiences, to extinguish the "freedom urge," and to induce neurotic behavior. All these achievements are visible in Canada. Moreover, virtually every theme of the movement's ideology was provided well in advance by the World Peace Council, as the documentation shows. The ideology of peace is indeed a Trojan horse. The most deceived are the many thousands of sincere peace group members.

An answer of sorts is almost certain to be offered. It will be something like this: It is quite possible to share certain views and policies with Communists without sharing their political goals and without being intellectually subordinate to them. Within rather cramped limits, this is a good answer. Indeed, when the Soviets make what seems to be a good proposal, all should applaud it. This defence reaches its limits, however, when the policies that are shared quite obviously contribute to the Soviet achievement of the goal that is theirs alone. For peace activists to adopt virtually every Soviet "peace" initiative over a period of eight years without ever pausing to consider where this might lead, was remarkable.

The evidence of intellectual subordination offered so far rests on the close identity between what Moscow has suggested and what the peace movement has done. In one important case there was an additional factor—timing.

In 1972 Marshal Grechko testified before the Supreme Soviet in favor of ratification by the USSR of the anti-ballistic missile (ABM) treaty. To overcome any *nomenklatura* fears that Soviet efforts to develop a "space shield" might be jeopardized by the proposed treaty, Grechko stated that the document placed "no limitation on research and experimental work aimed at solving the problem of defending the country against ballistic missile attack."[6]

The Soviet Union has apparently worked hard to develop defences against strategic missile attack or, more likely, against whatever response the West might be capable of after a disarming Soviet first strike. They maintain the world's only operational anti-ballistic missile system around Moscow, currently being updated to include long-range interceptors, high-acceleration interceptors designed to engage missiles in the atmosphere, and guidance and engagement radars, including a new facility at Pushkino. All the launchers are silo-based and reloadable. They have missile early-warning radars around the periphery of the USSR, a system that is also being updated. A sixth radar, under construction near Krasnoyorsk in Siberia, may provide complete early-warning coverage against ballistic missile attack. The Krasnoyorsk facility is in apparent violation of the 1972 ABM Treaty, which requires that ABM radars be located within a 150-kilometre radius of Moscow. Krasnoyorsk is 3700 kilometres distant.

It seems more than likely that the Soviets are developing a nationwide missile defence system. Reports tell of tests of new surface-to-air components apparently designed to intercept missiles, such as the SA-10 and SA-X-12. In the late 1960s the Soviets initiated a major research program into advanced technologies such as air defence lasers, including one capable of destroying satellites in orbit. Work is in progress on a gas-dynamic laser, the electric-discharge laser, and the chemical laser. There are further reports of research on excimir, free-electron, and X-ray lasers, in addition to visible and very short wave-length lasers. The Soviets claim to have developed the prototype of a 25-metre mirror that is necessary for any space-based laser weapon. Ground-based lasers are already operational. Work is also in progress on space-based weapons using particle beams, and there is research into radio frequencies that might cripple the electronic components of hostile missiles.

Currently, the USSR has the world's only operational anti-satellite system. Their somewhat primitive but effective satellite-mounted conventional explosive method has been tested. There are operational versions based at the Tyuratan Space Complex. Reginald Turnhill, editor of *Jane's Space Flight Directory*, writes that the Soviet Union has taken an "almost frightening" lead in space technology. The heavy lift booster system for the Soviet shuttle could be used for launching heavy military payloads, including ballistic missile defence weapons. As and when the fruits of this research and development are melded together, the Soviet Union could have a Strategic Defence. The Initiative has been in effect for more than twenty years.[7]

Naturally, Soviet leaders would prefer that their program, whether advancing swiftly as some observers fear, or slowly, should not face competition. When on March 23, 1983, President Reagan announced his country's Strategic Defense Initiative (SDI), the competition so heralded was unwelcome.

All new ideas for weapons and strategy have their good and bad points. Nothing in this field is ever perfect. The debate that erupted in the West as a result of Reagan's announcement was perfectly understandable and potentially constructive. The fact that it never reached its potential can be attributed to the pre-propaganda of the theme of fear. Indeed, whenever a new stage in the peace offensive is launched, all preceding themes and campaigns take on the form of pre-propaganda. They force their audience, the Western publics, to live in a particular psychological climate, in this case one where weapons are the enemy, defence is provocative, and straight-thinking about the Soviet threat is positively suicidal.

In the Soviet Union, discussion of the US SDI proceeded at two levels. For professional military men, it had to be seen for what it was, a defence initiative. *Aviatsiya i kosmonavtika*, a specialized monthly journal of the Soviet Air Force, ran six articles on the general subject of US military development in space between 1984 and 1986. In none of these was the phrase "strike space weapons" used to describe the US proposed technologies. A country which deceived its own armed forces over the military capability of its "main enemy" could not hope to succeed in war. The USSR has not made that mistake.[8]

The second level of discussion has been for the domestic and international public audiences. Propaganda has here been the order of the day. *Pravda, Izvestia*, and *Krasnaya zvezda (Red Star)*, and the wire services, TASS and Novosti, have made constant reference to "strike space weapons" and the ominous threat to peace posed by SDI. This was presumably useful in the constant mobilization propaganda for home audiences, as well as laying the foundations of the new components of the international peace offensive.

A few days after Reagan's speech, Yuri Andropov, then general secretary of the Communist Party, was quoted in *Pravda* as saying that SDI was not defensive but rather part of a US effort to acquire a first strike capability. He also warned of the damaging prospects for arms control. However, the World Peace Council's *Disarmament Forum* for May 1983 made quite mild reference to Reagan's announcement.

There then followed a twenty-one-month period during which the full power of the Soviet propaganda apparatus steered clear of SDI. Possibly the sickness and deaths of party leaders had something to do with this; there may have been conflicting voices in the Kremlin. Alternatively, the specialists of the International Department may have decided that the best course initially was to intervene at the intellectual level by trying to influence the arms control élites. They did, for instance, pay for a full-page advertisement in the *New York Times* on April 9, 1983, to publish the Soviet scientists' "Appeal to All Scientists of the World," which stated that SDI could never be made to work.[9]

But probably the major consideration was the forthcoming US presidential election. The Politburo presumably wished to see a liberal successor to President Reagan in the White House after November 1984. Such an individual might have been inclined to back off SDI, for his own reasons. After President Carter's confusion over the neutron bomb, which left him vulnerable to charges of having been deceived by hostile propaganda, a new president might have found it easier to cancel the research initiative if there had *not* been a massive propaganda blitz. No blitz came until after Reagan had been re-elected.

The Soviet timing was reflected in Canada. The Canadian Union of Public Employees' May 1984 special peace publication made no reference to SDI. The agenda for the Canadian Peace Congress' November 1984 "World Dialogue" excluded the topic.[10] Nor was SDI among the future "crucial questions" listed for consideration by delegates to the Toronto Disarmament Network's December 1984 conference.[11] Absolute silence in spite of the fact that SDI was obviously the most significant defence development of the decade.

With Reagan re-elected, the word came. Konstantin Chernenko, briefly in the highest office, was quoted by *Pravda* on December 6, 1984, as saying that "militarization of outer space, if not securely blocked, would cancel everything that has so far been achieved in the field of arms limitation," an appeal that reinforced the pressure on arms control lobbies in the West and also cleared the way for a major peace offensive blitz.

The World Peace Council's monthly, *Peace Courier*, No. 2, 1985, declared that "space defence is a first strike policy" and relied heavily on Western anti-defence sources to make the assertion seem credible. The March issue used the headline, "The US Space Offensive Threatens Us All." In April the theme was reinforced. The council's presidential committee issued a "No to 'Star Wars' Appeal to the Peoples of the World."

Beginning predictably enough with "Humanity faces the gravest danger: all life on our planet is threatened," the appeal alleged that SDI would accelerate the arms race, prevent negotiations, and generally upset the Soviet idea of peace. Also, early in 1985 the council issued a pamphlet entitled *The US Space Offensive: Road to Nuclear Annihilation.*

The reaction was as predictable as the blitz. On April 5, 1985, William Kashtan, the then secretary-general of the Communist Party of Canada, told his party faithful that any Canadian participation in SDI "spells real danger to Canada and the Canadian people,"[12] earning generous replay on Radio Moscow next day.[13] On May 20, the Toronto Disarmament Network co-sponsored a full-page advertisement in the *Globe and Mail.* Called "Stop Star Wars," the announcement consisted of an open letter to the Prime Minister, urging him: "Do not allow Canadian support for Star Wars." Other sponsors were Vancouver's End the Arms Race, the Winnipeg Co-ordinating Committee for Nuclear Disarmament, the Ottawa Disarmament Network, and the Christian Movement for Peace.

The Toronto Disarmament Network's de facto leader, Robert

Penner, had earlier launched the campaign with a press conference. Bob White, director of the United Auto Workers, and
economist Mel Watkins—one-time co-initiator of the New
Democrats' left-wing Waffle Group—assisted.[14] Project Ploughshares invited all its members to take part in the campaign. Dennis McDermott, president of the Canadian Labour Congress,
and John Fryer, president of the National Union of Provincial
Government Employees, endorsed the scheme.[15] The annual
Vancouver "peace" march on April 27 made "Stop Star Wars" its
principal slogan.[16] Thus, having done little or nothing in
response to SDI between its announcement in March 1983 and
the start of the World Peace Council's campaign early in 1985,
Canadian peace organizers suddenly moved like lightning.

Penner would write later: "In 1985 the Canadian peace movement achieved its first big victory for a specific policy . . . The
peace movement responded quickly and effectively on the ques-
tionable features of Star Wars and waged a significant campaign
of lobbying the federal government on the issue."[17] About the
Soviet space shield, and the twenty-one-month hiatus, Penner
wrote nothing.

Soviet propaganda, it would seem, played a dominating role in
mobilizing Canadians to support the peace offensive and in setting the agenda of the movement. This was achieved by the international and domestic Communist apparatus working together to create both psychological and physical channels for
ideas and material. So we must now examine the organizational
aspects: the means used to set the pace and the tone, the exercise of control by penetration, and the imposition of a Soviet
agenda from a minority position.

CHAPTER X

ORGANIZING FOR "PEACE"

"Radical change does not happen because of good ideas. It is the result of organizing effective power behind these ideas."

Robert Penner, de facto leader of the Canadian Peace Alliance[1]

The connection between propaganda and organization has been discussed in greater detail by Jacques Ellul:

Without organization, psychological incitement leads to excesses and deviation of action in the very course of development. Through organization, the proselyte receives an overwhelming impulse that makes him act with the whole of his being. He is actually transformed into a religious man in the psycho-sociological sense of the term; justice enters into the action he performs because of the organization of which he is a part.[2]

During the first half of the 1980s, networking was much encouraged within the Canadian peace movement. The exchange of ideas, material, speakers, and assistance helped prevent feelings of isolation and helplessness and promoted regional and national campaigns. The distinction between church and mainstream, used earlier for presentational convenience, did not long survive in any structural sense. Church halls often became the meeting places for secular peace groups, and church activists joined forces with nonbelievers. Such networking was horizontal; there was no superior authority.

In 1983, however, some eighty-three Toronto peace groups

formed the Toronto Disarmament Network; on the West Coast a similar process created Vancouver's End the Arms Race Coalition. These were a new type of network, vertical in form. Offices were opened, staff hired, newsletters published, campaigns directed. The component groups were like squads or patrols responding to orders from general headquarters. The Toronto Network and End the Arms Race can be viewed as regional coalitions with more clout than many national units. The Ottawa Disarmament Coalition and the Winnipeg Coordinating Committee were smaller versions of the same vertical networking trend.

In this process, many of the distinctions between the mainstream and Communist components crumbled. In their place arose a new dividing line between those whose sympathies were with the Soviet Union and those who favored a nonaligned political position, albeit, in most cases, a Marxist one. The first group struggled to impose vertical control by way of a central authority: themselves. The church component and the nonaligned or neo-Marxist radicals preferred horizontal networking and decentralization. ACT for Disarmament is a Toronto organization of the second type.

Early plans to create a national peace movement were discussed by Communist Peace member Nicholas Prychodko in *Communist Viewpoint* in October 1982: "The 35 [peace] organizations included many of the newer and smaller bodies which have emerged recently. The understanding of the need for unity is not as yet well developed on the part of some national groups and will require patient and persistent work."

Patient and persistent work by Communists and others led to a meeting of thirty-seven peace group representatives in Vancouver in March 1985, followed by another in Ottawa that June to prepare a draft paper as the "basis of unity" for a national movement. The Communist Gordon Flowers chaired one of the planning meetings.[3]

Communist support for this project was confirmed by Claire DaSylva in an article in the September 1985 issue of *World Marxist Review*. The author noted that an "important step" would be the formation of a "bi-national, all-Canadian peace coalition on the basis of a common program." This coalition would unite all peace movements under one umbrella and would be aimed at "transforming Canadian foreign policy." Finally, in November 1985 delegates met in Toronto under the auspices of the Toronto Disarmament Network and created the Canadian Peace Alliance.

The alliance's inaugural steering committee consisted of fourteen national organizations: Anglican Church Public Responsibility Unit; Canadian Labour Congress; Canadian Peace Congress; Congress of Canadian Women; Greenpeace; Physicians for Social Responsibility; National Farmers Union; Lawyers for Social Responsibility; Operation Dismantle; Performing Artists; Ploughshares; Veterans for Multi-lateral Disarmament; Voice of Women; and World Federalists, plus twenty regional organizations, many of them coalitions. The alliance was described by its creators as "an association of Canadian groups working for nuclear disarmament," and its published goals included a freeze of the arms race, Canada to be a nuclear free zone, the redirection of funds "from wasteful military spending," and strengthening of world institutions such as the UN. The alliance was officially a facilitating body, not a command headquarters. Nevertheless, its creation extended the vertical networking mechanism to the national level and represented an important stage in the political conversion of the Canadian peace movement.

Canada had been one of the first countries in the West to be organized for peace as desired by Moscow, receiving its peace congress in 1949. The United States was one of the last to be so blessed. Moscow used the 1970s to set in place the final link in its international chain of "peace" fronts. In 1975 the World Peace Council sent a delegation to ten US cities. It made contact with Communists and front organizers and worked to draw congressmen, church leaders, and non-Communist peace activists into a network that could be effectively controlled from Moscow. Three years later the council held its first meeting in the United States.

The event aimed to increase congressional and public opposition to new US weapons systems and to instil fear. Its "Washington Proclamation" announced that the "arms race grows with every hour—not just quantitatively but also qualitatively. Ever more deadly weapons of mass destruction are being perfected."[4]

The same year, 1978, a KGB officer called Yuri Kapralov was posted to Washington as counsellor in the Soviet embassy. Judging from his subsequent activities, his job was to control or at least influence the US peace movement.[5]

In 1979 the World Peace Council set up the US Peace Council with Michael Myerson, former secretary of the Peace Commission of the New York State Communist Party, as executive director.[6] The Kremlin had established a "peace" foothold in New York, commercial centre of the United States, which Moscow calls the "main enemy."

West Germany's Moscow-line Communist Party reportedly receives 50 million DM annually from the ruling Communist Party in East Germany to support fronts and "peace" initiatives. Some of this money was used to promote the successful Krefeld Appeal, which launched West Germany's peace campaign in 1980.[7] In Denmark the KGB agent Vladimir Merkulov gave money to finance in Danish papers advertisements favoring a nuclear weapon-free zone in northern Europe.[8] The Dutch threw out the TASS "correspondent" Vadim Leonov after he had boasted: "If Moscow decides that 50,000 demonstrators take to the streets in Holland, they will take to the streets."[9] Norway expelled two KGB "diplomats" for similar activity, and Switzerland, hardly the centre of NATO "warmongering," sent home a *Novosti* "news correspondent" who had organized peace demonstrations, drafted appeals, and collected signatures.[10] Soviet agents have a rather unattractive term for non-Communists in the West who believe what the agents tell them. They refer to them as shit-eaters.[11] Precisely how many Americans and Canadians deserve this title is unknown. From the European experience and from what we know of Kapralov's activities, there may have been thousands.

While the KGB's activities attracted media attention, the far more widespread involvement of domestic Communists within supposedly apolitical national peace movements tended to go unreported, out of incompetent journalism, fear of the McCarthyist label, or ideological complicity. Perhaps this neglect reflected the failure of educators in Canada and many Western nations to teach relative political values during the last quarter-century, leaving younger generations ignorant of the nature of communism.

Of the major Canadian newspapers, only the *Toronto Sun* regularly points to Communist sponsorship of the Canadian peace movement. Other papers print stories on this theme very occasionally, such as a report by Gordon Kent in the *Edmonton Journal* in 1986. According to this account, Communists were active not only in the party and the peace congresses, but also in a group called Youth for Peace and the Alberta Anti-Cruise Committee.[12] None of the electronic media seems to have faced this issue, with the distinguished exception of the CTV television network when it aired the Stornoway production "Agents of Deception."[13] Yet in Canada the Communists have probably been every bit as successful in assuming effective control over a mainly non-Communist and indeed apolitical peace movement as their opposite numbers in other NATO countries.

The main outline of the overt Communist organizational structure has been sketched in an earlier chapter. Its principal strength lies in the uniformity of thought and action of a disciplined ideological party and its fronts, backed up by the largest propaganda, subversive, and military apparatus the world has ever seen—that of the Soviet Union—and reinforced by the international network of Communists and far-left sympathizers, some of whom may be covert party members.

Of the International Department's assets, the World Peace Council is easily the most visible. It is supported by the KGB, the agent networks, the Soviet Committee for the Defence of Peace (known outside the USSR as the Soviet Peace Committee), and a host of supporting front organizations such as the Christian Peace Conference, the International Organization of Democratic Lawyers, the International Organization of Journalists, the International Union of Students—to list but a few.

These assets compensate, to a degree that most Canadians have not grasped, for the tiny size of the actual Communist Party of Canada. Paradoxically, its small size and weak electoral appeal may be seen as valuable assets if they fool us into underestimating the scope of the problem.

Covert organizations are difficult to describe for the obvious reason that many remain undetected. The various regional peace congresses disguise their Communist affiliations to greater or lesser degree, but are not really covert. A better example is the Toronto Association for Peace, reportedly set up by Gordon Flowers, which has operated as though it was independent, even though effectively controlled by Communists.[14]

The association organized the 1977 Toronto march against the neutron bomb, and in 1979 it distributed the Communist Party's peace program advocating withdrawal from NATO and NORAD. In 1982 the Toronto Association for Peace fronted for the Canadian Peace Congress and the party when it presented the petition "Peace is Everybody's Business." The Youth Coalition for Peace was another Toronto group reported to be under effective Communist control.[15]

For information about penetration, the left-wing (but non-Communist) press provides, in a purely matter-of-fact way, far more than the mainstream media. Many of these publications grew out of the so-called New Left—the Marxists who once denounced the USSR and orthodox communism and vowed to build anew. They are not opposed to speaking and writing frankly about the Communist Party of Canada, presumably because their far-left credentials protect them against charges of McCarthyism.

Writing in *Canadian Dimension* in September 1983, Bryan Palmer implied that the West Coast regional co-ordinating body, the End the Arms Race Coalition, was deeply penetrated. Praising the Communists for their "invaluable organizational accomplishments . . . [which had been] quite remarkable on the West Coast," he acknowledged: "The Peace Councils, like the Communist Party in the labour movement in the 1930s and 1940s thus perceive the disarmament movement as something on which they have a lock. Their concern is to keep the key."

According to a media report, the ubiquitous Gordon Flowers also joined the group called Operation Dismantle. By 1987, Pamela Ruth Fitzgerald, who ran for parliament on the Communist Party ticket in 1979, had become Operation Dismantle's chief executive officer. In 1980, Fitzgerald represented the Canadian Peace Congress at the Sofia conference.[16] The organization Veterans Against Nuclear Arms was energetically courted by Communists. They promoted its activities in their paper, *Canadian Tribune*, and veterans with Communist backgrounds started joining. When a Toronto branch was set up, two out of the eight-man executive had long-term Soviet links. Ray Stevenson had been a member of the secretariat of the World Peace Council and had been active with the Trade Union Peace Committee, an organization started by the Canadian Peace Congress in 1981. He had made financial contributions to the Communist Party of Canada. So had Bill Harasym, who is national secretary of the Association of United Ukrainian Canadians, a Moscow-aligned group.[17]

The Soviet embassy's information department has conducted an energetic mailing campaign. When in 1982 a New Brunswicker, concerned about peace but also disturbed by the tone of some brochures, wrote to the Toronto peace group that had distributed them, he was surprised to receive in reply a Soviet mailout.[18] But such propaganda activities are small beer compared with the flood of material issued free by the World Peace Council and the various propaganda agencies in Moscow. The Canadian Security Intelligence Service has stated that there is "pro-Soviet activity within the mainstream peace movement."[19] If this was not the case, Canada would be unique.

Ironically, confirmation of the Security Intelligence Service's assertion came, not from alert investigative reporters inside Canada, but from Moscow's *Literaturnaya Gazeta*. On May 23, 1988, *The Globe and Mail* reported an article in the Gazette by Professor Vyacheslav Dashichev of the Institute for Socialist Economics which blamed the Cold War of the 1940s and 1950s on Stalin's policy of imposing Soviet control in Eastern Europe.

Dashichev blamed Brezhnev for the breakdown of detente, cit-
ing the African adventures and the invasion of Afghanistan, and
also condemning the contradictory policy of deploying a new
generation of nuclear weapons in Europe, thus "increasing the
level of military danger," while *at the same time mobilizing and
funding peace movements.*

The second Reagan–Gorbachev summit meeting was held in
Reykjavik, Iceland, between 11 and 12 October, 1986. When
the Canadian Peace Alliance held its convention in Winnipeg
less than three weeks later, on October 31, delegates were
swamped by complex, well-presented Soviet material blaming
all the world's ills on the Americans and depicting Gorbachev as
the injured dove of peace. This emanated from the Novosti Press
Agency in Moscow and the World Peace Council in Helsinki
and illustrated both the size and the sophistication of the Soviet
propaganda apparatus, plus the easy access this apparatus enjoys
into its "target audiences." In contrast, the West had only limited broadcast facilities to reach Soviet audiences; in the Eastern
bloc, it has no "organization."

The last element in the Communist effort to dominate the
movement consists of dictating policy from a minority position.
One statement from the International Department and one example from the United States will illustrate the technique.

In November 1981 Boris Ponomarev, head of the department,
said:

> Then there is the question of the place of Communists in the
> antiwar movement. And today we must speak our minds on
> this. With all respect to the originality and independence of
> the various participants in the movement, one has to admit
> that Communists bear particular responsibility for it. A con-
> siderable role in the rise of the movement has been played by
> the emotional impulse, by people feeling the danger of war.
> Where does this danger come from and how can it be stopped?
> . . . Communists are called upon to give correct, precise and
> clear answers.[20]

Gerhard Wettig of the Federal Institute for Eastern and International Studies in Cologne, West Germany, has described the technique used to execute Ponomarev's orders:

> The communists' refusal to accept agreement and compromise with their peace "allies," is propagandistically masked by the assertion that all the "peace forces," whatever their ideological orientation, share a common political interest in combatting the arms race. For this reason, the Kremlin and its local communist agents keep explaining, they should unite for common action, emphasize their common interests, and neglect what divides them. That rationale does not only serve as a justification for cooperation between communists and non-communists in general. It also entails the specific operational guideline that only those actions should be taken which can be based on mutual consensus. This has far-reaching practical consequences.[21]

A classic example of the technique described by Wettig was to be seen in 1982, when on June 12, 165,000 people marched along First Avenue in New York City past the United Nations and the US Mission. When the marchers reached Central Park, they joined an estimated 400,000 people already assembled. The stated purpose of the demonstration was to apply additional pressure on the United States during the UN Second Special Session on Disarmament. Although many of the demonstrators were not Communists and would presumably have welcomed an even-handed appeal to East and West for disarmament, the focus of the march, the rally, and the propaganda that accompanied these events was almost exclusively anti-West. Nevertheless, the media informed the public that the demonstration reflected broadly based social forces; anyone who suggested that Communists were behind it risked being labeled a McCarthyist.

Interviewed for television in December 1984 by the Toronto journalist Les Harris, Michael Myerson, head of the US Peace Council, admitted quite openly that the entire event had been orchestrated by his group—that is to say, by Communists acting on Moscow's behalf.[22] Other reports have shown that the Peace Council adopted the technique described by Wettig: seek consensus on the basis of slogans and demands acceptable to all component groups. When it is proposed that the United States be condemned, all will agree; but if it is suggested by some non-aligned group that the Soviet Union be criticized, the Communists or their covert allies object, and in the interests of a united front the proposal is rejected—brilliantly simple and remarkably effective. Myerson had only five Communists on a co-ordinating committee of twenty-seven, yet was able to control the agenda and its outcome.[23]

The Soviets used the event to demoralize their own people as well as Western audiences. "But it is a fact," wrote *Pravda's* special correspondent A. Vasilyev from New York, "that during the seven hours of the demonstration and rally attended by a million people on the day I did not see a single anti-Soviet placard." The West's resistance to communism is the sole source of strength and hope for the suffering populations of the East. Reports like Vasilyev's undermine this hope by depicting the West as a traitor to democracy.

Peace movement organization, Communist organization, techniques of penetration and dictating policy from a minority position—all were in evidence at the first convention of the Canadian Peace Alliance.

The preliminary process had ended with a meeting of national and regional representatives in Ottawa in August 1985, where the ground rules were agreed for a founding convention to be held in Toronto that November. It was immediately clear that delegates divided into those who favored a vertical command structure and those seeking only a horizontal co-ordinating body. Generally speaking, it was the Communists and the four main coalitions who wanted centralized power. Those who resisted centralization were non-Communists, including the non-aligned radicals ACT for Disarmament and La Coalition Québécoise pour le désarmement et la paix; the World Federalists; Project Ploughshares; and the majority of grassroots groups that had not been swallowed up in regional networks.

A surprising supporter of centralization was the Department of External Affairs. One of its officials was quoted by the *Globe and Mail* as saying: "It is to our advantage to see that the convention is a success. If it works, the peace movement will be able to speak with one voice—and that should make things easier for us."[24] Presumably the spokesman was unaware of the implications of "one voice"; his remark suggests a rather disturbing naivety in the department over the true nature of the movement it was funding so generously, including $25,000 for the forthcoming convention.

Prof. E. P. Thompson, the British champion of nonaligned activism, had been invited to address the founding convention of the Canadian Peace Alliance as honored guest. But when Communist Gordon Flowers was in the chair, he tried to have the invitation cancelled. Although the motion was defeated, the Communists were compensated by an agreement that Thompson's "keynote speech" would be deferred until an hour and a half into the Friday night's agenda and be confined within an insulting fifteen-minute limit.[25]

Consequently the November convention began not with Thompson, but with a remarkable diatribe by the Physicians for Social Responsibility's Dr. Thomas Perry. After introducing the theme of fear, Perry justified the "no evil" concept with the assertion that "there is not a shred of evidence that they [the Soviet leaders] threaten us with invasion or with the destruction of our way of life,"[26] a view that would certainly surprise Poles, Latvians, and Afghanis, not to mention the many thousands of Russian scientists put to death by Lenin (not Stalin) in the aftermath of the 1917 revolution.

Perry went on to caution the delegates about the dangers of red-baiting, so destructive of consensus. He was apparently unconcerned by the report of his medical colleague, Dr. Abdullah Osman, former professor at the University of Kabul, Afghanistan, that in the aftermath of the Soviet invasion of his country, "almost all doctors and health personnel have been killed, imprisoned or driven out of the territory."[27] Perry's remarks apparently set the tone for the entire proceeding, which by all accounts provided an excellent case study of Gerhard Wettig's analysis of Communist coalition tactics and their "far-reaching practical consequences."

A grassroots delegate, Alan Silverman, complained in *Peace Magazine* that whenever anyone raised the question of superpower behavior and its effects on peace, "people were suddenly rushing to the microphone talking about 'unity', 'divisiveness,' 'not relevant,' and so on."[28] Stephen Dale recorded in *Now* magazine that ACT "was bitterly disappointed that the alliance had routed its call for a more explicit statement of support for dissident peace activists in the Soviet bloc—thereby failing to place itself within the nonaligned school of peacemaking."[29] *Canadian Dimension* reported the Quebec pacifist Jean-François Beaudet as saying that a Communist called Mark Solomon (who is chairman of the Department of History at Simmons College, Boston) distributed a "silly diatribe" against Thompson. Beaudet had nothing good to say about "people who profess to seeking 'unity' but who work to stifle discussion."[30]

Alas, the technique of seeking unity while stifling discussion was a quintessential Communist tactic in the shaping of the Canadian Peace Alliance. Dimitrios Roussopoulos assessed delegates as consisting of "the liberal, left-of-centre, 'progressive' and also the pro-Soviet constituency of the 'peace movement.' " He went on to say that estimates had indicated that up to 35 to 40 percent of those who attended were delegates from organizations sympathetic to Soviet foreign policy—meaning, presumably, Communists and their close allies.[31] One year later, at the second convention, he increased his estimate by a further 5 to 10 percent.[32]

Anyone who has worked in committees knows that 25 percent of voters can control the agenda and its conclusions if that minority is united, knows exactly what it wants, and has a disciplined and ruthless approach. The Communists in the alliance were restrained, however, by the need to avoid a split that might have left a rump Canadian Peace Alliance virtually indistinguishable from the Canadian Peace Congress. They accepted compromises—at least for the time being—which limited the alliance to a networking, information-sharing, debating, and "facilitating" role. The last left the door open wide enough, bearing in mind that the four coalitions and like-minded groups could presumably be relied upon to request alliance facilitation of any programs that the "action caucus" within the movement had decided upon.

ACT's Bert Keser was critical of proceedings. He reported in *Canadian Dimension* that "decentralization proposals were put at the bottom of the agenda. Then, with less than a third of the agenda completed, a quick vote transformed the Conference Planning Committee into the new Steering Committee."[33] He noted that there was virtually no plenary discussion on political issues, especially East-West.

Delegates contributing to the same article who seemed satisfied with the convention included Toronto Disarmament Network's Wendy Wright; End the Arms Race's Gary Marchant; John Morgan, Peace Congress; and BC Federation of Labour's Cliff Andstein. Marchant was disappointed only that political parties had been excluded from membership.[34] This satisfaction presumably sprang from the Soviet-aligned centralists' success in controlling the convention, at least over essentials.

Satisfaction was certainly expressed by Communist Party of Canada general secretary William Kashtan, who wrote about the alliance in March 1986: "This unity was also shown in the desire of the convention to push aside questions which might divide, such as anti-Sovietism and red-baiting, and to focus rather on what unites the all-out fight for peace."[35]

Science for Peace did not join the alliance. Like the physicians, who joined and rather quickly quit, they may have found its political alignment too blatant. In general, however, the alliance could claim a membership that represented the great majority of Canadian peace activists, including Giff Gifford's Veterans for Multi-lateral Disarmament. Gifford, a strong supporter of the alliance, stressed the need for centralization.[36] He changed the title of his organization to Veterans Against Nuclear Arms, a name that fitted more comfortably within an alliance that had little patience with multilateral anything.

The Canadian Peace Alliance might well have come into being with no Communist component, or without Communists as prime movers. Nationwide movements frequently form umbrella groups for obvious reasons. Yet the record shows that Communists saw in vertical structures the means by which a tiny minority at the national level could become a powerful force in the committee and convention level, so magnifying a hundredfold their influence over policy. They moved in and, at the least, accelerated and shaped the process. Thus the propaganda of which they were also the main providers would not go to waste in excesses and deviation of action. Instead, it would provide peace activists with the overwhelming impulse to act with the whole of their being.

CHAPTER XI

TRANSMISSION BELTS

"The question that must always be asked is: 'Who stands to profit?' In politics it is not so important to know who is championing certain opinions. What is important is to know who stands to profit from those opinions."

Lenin, quoted in *Kommunist* 6, 1983
in relation to Western peace movements.

Until 1935 Soviet ideological penetration of the West was mainly conducted by straightforward "class warfare"; blindly obedient Communists struggled for power against all comers, social democrats being identified as the worst enemy, being branded with the name social fascists. In this form of conflict there was no place for compromise, and in the rush to appear uncompromising and pure, Communists lost sight of Lenin's advice about tactical alliances and benefiting from "certain opinions," regardless of their origin. Not that Lenin's methods involved real compromise—that would have been a contradiction in terms—they simply sanctioned any devious means that led toward the great socialist utopia.

At the Communist International's seventh and last conference in 1935, the concept of the popular front was formally sanctioned. It has provided the framework of Soviet propaganda and deception ever since. In 1949 the Comintern's successor organization was using it in the cause of "peace," as ordered in the *Cominform Journal*:

Particular attention should be devoted to drawing into this movement trade unions, women's, youth, co-operative, sports, cultural, educational, religious and other organizations, and also scientists, writers, journalists, cultural workers, parliamentary and other public leaders who act in defence of peace against war.[1]

Just as the anti-fascist popular front offered the "either/or" choice of backing communism or siding with fascism, so the postwar peace offensives have tried to force Western publics to choose between peace and war—or rather, death, the latter option to be subconsciously identified with resistance to communism. Moscow is aware of the West's fickle, fashion-dominated culture in which today's wild enthusiasm is tomorrow's stale joke. Communists feel secure only when their ideological gains are consolidated through political, and eventually military, power. So, while Moscow has tried to widen the peace movements by drawing in ever more segments of Western society, it has simultaneously tried to tighten its control over this constituency. Particular attention has been directed toward radicals and social democrats in the West. In 1971 Ponomarev observed that, while the New Left was "neither ideologically nor organizationally homogeneous," it was nevertheless worth cultivating because of its "overall anti-imperialistic direction."[2] Fourteen years later Pravda was saying: "A major role in the defence of peace belongs to the joint actions of Communists and Social Democrats."[3]

To widen the social base of Western peace movements and at the same time tighten its control over these organizations, the International Department has used two principal methods: first, the creation of transmission belts, and second, the assumption of overt and covert Communists of control over Western movements.

Transmission belts act as intermediaries between sources (or fronts) identified in the West as Soviet or Communist and Western audiences. They transmit ideas, programs, people, and material. Unlike the front, which is fully controlled, and whose staff knows perfectly well what they are about, the transmission belt is often staffed by "innocents." Although belts are not

securely under Soviet control, this defect is more than offset in
the Kremlin's eyes by their credibility. During the Vietnam War,
the Stockholm Conference was a classic transmission belt. In
the 1980s the popular Greek daily newspaper *Ethnos*, covertly
influenced by the KGB, is another.[4]

For all its efforts to pretend otherwise, the World Peace Council's condition as a totally controlled front was fairly widely
recognized in the West even at the start of the 1980s offensive.
This did not diminish its value as an organizational tool and the
source of material that the faithful in foreign lands could use and
transmit locally. The Third World and the UN, too, seemed anxious to accept it at face value, perhaps as a means of snubbing
the West. However, its identification with Moscow did severely
curtail its usefulness for directly influencing the opinions of
Westerners. Consequently, any informal group that could bridge
the credibility gap would be welcome.

Generals for Peace and Disarmament is a self-selected group of
former NATO generals and admirals, which came into existence
in 1981. There is nothing original about senior retired servicemen assisting the cause of peace: the best way of learning to hate
war is seeing it in close-up. After World War I, the British brigadier-general Frank Crozier joined the Peace Army. Today many
retired soldiers, sailors, and airmen become involved in strategic
and other studies because of a concern about war's destructive-
ness. Without doubt, half at least of the members of Generals for
Peace belong to this apolitical category. They are the innocents.

The core of the organization, however, is not innocent at all
in the political sense: generals Francisco da Costa Gomes of
Portugal; Giorgios Koumanakos and Michalis Tombopoulos of
Greece; Antoine Sanguinetti of France; and Italy's Nino Pasti.
Costa Gomes is a World Peace Council vice-president; Sanguinetti, Pasti and Koumanakos are council officials; Tombopoulos
is vice-president of the Greek Committee for the Struggle
against the American Bases. All these appointments point to an
anti-NATO commitment.

World Peace Council membership does not necessarily imply
Communist Party membership. It does imply acceptance of the

party line that military, including nuclear, strength is "a good thing" in Soviet hands and a danger to peace in Western, a line that infuses Generals for Peace also. Pasti reportedly told a Paris audience that "the Soviet SS-20 is a weapon for peace in Europe." None of the pro-Soviet generals would have countenanced setting up a group without prior consultation with World Peace Council's president Romesh Chandra. Indeed, it was at the 1980 Sofia meeting that the generals who were council members first floated the idea.

The output of the Generals for Peace has been, without exception, indistinguishable from normal Soviet propaganda. Most of it has been published in Helsinki by the council, and other books by the generals, writing either collectively or as individuals, have been handled by Pahl-Rugenstein Verlag in Cologne, a West German Communist Party outlet. Ponomarev in 1981 helped launch the generals' group by saying: "The most characteristic feature of the antiwar movement is the breadth of its socio-political base. Take, for instance, the speeches against war made by former military officers. I have in mind the series of generals and senior officers who, until recently, occupied prominent posts in their national armies and in NATO."[5]

In spite of all this evidence of Soviet indirect control, the transmission belt system works. The generals' books and pamphlets are recommended by several Canadian peace groups.

In 1985 the generals issued a poster beginning, "Let there be no illusions about space weapons: they are not for 'Star Wars' but for nuclear war on earth." The statement did not condemn Soviet space weapons.[6]

In his book, A General for Peace, Leonard Johnson describes his conversion to the peace ideology that caused him to join Generals for Peace and Disarmament in 1984. Following a 1979 visit to the NORAD Command Post at Colorado Springs, he "rejected nuclear deterrence outright." One year later, Moscow's point man in its peace offensive, Georgi Arbatov, accompanied by the Soviet ambassador to Canada, veteran propagandist Alexander Yakovlev, told Johnson what he wanted to hear: the USSR poses no threat to anyone. The enemy was redefined and all the pieces of the ideology fell into place. After such a conversion, it was perhaps inevitable that Johnson should write that the Soviet rape of Afghanistan was "by no means a clear case of Soviet aggression."[7]

As with others in the peace movement, Johnson's conversion began with an emotional reaction. As argued earlier, deterrence works because the risks it presents to any potential aggressor are unacceptably high. Therefore a determination to retaliate if attacked must be built into the system. Yet when Johnson witnessed a procedural exercise at Colorado Springs during which retaliation was simulated, he allowed his emotion to overwhelm his sense. His explanation: "I had stumbled onto one of the fundamental problems of nuclear deterrence, which is that retaliation, *the certainty of which is intended to deter attack*, is no longer rational after deterrence has failed."[8] The emphasis that has been added underlines the contradiction in Johnson's argument.

The building of transmission belts resembles nature's way with the creation of calcium columns from floor to ceiling in caves. Stalactites form downward from the roof, while stalagmites rise upward from the floor. If we see the ceiling as the USSR and the floor as the West, it is as much to Moscow's advantage to augment indigenous Western stalagmites as it is to rely entirely on forming stalactites. Indeed, once the column, or transmission belt, is complete, it will be stronger and more credible if at least half the building has been done in the West, from the floor up.

The Institute for Policy Studies was formed in Washington, DC, in 1963 as an avowedly radical organization under the sponsorship of Richard Barnet and Marcus Raskin. It can be seen as a transmission belt, of the stalagmite variety, since no one has been able to demonstrate direct Soviet sponsorship or control. In his book *Real Security*, Barnet stated that "Soviet ideology categorically rejects the idea of expansion by military force." Given such a starting point, who needs Soviet sponsorship? Almost everything the Institute for Policy Studies has ever done is anti-Western, anti-defence, and pro-Marxist. Yet their presentational standards are high and their influence is great. The *Globe and Mail* is one of the many newspapers that regularly carries their material.[9]

Institute Fellow William M. Arkin has been active with the Canadian peace movement as part of his crusade to convince Iceland, Puerto Rico, Bermuda, the Azores, Diego Garcia, the Philippines, and Canada that "each one of these countries is earmarked to receive US nuclear weapons in wartime," a story that reinforces the theme of fear and undermines alliance confidence.[10] Arkin is a darling of the Canadian peace movement and regularly speaks to conferences. In Edmonton in November 1986 he heaped scorn on the Canadian government, saying "one would have to be a moron not to realize that secret links are being forged between Canada and SDI." The official Canadian assessment of the Soviet challenge was scathingly dismissed as "the bogey man and other horrors too unmentionable."[11]

The Center for Defense Information was formed in 1973 and maintains close links to the Institute for Policy Studies. Although the center claims that it "supports a strong defense but opposes excessive expenditures of forces," in practice it has opposed every major US weapons system or policy developed since its inception. It, too, is the ideal transmission belt. Its newsletter, *Defense Monitor*, publishes carefully selected data that present the USSR as a weak opponent. The director is retired rear admiral Gene La Rocque, and his deputy is Eugene Carroll, of the same rank.[12] The Dutch analyst J. A. Emerson Vermaat reports that in 1982 La Rocque made an extensive tour of Eastern Europe and the Soviet Union. "Although not officially affiliated to the GDP [Generals for Peace], La Rocque and his Center for Defense Information indulge in similar activities and there are signs of coordination between them."[13]

At the Edmonton conference no less a figure than George Ignatieff advocated the establishment "with the help of the Veterans for Nuclear Responsibility [*sic*], a centre for defence information . . . modelled on the Center for Defense Information in Washington." Giff Gifford of Veterans Against Nuclear Arms quickly reassured Ignatieff that his Canadian Defence Research and Education Centre would, indeed, become Canada's equivalent of the US center.[14]

It was suggested earlier, in connection with propaganda and ideology, that the peace movement's rejection of Western defence is total and that the so-called issues of cruise testing, SDI, and the like are merely vehicles toward the desired end of defenceless "neutrality." It was also argued that blind faith of this sort does not require rational arguments and that adherents are frequently beyond the reach of logic. However, in moving from point A to point B, peace activists do require spurious arguments to impress the public, attract recruits, dumbfound critics, and convince the rank and file that they are, after all, acting rationally. Whether witting or unwitting, the Institute for Policy Studies and the Center for Defense Information aided and abetted by the Generals for Peace, are key sources of such spurious argument, vital instruments in the operation to disarm the West.

Early in 1986 CDI devoted an entire issue of its *Monitor* to resurrecting Liebknecht, or rather to depicting the contemporary United States as the Doppelgänger of the Germany of 1907. It was as though the notion of militarism was so important to the anti-defence rhetoric that no limit could be set on the inventiveness or outright mendacity permitted in its portrayal. According to the resulting report, the United States was a "national security state" on a "permanent war economy" in which the "military-industrial complex" enjoyed "unwarranted influence," employed "rising secrecy," and turned campuses into tools of the "defense establishment." "Rambomania . . . promotes a sort of war hysteria that desensitizes Americans to the gravity of military action as a means of foreign policy."[15] This about a country that has turned its back on the draft, spends about one-third as much as the USSR of its gross national product on defence, and permits the Center for Defense Information to exist and publish.

The output of the center permeates every North American

peace research institute, peace group, school, and university, as well as many public libraries. Almost every Canadian peace organization makes respectful reference to the output in its own pamphlets and writings. The center provides precisely what the faithful want to hear on every related issue. It is the Word.

Physicians for Social Responsibility, Canada (later, Canadian Physicians for the Prevention of Nuclear War) and Science for Peace were formed in 1980 and 1981 respectively. The physicians are committed to public education on the health implications of high technology, with a present focus on nuclear war; the scientists seek to raise awareness, especially among Canadian scientists and educators, of the dangers of war, especially nuclear war. These are socially beneficial agendas, always provided that they do not descend into scarce tactics, which unfortunately they sometimes have. In the United States, for instance, Helen Caldicott has been president of the equivalent physicians' organization, using her considerable talents to generate nuclear neurosis. Moreover, she committed her physicians to a political movement: the freeze campaign.

The physicians' movement is a stalagmite. It was begun in the United States in 1960 by Dr. Bernard Lown, although it did not become large and influential until the 1980s. The Soviets picked the idea up in 1980. Among those involved in its subsequent "internationalization" were the ubiquitous Ponomarev, Georgi Arbatov, and retired military intelligence general Michael Milstein, none of them medical doctors. In 1981 Yevgeniy Chazov, Brezhnev's personal physician, member of the CPSU Central Committee, Hero of Socialist Labor, and a member of the USSR Academy of Sciences, was named president of the Soviet Committee of Physicians for the Prevention of Nuclear War. The Russian group was necessary to legitimize the founding of the International Physicians for the Prevention of Nuclear War (IPPNW), with Chazov as co-chairman and Bernard Lown as his partner.[16]

As chief of the Fourth Directorate of the Ministry of Health,

Chazov oversees, among other things, the so-called Kremlin hospitals, which cater exclusively to the *nomenklatura*. One of his medical bureaucratic colleagues, Marat Vartanyan, supervises and attempts to excuse the abuse of psychiatry in the USSR to punish and destroy political dissenters. In 1973 Chazov was one of the signatories of a letter expressing outrage at Andrei Sakharov's criticism of the Soviet Union, which went on to declare that the authors "wholly and completely" approved and supported Soviet foreign policy.

The international movement spread rapidly to forty-one countries, collecting a hotly debated Nobel Peace Prize in the process. But whereas the non-Communist affiliates performed as Ponomarev had doubtless intended, fueling the nuclear fear theme and adding new horrors about postnuclear war conditions, Chazov and other Communist doctors issued only token warnings to Soviet bloc publics.

In Canada the physicians' movement has been rent by the human rights issue. The founding president, Frank Sommers, raised the subject politely with Soviet counterparts during a 1983 tour of the USSR. The response was rude, arrogant, and predictable, ending with a warning that there was no place for ideological conflict in the movement against nuclear war. The incident highlighted the political nature of the Soviet campaign and gave an inkling of the Soviet meaning of "peace."

In 1985 Vladimir Brodsky, a Soviet physician with the courage to join a non-party-sponsored Russian peace group, was sentenced to three years' imprisonment in Siberia on the charge of "malicious hooliganism." The Canadian physicians' failure to support him has already been noted. Chazov, however, saw a way of exploiting the concerns of Frank Sommers and other members of the Canadian delegation who valued human rights and freedom.

The 1986 conference of International Physicians in Cologne included a press conference where, according to Metta Spencer's account in *Peace Magazine*, a Dr. Pastore read an important announcement: the release from prison of a member of the Moscow Group for Trust, Alexander Shatravka. He added that Dr.

Vladimir Brodsky's case was being favorably reviewed and that his release was also expected. The statement was explicit that these actions were in response to the concerns of members. It was an unsurpassed public relations gesture, the unique act that could heal the breach in the organization and restore trust. That evening, the exultant delegates rejoiced over the prospects of détente implied by this single act. Dr. Donald Bates, the Montreal councillor of International Physicians, expressed his delight to Dr. Chazov, who smiled and sent a message. "Tell Frank Sommers," he said, "that this is my present to him."[17]

Two years earlier, Metta Spencer had courageously supported the independent Moscow peace activists against KGB persecution at a Soviet-sponsored conference. For breaking the rules as enforced by her Communist hosts, she was unceremoniously expelled from the USSR. How remarkable that she could celebrate an incident that demonstrated in the most dramatic manner imaginable the cold, calculating methods of Chazov and his comrades in the KGB. In the *nomenklatura*'s world, an individual who dared to speak out of turn could be banished, imprisoned, and, if necessary, tortured within a fake system of justice that pronounced guilt according to political needs and, if convenient, released its victim for a public relations advantage.

Would Bates be empowered to order the release of some prisoner from a Canadian jail as a present for Chazov? One wonders in what regard the Soviets held Canada's "exultant delegates," and what lessons they learned for future psychological operations.

According to the *Canadian Medical Association Journal*, Bates characterized Western leaders Reagan, Thatcher, and Kohl as the "unholy trio" and considered that the United States deserved more criticism on the issue of disarmament than the Soviet Union. In contrast, the University of Toronto's Dr. Rakoff, who has not joined the physicians' movement, stated that: "It slowly [became] apparent that peace consists of hammering the West. Not a single criticism of the Soviet Union is permitted . . . How come it is only North American missiles that are wicked?"[18]

When the Canadian movement held its annual meeting in Calgary in April 1986, fewer than fifty of its three thousand members attended. The politically motivated had evidently taken over, and the remainder stayed away. In these circumstances it was inevitable that Sommers would be defeated on the human rights issue. The physicians' board stood firm on its narrow nuclear war focus, a decision that was bound, inevitably, to convert it into part of the anti-defence lobby. Yet paradoxically, one month later the group's new president, Van Stolk, wrote to the Canadian Peace Alliance withdrawing affiliation. He explained to the CMA *Journal* that he had misgivings about the alliance's leftist leanings and wished to distance his professionals from "all these numerous peace groups."[19]

The physicians even went so far as to invite the Klaus Barbie of psychiatry, Prof. Marat Vartanyan, to be their guest. Rakoff remembers encountering him at a Toronto meeting where, as soon as awkward questions were asked concerning psychiatric torture, Vartanyan was "whisked away."[20]

The concept of mobilizing scientists against the arms race was given early impetus by Leonid Brezhnev in 1982, when he proposed setting up an International Committee of Scientists for Peace. This call reiterated a 1981 appeal in the Moscow journal *New Times*, and soon there was an organization headed by Ponomarev, Arbatov, and Chazov to get the show on the road.[21]

The Soviets use only the most politically reliable members of their scientific community to influence Western scientists. Contacts are controlled by the Directorate of Foreign Relations of the Academy of Sciences, under directions from the International Department and KGB. Enormous efforts have been made to prepare Soviet professionals of all kinds for operations in the West. A new lexicon of words and phrases, ideas and responses, is taught, so that people whose political beliefs and social attitudes are utterly opposed to everything the West stands for can nevertheless present themselves as nearly as possible as the mirror images of their Western counterparts.

On historical issues they are instructed to play dumb, adding, for example, that all has changed for the better since the

Ukrainian famine or Stalin's mass murders, if indeed they admit knowledge of those events. On political matters they are trained to mix apparent frankness with mendacity. They will agree that newspapers in the USSR reflect party policy, then argue that this is the way Russians like it. Under glasnost, the Russians presumably like something else. Anything bad is a relic of the past and is being phased out; everything in the future will be good because the future will be socialist. Afghanistan is dealt with in one sentence before the discussion is turned to Lebanon or El Salvador. Only when the subject of human rights in the Soviet Union is raised will the shutter crash down.

The Academy of Sciences is heavily involved in weapons research, and most influential Soviet scientists undertake military work. Academician Yevgeniy Velikhov, a central figure in Soviet laser and particle-beam efforts, is a key contact between the academy and Western scientists. N. G. Basov and A. M. Prokhorov work on laser weapons. Soviet nuclear physicist V. Yemel'yanov is a frequent participant in Pugwash meetings. He is also prominent in the defence industry.[22] None of this is surprising, given that advancement in any field in the USSR depends largely on Communist Party loyalty, and party ideology decrees that the strengthening of Soviet military power and the strengthening of peace are one and the same thing.

Interviewed by *Peace Magazine*, Derek Paul, research director of Science for Peace, expressed the opinion that his host at a May 1986 Moscow conference, Yevgeniy Velikhov, was "an excellent person." Paul continued: "Velikhov seems to be sincerely committed to disarmament. He said that Chernobyl had affected him profoundly and deepened his commitment, and I believe him."[23] Paul is another Canadian who speaks his mind to Soviet hosts; neither he nor his Science for Peace companions Eric Fawcett and Arthur Forer could be accused of moral weakness. As delegates to an International Forum of Scientists to Stop Nuclear Tests in Moscow in July 1986, however, the group experienced a new and sophisticated phase in Soviet efforts to persuade Western professionals that their desire for peace and disarmament was shared by their Soviet opposite numbers.

To disarm the human rights objection, the hosts permitted the Westerners to visit the families of certain dissidents who were in prison; David McTaggart and Daniel Ellsberg, who had offended the Soviets in 1982, were allowed to attend; when Fawcett expressed the wish that Sakharov be invited to join the conference, the Soviet chairman turned the question gracefully away rather than insulting the speaker.

Then eighteen delegates were permitted to meet General Secretary Gorbachev, who spoke of a "new way of thinking," a phrase lifted from a 1955 Russell-Einstein manifesto and therefore likely to impress the guests. It did. Eric Fawcett is quoted by Spencer as being certain that the Soviet Union "can change. It will change. It is changing."[24] What these visitors were witnessing was the start of a new Soviet psychological campaign, "New Thinking," about which more will be said in the concluding chapter.

CHAPTER XII

GRASSROOT POLITICS AND PEACE

"The policy of the Soviet Union towards the West serves to exploit for its own purposes the 'solid anti-war potential' grown up in Western Europe."

G. Voronzov, *Mirovaia ekonomika i mezhdunarodnye otnosheniya* [World Economy and International Relations] (Moscow) 11, 1981

The Soviet desire both to widen the base of Western peace movements and to bring the movements under tighter control found expression in demands that the fight for "peace" be translated into a fight for "socialism," which in turn would enable Communists in the West to co-opt their local social-democratic parties. Ponomarev briefed Communist delegates to this effect at the April 1980 conference in Paris; one year later he told East Germans that "our Party calls on all parties active in the labour movement to concert their efforts against the war danger" and went on to emphasize the "immense responsibility for peace" of Western social democrats.[1] An editorial in *Kommunist* in December 1983 argued that the struggle for peace had become the cardinal struggle, the main battleground on which the class struggle was being fought, "and the struggle for peace can therefore be transformed into the struggle for socialism." Thus the peace offensive widened its objective from merely hindering Western defence and undermining morale to include the recruitment of fifth columns in Western nations.

During 1984 and 1985 Moscow constantly chided Communist parties in the West for failing in their "vanguard role," for neglecting to take control of the peace movements, and for falling down in their duty to convert the peace movements into wider revolutionary forces. Criticism was larded with optimism, such as the following from V. Orel in *Kommunist*, August 1984: "The struggle for peace . . . has a tendency to develop into a struggle with a broader social content. The protest against nuclear war may, in certain conditions, also turn against the society that begets wars."

In Britain the New Left peace organization European Nuclear Disarmament, or END, refused to co-operate in this Soviet strategy. The group's leader, historian E. P. Thompson, may have known from his earlier experience as an active member of the Communist Party of Great Britain how these things were managed.

END is nonaligned; it provides the inspiration for Quebec's Coalition Québécoise pour le désarmement et la paix and Ontario's ACT for Disarmament. It has encouraged independent peace activities in Soviet bloc countries, anathema to Moscow. In consequence Thompson and END have been savagely attacked by the *nomenklatura*. V. Matveev said that "some are trying to batten on the antiwar drives and use them for aims that have nothing in common with the defence of the world against a nuclear catastrophe. I am speaking of attempts by some people like Thompson in England to bring cold war motives and tendencies into the antiwar movement."[2]

Considering that Thompson had asked, "Is nuclear war preferable to being overcome by the enemy? Is the death of fifteen or twenty millions and the utter destruction of the country preferable to an occupation which might offer the possibility, after some years, of resurgence and recuperation?,"[3] Matveev's assertions about cold war motives were absurd. Thompson's sin, in Soviet eyes, had been his independence, his unwillingness to subordinate his agenda—Marxian and defeatist though it was—to the Communist line, which depicts Soviet power as good, any resistance to the Moscow line as evil. The END experience marked the limit of Soviet tolerance of idiosyncratic elements within any popular front, at least until the onset of the Gorbachev New Look.

While the Soviets were trying to co-opt Western peace movements for Communist purposes, various factions within the Canadian body politic were pursuing quite separate but parallel
policies of co-option. A contributor to the journal *Canadian
Dimension*, David Langille, wrote in two issues during 1985:

> As activists we are concerned about how to build and
> strengthen the Canadian peace movement so that it can have
> more influence over public policy. As socialists we need to
> ensure that progressive social movements become powerful
> enough not only to challenge existing power structures but to
> fundamentally transform our society . . . Socialists active
> within the peace movement can assist in political education,
> build on organizational resources, and unite with activists in
> other social movements so as to gain power in the municipal
> arena. When we have a multitude of small groups which share
> the same vision and are capable of united action then we will
> be in a position to put socialism on a national agenda.[4]

The principal actors in the process described by Langille seem
to have been:

• The New Democratic Party—the social democrats whose
traditional defence policies are roughly in line with the "peace
ideology," but whose policy line is hotly debated between the
neo-Communist left wing and the democratic right, some of
whom see the neutralist slant as an election liability; and
• The Canadian Labour Congress, composed of constituent
unions and their members from all parts of the political spectrum
but led by activists varying from centre-left to extreme left and
with opinions on defence somewhere between the New Democrats and the Communists.

Naturally the Communist Party of Canada used its position of
influence within the peace movement to push the political struggle in the direction desired by Moscow. Covert Communists and
close allies within the New Democratic Party and Canadian Labour Congress have established so-called Action Caucuses.
William Kashtan, as chief Canadian Communist, stressed the

importance of these groups in his report to his party's Central Committee in November 1985.

Social democrats differ from Communists in many ways, but none is more important than the recognition of individual responsibility. It might have been hoped, therefore, that something would have been learned from the post-Vietnam experience about the need to consider the likely consequences of policies and actions. Instead, there seems to have been a steady, mindless drift to the left.

From the outset, the New Democrats and Labour Congress flirted with the 1980s peace movement; after 1983 they tried to use it; during 1985 and 1986 they appeared to be endeavoring to control it. It must be assumed that the purpose of these advances was to enhance the social democratic electoral chances: an international issue was manipulated for domestic political ends. Within the domestic arena, it was no doubt argued, the Communist Party of Canada could be used and then abandoned, so close co-operation between the social democrats and labor on the one hand and the Communists on the other on the issue of peace could be seen as harmless.

However, since the Communist Party has no choice but to toe the Moscow line over peace, co-operation with that party comes at high cost: disregarding past disasters and ignoring consequences except in the short-term domestic sense. The price of co-operating with an inflexible partner is the abandonment of principle, and this seems to be a price the New Democrats and the CLC have been willing to pay.

In his 1982 article about the peace movement, Communist writer Nicholas Prychodko noted with satisfaction that various trade unions, notably the United Electricians, Canadian Union of Public Employees, the postal workers, the United Auto Workers, the Quebec Confederation of National Trade Unions, and the Quebec teachers' union—all known for their left-wing leaderships—had boarded the peace bandwagon. While congratulating the Labour Congress on the "positive statement" on peace at its recent conference, Prychodko nevertheless chided it for failing to play a more active role in initiating and supporting peace activities. The New Democrats were damned with faint praise; their reaffirmed opposition to NATO and NORAD was fine, but the party "can yet do much more in and outside Parliament and other elected bodies to assist the peace movement."[5]

While Prychodko's message was being published, James Stark's Operation Dismantle was conducting the municipal referenda exercise mentioned earlier. The technique of confronting political figures publicly with either/or questions related to peace seems to have been noted with approval not only by Project Ploughshares but also by the politically minded.

In her 1985 article in *World Marxist Review*, Claire DaSylva, Central Committee member of the Communist Party of Canada, discussed the political issues. It is true that Communists are apt to claim more for their actions than is justified and that the claims in the report deserve a pinch of salt. Nevertheless, they are instructive, for this article describes the methods by which the Communist Party intended to hijack the Canadian peace movement.

After boasting of the size and diversity of the movement, DaSylva noted how Canadian municipal councils across the country had played important roles in "widening the struggle against the threat of a world war." She was referring to the Project Ploughshares–sponsored nuclear free zones campaign, which she claimed had persuaded over ninety towns and cities and the province of Manitoba to declare themselves nuclear free. Next she turned to the Peace Petition Caravan Campaign, which had

> collected 430,000 individual signatures from all over the country, marked the beginning of a coordinated effort by peace movements in English and French Canada together with the organized labour movement around a common programme. The increasing involvement of the labour movement in particular in the struggle for peace is of special importance. This cements the mass base of the movement and makes it more effective.[6]

DaSylva went on to describe the "growing cleavages" inside

the "bourgeois" parties and the "ruling class," pointing to Liberal MPs Lloyd Axworthy and Warren Allmand, and Leonard Johnson, the general for peace, as examples. She acknowledged that some peace activists still wanted to blame the war danger on both superpowers, an error to be corrected by the Communist Party, which would

> help Canadians come to the conclusion that the threat to Canada's security does not come from the Soviet Union but from the USA. While we need ongoing exchanges of views on this subject, we need as well to unite everyone possible in a country-wide campaign against the threat of nuclear war. Discussion on the source of the war danger should not lead to divisions within the peace movement. Patience and tact are called for.[7]

The campaign for Canadian provinces and municipalities to declare themselves nuclear weapons-free zones was supported by many elements in the peace movement but was largely the child of Ploughshares. As such, it sprang from the apolitical "peace ideology" rather than from the left. Nevertheless, the left played its part in a campaign that was precisely in accord with the Communist Party's oft repeated 1971 call for Canadian nuclear free status. For while such declarations at levels below federal were largely symbolic, they could be counted on to provide pre-propaganda conditioning for voters for a subsequent initiative at the federal level.

Relatively early in this campaign, in 1983, New Democrat member of the Ontario Legislature Richard Johnston introduced a resolution to declare the province nuclear free; it was defeated 63 to 38. Within municipalities, the campaign progressed steadily, and by April 1986, seventy-eight had joined the club. The Northwest Territories also declared itself nuclear free. The first province to make the declaration was Manitoba, whose New Democratic government followed the lead of Premier Howard Pawley in May 1985.

In November 1986 Johnston returned to the charge in an Ontario assembly now dominated by Liberals and socialists. This time he won by 61 votes to 9. Although it was pointed out that the resolution was merely a nonbinding private member's statement of principle without legal power, the fact that so many members, many of them so-called Liberals, should share the defencelessness principle illustrated the power of the peace culture. The resolution itself would provide a springboard for future psychological operations.

In April 1983, the Office of the President of the Canadian Labour Congress assumed direct responsibility for liaison with the peace movement. By this manoeuvre, the left wing succeeded in outflanking the moderate director of international affairs, John Harker, who, according to *This Magazine*, was so reactionary as to believe "in reform, not revolution." The Ottawa Disarmament Coalition noted with satisfaction that after the reorganization "the situation totally changed."[8]

The congress had provided the major share of the Peace Petition Caravan Campaign, supported anti-cruise and Stop Star Wars campaigns, and participated in the setting up of the Canadian Peace Alliance. The Peace and Disarmament Committee of the Ontario Federation of Labour held its first meeting in January 1985, intended to stimulate activity in the world of "peace" by member unions of the federation. To greater or lesser extent unions across the country followed the lead, providing financial and other assistance to the peace movement. Again according to *This Magazine*, by mid-1986 "over one-third of the Canadian Labour Congress's overall budget now comes from government, and this figure is increasing,"[9] so the CLC was presumably well placed to finance "revolution, not reform."

Writing in *Canadian Dimension* in December 1984, Donna La Framboise described some of the in-fighting that attended the planning and execution of the first major project jointly managed by the peace movement and the Labour Congress—the Peace Petition Caravan Campaign. Besides the CLC, the campaign was sponsored by Greenpeace, Operation Dismantle, Ploughshares, Voice of Women, and the Canadian Peace Congress fronting for the Communist Party. Bob Penner of the Toronto Disarmament Network was a leading figure, along with the congress' Prychodko, Ploughshares' Simon Rosenblum, Angela Browning of ACT for Disarmament, Joe Flexer, United Auto Workers, and the Labour Congress representative and evident campaign controller, Neville Hamilton. The petition that was to be hawked from coast to coast included the inevitable current issues of cruise testing, nuclear free zones, and the redirection of defence dollars.

Acceptable though these items were to the Communists, the Toronto Disarmament Network, and the Labour Congress, the absence of a more or less nonaligned appeal for a "freeze" by both East and West offended Simon Rosenblum. But when he raised the matter with Hamilton, the latter refused to permit a vote. *Canadian Dimension* reports that Rosenblum accepted defeat, and quotes him as realizing that "all hell would have broken loose [if Ploughshares had won its argument]. I don't know what the CLC or the Peace Congress would have done . . . They probably would have packed their bags." The apparent Labour Congress determination to block any modification of the Communist-approved agenda is instructive. It would seem that other major figures in the campaign's direction, such as Bob Penner, went along with the Labour Congress–Communist Party position.

Two years after the event the Communist-sponsored front, the Toronto Peace Association, held a meeting on labor and peace. Among those present were Grace Hartman, Murray Randall, the Labour Congress's peace co-ordinator, Toronto Disarmament Network's Wendy Wright, and the Canadian Peace Alliance's Robert Penner. Of the Caravan, Penner said that "without the CLC the Peace Petition Caravan would never have happened."[10]

The Caravan adopted the technique of confronting political and public figures with either/or questions on the motherhood issue of peace, immediately prior to the 1984 federal election. The Canadian Labour Congress was apparently willing to cooperate with the Communists on the latter's terms so far as the wording of the pledge went, in exchange for organizational and ideological backing in the actual implementation of the campaign. In the domestic sense, the Labour Congress seems to have been fronting for the New Democrats. The Canadian Union of Public Employees and the National Union of Provincial Government Employees—the two major civil service unions—each published material supporting the caravan. Yet Linda Hearst, a CUPE Local 79 executive board member, thought very little of the Caravan as a peace movement exercise. She, too, was quoted, saying: "Labour officials candidly asserted that the major reason for supporting the PPCC was that the project would train door-to-door canvassers. The assumption was made that these canvassers would then be recruited by the NDP."[11]

The Women's International Peace Conference, held in Halifax in June 1985, was sponsored by a multitude of groups, with Voice of Women in the forefront. Judging by the contents of the statement issued at its conclusion, and the mass of "affirmations" appended, the Voice of Women's efforts would not have disappointed the organizers of the Prague conference five years earlier.

The entire document might have been the work of the World Peace Council; all the appropriate Marxist revolutionary movements received endorsement. The conference was assisted by the Labour Congress, who provided female organizers. For many grassroots, apolitical women activists, this was their first encounter with "machine politicians." *Peace Magazine* wondered how well the intruders were received. "They [the union organizers] used expressions such as 'fight for peace,' or 'struggle,' and they spoke of gaining 'power'—terms that many Canadian peace movement women avoided altogether."[12] Revolution, not reform, seems to have been the Labour Congress formula, whether the grassroots peace activists liked it or not.

The full-page advertisement in the *Globe and Mail* on May 20, 1985, opposing Star Wars, was mentioned earlier. Based organizationally on Penner's Toronto Disarmament Network, sponsorship was shared between the Christian Movement for Peace and the four regional peace networks that had come into existence over the previous two years: British Columbia's End the Arms Race, Winnipeg's Coordinating Committee, the Ottawa Disarmament Coalition, and the Toronto Network.

The Christian Movement succeeded in attracting only one church signature, that of the United Church Peace Network, Toronto. The coalitions gathered in more than five hundred endorsements. These included many peace groups; some distinguished Canadians signing as individuals, the Hon. Walter Gordon being one such; sixteen members of Parliament, the majority of them New Democrats but also Lloyd Axworthy and Charles Caccia from the Liberals; and a hefty twenty-five unions and labor councils. The Labour Congress's Dennis McDermott, Postal Workers' Jean-Claude Parrot, Public Employees' Jeff Rose, and Provincial Government Employees' John Fryer signed personally, along with Alberta's David Werlin, British Columbia's Art Kube, and Ontario's Cliff Pilkey.

If the networking and the heavy union presence reflected one aspect of recent political developments, the inclusion of Communists in the appeal seemed to reflect another. William Kashtan signed for the Communist Party; thirteen other endorsers were from either the same party or its clubs or fronts. The sponsor groups' readiness to incorporate the Communist peace offensive within the mainstream Canadian movement, in the process compromising many non-Communists, seemed to demonstrate a determination to demolish mental and political barriers and to legitimize the Communist concept of peace as the universal triumph of the creed. They were following precisely *Kommunist*'s advice to convert the peace concerns of Westerners into the cardinal struggle, the main battleground on which the struggle for peace can be "transformed into the struggle for socialism."

The advertisement attracted the ire of the MP for Mission–Port Moody, Gerry St. Germain. The following day he drew Parliament's attention to the Toronto Disarmament Network, calling it a "left-wing advertising co-operative" formed in Canada "to disseminate inaccurate, alarmist propaganda." He went on to name some of the signatories and concluded, "It is interesting to see this polarization of like minded people."[13]

Although supportive of the peace movement, Labour Congress president Dennis McDermott was generally regarded as a moderate. No one ever looked to him as a likely sponsor of revolution rather than reform. His successor in office, Shirley Carr, is regarded as far more radical. She demonstrated her commitment on the last day of July 1986 in a letter to her executive council, affiliated organizations, provincial and territorial federations of labor, and local labor councils. After recapitulating the congress' earlier support for the Canadian Peace Alliance and "our well known views on nuclear disarmament," Carr announced that she had appointed her executive vice-president Dick Martin to be her man on the alliance's executive committee and "Brother Murray Randall, CLC Senior Researcher," to serve on the administrative committee of the alliance. Randall had been heavily involved in the Peace Petition Caravan. Then Carr came to the point of the letter, which was to encourage "your union to affiliate to the Peace Alliance," encourage other unions to do likewise, and to pay membership fees.

By the time of the Canadian Peace Alliance's second convention, held in Winnipeg in November 1986, the steering committee was able to report that of the 280 member groups, twelve were national and another thirty-seven were regional labor organizations. In view of the fact that most peace groups that wanted to join had presumably done so, a steady recruitment of fresh members from the labor movement could change the voting pattern in the alliance. Given the Labour Congress' record of solidarity with the far-left position, this may bode ill for peace activists who had hoped that their alliance might remain a co-ordinating body open to all strands of peace movement opinion, even the subversive notion that the Soviet Union, as well as the West, bore some responsibility for the arms race.

The steering committee also reported on the projects that the alliance had co-ordinated during its first year, notably the No to

Star Wars campaign, and opposition to NATO air force training over Labrador. Bob Penner had moved up from the Toronto Network to run the alliance, and the organization had begun to establish itself as a national body. The convention reopened the issues that had dominated its founding meetings: whether the alliance was to be a vertical command structure or a horizontal co-ordinator. Dick Martin, speaking for the Canadian Labour Congress, urged the delegates to allow the alliance to undertake campaigns in its own name. Peter Langille of the Ottawa Disarmament Coalition was joined by Nicholas Prychodko of the Canadian Peace Congress in a bid to abolish the rule requiring 70 percent of delegate votes to pass a resolution. Gordon Flowers, also of the congress, and the representative from the Northwest Territories, advocated opening the alliance to political parties.

These centralists were opposed by delegates of groups such as the Orangeville Citizens for Peace, the First Unitarian congregation of Toronto, Veterans Against Nuclear Arms, and the Pembina Institute. The line-up was unchanged from the founding convention: the Communists and the major coalitions favored centralized authority; the churches, the apolitical, and the grassroots groups opposed.

The balance had, however, shifted slightly in favor of the first group. The union presence—decidedly in the centralist camp—was growing, and the leadership of the alliance itself, composed of committed networkers, was now a force in its own right. As Penner described it, the "new alliance has tremendous potential to propel the movement forward, but it will have to prove itself to move the hesitant among its ranks, so that it can strengthen its mandate to the point of becoming a truly effective vehicle for change."[14]

The centralizers succeeded in mustering an estimated 60 percent of votes in the divisions over voting rules and political parties, a clear majority but not enough to carry the day. On the topic of alliance sponsorship of campaigns, rather than risk a similar defeat or a victory that might split the movement, the chairman deferred discussion while an ad hoc committee worked out a compromise. This carried the centralizers some of the way toward their goal, without alarming the others. It was as though a psychological conditioning process, once started, picked up its own momentum, reinforcing its myths in the manner described by Jacques Ellul:

> He who acts in obedience to propaganda can never go back. He is now obliged to believe in that propaganda because of his past action . . . He is what one calls committed—which is certainly what the Communist party anticipated . . ., he has disturbed a certain order; he needs justification for this—and he gets more deeply involved by repeating the act to prove that it was just.[15]

It follows that, however apolitical the peace ideology might have been in its beginnings, the only source of reinforcing propaganda for undiluted "peace" is the left, and the left looks to the Soviet Union. Thus non-Communists in the peace movement, including Christians and believers in democracy, wittingly or unwittingly close down their critical faculties and absorb Soviet propaganda in the way that a man dying of thirst might drink poisoned water.

At the Winnipeg convention a young man from Alberta, identified in the minutes as Jim Stanford of the Calgary Disarmament Coalition, waved his Communist Party of Canada membership card in the air and declared that he was, had always been, and always would be, a Communist. The banning of political parties, he felt, was "like initiating the Cold War here. Communists know that you can't play along with the Cold War mentality; you have to fight a Cold War mentality."

Other delegates assured him that the ban on parties did not mean that Communists were unwelcome; "let us not mix up the distinction between allowing persons and allowing political parties to join." Stanford's blatant statement may have been less than welcome to the 45 percent of delegates who were Communists or pro-Soviet, who presumably preferred to preserve the illusions of those present who were apolitical. But no one questioned the words about a "Cold War mentality." This is coded

language for resistance to Communist hegemony; those who resist are labelled cold warriors.

The chief preoccupation of the Canadian Peace Alliance in
1987 and 1988 has been the Peace Pledge Campaign. This may
be seen as the climax of the political takeover of the peace
movement, in which many thousands of supposedly apolitical
peace groups and individuals across the country are mobilized, as
a *Globe and Mail* reporter put it, "to try to make Canada end
cruise missile testing and revamp its current defence policy."[16]

A planning chart prepared by the Peace Alliance showed the
intended sequence of events culminating in "intensive political
lobbying at CPA convention in Ottawa," which took place in
June 1988.

At this third convention the role of the Alliance was again
debated and change was again deferred. Priorities were listed:
the Peace Pledge Campaign; an Election Priorities Project;
and opposition to Canadian defence policies, especially nuclear
submarines. It was decided to establish a Youth Section of the
Alliance.

To the encouragement of all Canadians who value peace with
freedom, the Peace and Security Institute had refused to subsi-
dize the convention with the $50,000 demanded by the organ-
izers. This refusal was the subject of much resentful comment,
letters to ministers, and grumbling. It transpired in the course of
this discussion that the Canadian Peace Alliance was strapped
for cash and looked increasingly to what was called "daddy" to be
bailed out. Daddy is the Canadian Labour Congress.

Meanwhile, activities at the municipal level have continued.
With more than 150 Canadian cities and communities declaring
themselves nuclear free, Toronto councillor Jack Layton formed
an association of municipal nuclear free zones.[17] This was in line
with other Western countries, where far-left and Communist
groups have co-operated to undermine morale and defence in
this way.

The international movement held major conferences in Manchester, England, in 1984, Cordoba, Spain, in 1985 and
Perugia, Italy, in 1986. Canada was represented for the first time

at the third meeting. The destruction of loyalty from, so to speak, the grassroots up is now a finely tuned, international operation.[18]

The movement also encourages "town twinning," in which Western cities twin with Eastern ones, in the manner pioneered by Vancouver and Odessa. This provides the Soviets with another conduit for deception and propaganda, since their end of the operation is controlled by "organs of the state," while the Western visitors or hosts are conniving Communists or "innocents." Pravda is constantly lauding these developments, which serve the cause of Soviet "peace," and at the same time help persuade Soviet citizens not to expect moral support from the West.[19]

CHAPTER XIII

FEDERAL POLITICS AND PEACE

"The evil that is in the world always comes of ignorance, and good intentions may do as much harm as malevolence if they lack understanding."

Albert Camus, *The Plague*

In the period from about 1968 to 1985 Canada's commitment to deterrence and defence wavered, in both philosophical and material terms. The dominant Canadian culture of the period tended to reject assessments of the threat, however well documented, and to denigrate those who uttered them. Both were portrayed as outdated—creatures of the cold war mentality. It was much more fashionable to see tensions in East–West relations as the outcome of mutual misunderstandings.

On his election as Canada's prime minister, Pierre Elliott Trudeau attempted to lead Canada out of NATO. His cabinet and party rebelled, and he was obliged to give way. Instead, he accelerated the process that reduced Canada's Armed Forces from 120,000 members to less than 75,000, decimated the reserves, halved the contingent in Europe, and denied what was left the equipment it needed for combat readiness. Shortly after the Soviet invasion of Czechoslovakia, Trudeau said, "We are hoping that Europe—and the world—will evolve beyond the political partition of spheres of influence, and our foreign-policy review is an attempt to go beyond that."[1] In other words, Canada was to live in an imagined world, not the harsh one that surrounded her.

Speaking in Kiev, USSR, in 1971, Trudeau equated the constitutional structure of the Soviet Union with Canada's. He told his official audience that Canada was befriending the USSR to counter the US threat "to our identity from the cultural, economic and perhaps even military point of view."

Some months after the USSR invaded Afghanistan, Trudeau told the French on a radio program that the West could not win a political or military victory over the Soviet Union in Afghanistan. "I don't think we can help the Afghan rebels militarily in any useful fashion," he reportedly remarked. And he went on: "If to help them means to kill them, I don't find that useful; if to help them means involving the whole world in a new global and possibly nuclear conflict, then I don't find that wise either."[2] Thus the liberal ethos is reduced to defeatism and surrender.

Yet for all these flirtations with the Brave New World of the killing fields, Trudeau never completely abandoned his rationality over East–West relations—witness his open letter to the peace movement, quoted earlier. It was as though the emperor reserved to his own intellectual self the right to make decisions on Canada's alignment and resented pressures from what Ponomarev might have termed Canada's "peasantry." Certainly, Trudeau was rational when he appointed Robert Ford as special consultant on Soviet affairs after the latter's return from Moscow, where for the previous sixteen years he had been our ambassador.

An extraordinarily gifted and dedicated man, Ford was outraged on his return to Canada by the arrogant, even militant ignorance of several Canadian journalists who interviewed him. Although deeply attached to the Russian people, Ford was acutely aware of the harsh realities of the Soviet regime that exploited the people and deeply mistrustful of the Kremlin's intentions. Unaware, perhaps, of the sea change in Canadian attitudes that had occurred while he was serving our interests in Moscow, Ford told it like it was, and the media would not hear him. The culture of self-deception discounted empirical evidence. Of the Canadian peace movement in 1982, Ford observed that it was "a primarily anti-western movement," one that could not be taken seriously unless it was "marching in the streets to protest against the presence of Soviet nuclear submarines in . . . Swedish territorial waters."[3] For his opinions, he received abuse and threats.

Ford's successor in Moscow was Geoffrey Pearson. Geoffrey, son of Nobel Peace Prize–winner and former prime minister Lester Pearson, was the embodiment of the essentially optimistic, infinitely trusting culture that his father had begun to generate two decades earlier before handing the torch to the eager hand of Trudeau. According to well-informed Ottawa gossip, Pearson's blithe interpretations of Soviet policy were often 180 degrees off course from the sober assessments provided by the experienced Ford. Trudeau's own optimism was presumably curbed by the latter's wise counsel. Ford's low opinion of the Soviet political system was matched by his commitment to dialogue. In 1986 he told the *Globe and Mail's* John Fraser that such dialogue must be backed up by Western vigilance. The commitment to dialogue is shared by all three Canadian political parties and the foreign affairs community in Ottawa. The need for vigilance is nothing like as widely recognized.

The widespread desire to maintain dialogue with Moscow has manifested itself mainly in an enthusiasm for arms control and disarmament negotiations. The creation of a special section within the Department of External Affairs to deal with the matter illustrated the importance attached to the subject. Arms control can be an important component of national security, but only within its original purpose of improving stability. It cannot go beyond that limit unless there is mutual trust. Those who are captives of the optimistic culture are apt to deny the need for vigilance; they embrace unconditional trust. Like the peace movement that in some respects they resemble and overlap, they form a pressure group forever urging governments to throw caution to the winds, to follow their hearts and not their minds.

Responsible officials and negotiators, equally anxious to conclude beneficial agreements but concerned too about maintaining the balance of deterrent forces on which peace depends, are accused of dragging their feet. A climate is created in which it is politically necessary to have agreement—almost any agreement—rather than admit to stalemate. The advantages accruing to the Soviets are obvious. When two unequal powers are in dispute, and the weaker is eager to negotiate, any "compromise" is likely to weaken it further. The cynical might suspect that some of this eagerness stemmed from a sense of guilt in governing circles about Canada's weak contribution to the other major component of security—defence. Instead of being seen as a complement, arms control might become an inexpensive substitute.

The interface between the arms control lobby and the peace movement is complex and subtle. Arms controllers who acknowledge the need for vigilance may be interested in the message of the peace movement while rejecting its basic premises. Even so, they are not immune to political pressures. Arms controllers captured by the Pearson-Trudeau-Pearson optimism might be less inclined to heed the restraints of vigilance. Insofar as the peace movement's theme of "see no evil, hear no evil, speak no evil" strengthens their inclination to throw caution to the wind, their commitment to national security is weakened. They become covert peace activists—apostles of defencelessness—in arms controllers' clothing. The arms control community does not as a rule take to the streets or reduce their argument to crude slogans. Theirs is the intellectual end of the debate, where rational discussion, research, and lobbying are the acceptable weapons.

Arms controllers and peace activists meet regularly at conferences ostensibly discussing peace and security. Together they represent, so to speak, the intelligentsia of the movement. To attract funding, high-profile speakers, and mainline media attention, the organizers "balance" the agenda between the pros and antis, while in fact stacking the cards heavily on the side of the anti-defence lobby. Audiences are composed largely of peace movement supporters, the left, and the "new nationalists." The events become festivals of anti-Americanism and defencelessness. They are useful to the peace movement because they draw university faculty and students, professionals, and "pop academics" into the net, generate media coverage, and make the anti-defence message respectable. One such conference was held at Guelph University in October 1983.

Prime Minister Trudeau chose this event to launch his peace initiative. According to a detailed account by Richard and Sandra Gwyn in *Saturday Night*, Trudeau's decision to set out on his crusade was inspired by a meeting with Helen Caldicott, arranged by his "young, beautiful . . . 'date,'" actress Margot Kidder, a peace activist. Trudeau had also read Jonathan Schell's best-selling nuclear horror story, *The Fate of the Earth*.

The Gwyns tended to characterize those who advised Trudeau to exercise vigilance in his negotiations as "hawks" and wondered whether, in deciding to address world leaders rather than world opinion, Trudeau had set his sights too low. The prime minister used Geoffrey Pearson, who had just completed his three-year stint in Moscow, to persuade the Chinese leadership to receive the Trudeau team. The delegation was received there politely—as it was around the world—without any visible results.[4]

In his *Globe and Mail* interview Robert Ford said that the "peace initiative was a total absurdity, and the Russians just laughed at it. Oh, I'm not saying it wasn't noble and all that, but the way he [Trudeau] went about it and the lack of common sense and logic was self-defeating." Yet just these qualities of the wish to live in an imagined world underwrote the whole optimistic and irrational worldview associated with the Trudeau era, one that remains deeply imbedded in the Canadian psyche. The Gwyns rhapsodized over the episode: "This Canadian factor illuminates something about the nature of the peace initiative. It may also illuminate something about Canada." Sadly, they may have been right.

The pervasive effect of the optimistic worldview was dramatically illustrated in the aftermath of the Progressive Conservative victory in the 1984 federal elections, which gave that party a record parliamentary majority. Conservatives who sought to reverse the foreign and defence policies of previous Liberal governments found themselves in a minority. Either because they were themselves captives of the culture, or because they lacked the will to challenge the popular Liberal myths, the majority of governing Conservatives continued to act as though good intentions, even when they lacked understanding, were certain to produce good results. Canada continued to live in an imagined world. The Conservatives appointed a New Democrat, Stephen Lewis, to represent Canada at the United Nations. They appointed an elder statesman of the peace movement, Douglas Roche, as Ambassador for Arms Control and Disarmament.

A sincere and serious man whose dedication to the cause of peace cannot be questioned, Roche typifies all that is best in the apolitical, grassroots movement. Nevertheless, his utopian internationalism seems to have led him into that maze that is the peace culture: the intellectual prison of the peace ideology. Blissfully unaware of the degree of Communist psychological and organizational control over the agenda and actions of Canada's peace movement, Roche distributes collections of his speeches and the "peaceful" remarks of various Canadians at taxpayers' expense, and he praises everything the movement does. At a peace conference in Edmonton in November 1986 he urged his audience to find new ways to inspire young people and to work to create "the world of our dreams." In December 1987 Roche told a Hamilton audience that "Canada's peace movement has taken on a sharp new 'professional look' that goes far beyond the days of peace protests and ban-the-bomb placards."[5]

It was as though the ambassador was trying to reassure Canadians that, although the peace movement had peaked in 1985, and was no longer a highly visible presence in national affairs, its political clout was undiminished. He gave a special briefing to the *Toronto Star*'s editorial board, in which he said that, for the first time, politicians in Canada and elsewhere had to reckon with a popular, stable, and broadly based yearning for action on disarmament.[6] If Roche had understood Soviet negotiating strategy and revolutionary technique, he would have recognized the situation he had described for what it was: the prize most sought after by the Soviets.

As head of the official arms control establishment, Roche provides the ideal conduit into government policy-making for the movement and their covert allies within the arms control lobby. He reconstituted the Consultative Group on Disarmament and Arms Control Affairs, composed of some fifty individuals, many of them arms control lobbyists or peace activists. One of the topics discussed was Canada's reaction to the US Strategic Defense Initiative.

In April 1985 Roche invited specialists from the nongovernmental Canadian Centre for Arms Control and Disarmament to a two-day seminar on this issue. The papers presented were impressive: as the work of scholars committed to arms control, they naturally emphasized this half of the security mix. The final paper, by Lawrence Hagen, provided policy options for the Canadian government and hinted at the desirability of selecting the compromise answer in which Canada would refuse official participation in SDI development while leaving the door open to private participation by corporations.

Centre staff later testified before the Special Parliamentary Joint Committee on Canada's International Relations, which invited input on SDI. The committee toured the country, hearing from numerous groups and individuals, the peace-at-any-price lobby being the best organized and most numerous. As Robert Penner put it, it was here "that the peace movement made its most effective intervention, swamping the committee with well presented and well researched arguments against Star Wars."[7] At the end of this extraordinary performance the committee recommended—and the government accepted—the compromise.

Writing in *Peace Magazine* in November 1985, Toronto Disarmament Network co-ordinator David Kraft exclaimed: "Groups from across Canada have enthusiastically participated in a Stop Star Wars Campaign which forced Brian Mulroney to send an official 'No' to Washington's invitation for government-to-government participation in the Star Wars program."

Unlike the major NATO allies, Canada had distanced herself from research into the possibility of defending communities from nuclear attack. By implication, she had also distanced herself from Western values generally. The outcome was apparently due to a combination of factors: the continuing Canadian government flirtation with unreality; a not always vigilant commitment to arms control that saw defence as a rival rather than a partner in national security; and the pressure from a government-funded peace movement that had been unable or unwilling to distance itself from Communist and therefore Soviet influence. The number of Canadians who had argued for this decision out of a duty to serve Soviet interests was minute. The great majority believed that the decision served the interests of "peace." Caught in the web woven by the peace ideology, they were as much victims as perpetrators.

The Canadian Centre for Arms Control and Disarmament is an excellent example of public-spirited citizen advocacy. Whatever might be felt about the need for arms control to be balanced by vigilance and a strong defence, the importance of arms control cannot be questioned. It deserves a powerful intellectual lobby, just as the subjects of defence, terrorism, revolution, and propaganda deserve theirs. In Canada's tradition, however, supposedly independent institutes all too often expect and receive the best of both worlds: the appearance of independence plus the security of government funding. To be sure, independent groups can provide government with valuable research and advice; payment for such services is perfectly in order and does not undercut credibility. Large subsidies that keep an organization alive, on the other hand, may lead to one of two situations.

In one, the government is financing activities that are deemed irrelevant or counterproductive, in which case it is wasting taxpayers' money; in the other, it is bankrolling a project that seems to be needed by the government, in which case independence becomes tenuous. External Affairs already has substantial resources devoted to arms control, so what purpose can the funding of a supposedly independent agency serve, other than to undermine its nongovernmental credentials? It is hard to escape the conclusion that such funding meets the desire of a faction within the department, or within the political direction, to propagate views that the faction prefers not to initiate in its own name.

The question goes far beyond the Centre for Arms Control and Disarmament; indeed, it goes beyond the subject of peace and war. Canadian government funding agencies have certainly consolidated the hold of liberal-nationalism with all its faddish, left-of-centre notions over the past fifteen years.

In December 1986 the *Globe and Mail* reported that a pro-family feminist group had accused "radical feminists" in the Secretary of State's department of using their supposedly nonpolitical civil service positions for political ends by recognizing and funding only radical feminist movements. In January 1987 Secretary of State David Crombie apologized for the way the pro-family organization had been treated by his department's officials, who had ignored or delayed requests for assistance and denied the applicants "competent, fair and courteous treatment."[8]

Securing government grants is one of the most developed art forms in this country. It may have contributed to Canada's intellectual decline, because independence of thought has been a handicap for those benefiting from the patronage system, while the existence of the system has inhibited the growth of alternative funding sources. Be that as it may, the Ambassador for Arms Control and Disarmament has at his disposal a $1-million-a-year pork barrel called the Disarmament Fund. It is used for a variety of causes, the three most favored in the accounting years 1984/85 and 1985/86 being the centre, the United Nations World Disarmament Campaign, and the Halifax women's conference.

When subsidies and research grants are combined the Centre for Arms Control and Disarmament received a total of $335,700. The UN World Disarmament Campaign is one of the many UN projects to have suffered Soviet misdirection, mainly through the World Peace Council. It received $200,000. The $150,000 given to the women's conference might just as well have been handed over to Boris Ponomarev, so well did it serve his purposes. The fund also devoted some $350,000 to arms control and peace research, $222,000 to conferences on these subjects, $115,000 to church peace groups—almost entirely to Project Ploughshares—about $283,000 to mainstream peace groups, and a small but significant $40,000 to peace education.

Ambassador Roche's largesse is small beer compared to that of the Department of the Secretary of State, which has seventy-five times as much public money available inside the Citizenship and Culture Program as the Peace Fund's relatively meagre $1 million per year, and it is extremely guarded about its beneficiaries. We do know that the department gave another $64,000 to the Halifax women and that more than $13 million flows annually to various feminist groups from this source. The very unrepresentative National Action Committee on the Status of Women, which calls itself nongovernmental but survives with the help of a government subsidy that has risen from $15,000 in 1975 to $411,000 in 1985/86 and to $1 million a year in 1988, has been successful in setting the agenda for many of the other feminist groups.

NAC's annual report for 1985 set out its positions on Canadian defence. It advocated withdrawal from NATO and NORAD and from the Canada-US defence sharing agreement, halving Canada's defence budget, declaring Canada a nuclear free zone, and rejecting any Canadian participation in SDI. In April 1988 NAC wrote to Prime Minister Mulroney calling on the federal government to withdraw the 1987 White Paper on defence "in light of the new spirit of co-operation between the USSR and the US."[9]

If, as reported, the Canadian Labour Congress gets more than a third of its funding from the government, then much of what is donated to the peace movement from the unions represents another form of government subsidy. The provincial government employees, for instance, gave $10,000 to the Peace Petition Caravan and another $8,000 to a Cruise Injunction Defence Fund. Other government departments to which the movement can turn for funding include Employment and Immigration ($8,443 to Conscience Canada for a Children and Peace project), the Canada Council, the Canadian International Development Agency, Health and Welfare, Justice, Labour Canada, the National Film Board, and, by far the most important, the Canadian Institute for International Peace and Security.

One of Pierre Trudeau's last actions as prime minister was to set up a new organization devoted to "peace," which Geoffrey Pearson would direct. The Canadian Institute for International

Peace and Security was established by act of Parliament on August 15, 1984, with Pearson in charge. The act requires the institute to "increase knowledge and understanding of the issues relating to international peace and security from a Canadian perspective, with particular emphasis on arms control, disarmament, defence, and conflict resolution." It goes on to say how this is to be done: by fostering, funding, and conducting research; promoting scholarship; studying and proposing ideas and policies; collecting and disseminating information; and encouraging discussion.

During the debate that preceded the establishment of the Peace Institute, fears were expressed that the new institute might be less than independent, becoming instead a servant of the political party in power. To guard against this, a board was formed, representing various parties and points of view which would act as a buffer between government and the institute. Funding was provided on a scale that helps explain why Canada cannot control its public debt.

By way of contrast, let us look at how the London (UK)–based International Institute for Strategic Studies was funded. Few would question its pre-eminence today in the field of security studies, and it is instructive to note that IISS was set up privately by people who were concerned about the world's future. They raised money from publics, not governments. To justify their requests for funding, they had always to perform to the highest scholarly standards while at the same time addressing key issues and presenting relevant material in a form that nonspecialist audiences could understand. After more than a decade of making ends meet, IISS earned a matching grant from the Ford Foundation. A campaign to match the grant succeeded, and the institute now has investments that, together with other income, bring in some $2 million per year. Because of the imperative to make the most of every penny, the institute is economically productive, self-supporting, and enjoys an enviable reputation.

The idea that problems can be solved by "throwing money" at them is, however, deeply entrenched in Ottawa. So when the

Peace and Security Institute was put together, public money was, indeed, thrown at it, presumably in the hope that world conflict could be "solved" by largesse. The budget was to be $3.8 million for its first full year of operations, rising over the next couple of years to a fixed annual budget of $5 million.

In its first year, the institute gave a modest $10,000 to the Halifax feminists, $55,000 to the Canadian Centre for Arms Control and Disarmament, $38,000 to UN disarmament propaganda, $34,800 to Project Ploughshares or one of its researchers, and $25,000 to the North-South Institute, another supposedly independent lobby. Overall, research and conferences between them received some $346,000, and mainstream peace groups got $395,000. The amount of $82,000 was devoted to peace education. Considering what we know about the ideology, agenda, and organization of the mainstream, and the tendency of many committed researchers to assemble material to support preconceived conclusions, this single-minded allocation of public money is curious, to say the least. It is almost as if the Peace Institute had been created for the purpose.

In July 1986 an article appeared in the *Globe and Mail* airing criticisms of the institute's funding policy. George Bell, a member of the institute's board, university vice-president, and former brigadier-general, was quoted as saying that he was "increasingly concerned about the amount of money and the nature of the projects being supported."[10] He thought that the "security" part of CIIPS's mandate was being neglected, but agreed that this might be due to neglect on the part of defence advocates to apply for money as aggressively as had the anti-defence lobby.

With a government trying to maintain its distance and a board divided into defence and anti-defence camps, the policy and performance of the institute inevitably reflected to a large extent the attitudes and ambitions of its executive director, Geoffrey Pearson. His was an unenviable task, in the sense that he could never hope to satisfy everyone; more serious in the structural sense, he would have the gravest difficulty in reconciling the competing elements in his charter. However, for an optimist determined to "study and propose ideas and policies for the enhancement of international peace and security," as required by Parliament, the position of director provided a great opportunity.

Canada was certainly overdue for a lively public debate on the related issues of peace and security at the time the Peace Institute was set up. The agenda should have been as wide as possible, welcoming opinions across the board. The spectrum might have stretched from, on the one hand, the prospect of a non-aligned, disarmed Canada to, on the other, proposals for a Canada contributing to her own and to the West's defence at least on the pre-1968 scale, but with the latest equipment, including nuclear-powered submarines. Questions of deterrent policy ought to have been discussed from both sides, with the case for the current NATO policy receiving the wide public attention so long denied it in Canada, as well as the case against. Insofar as Canada wished to show leadership in making recourse to nuclear weapons to halt any renewed Soviet aggression in Europe less likely, an emphasis on improved conventional defences—expensive though these are—combined with really effective limitations on the forward deployment of offensive power would surely have been in order.

The debate could be effective only if it included well-informed and unbiased assessments of Soviet and other threats to the Western democracies, noting the various components—military, political, ideological, psychological, and economic. It would also need to assess the means of delivery—the balance of military power, the dual party-government approach by the USSR, providing that power with a one-sided ability to fight the political and psychological battles on the West's home ground, proxy warfare, and so on. Examination of front operations by West and East, of propaganda and deception, would illuminate a severe asymmetry. It would also expose the work of the World Peace Council and its affiliates, domestic Communist parties, and the entire Soviet apparatus for using "peace" as a political weapon. This huge area is "essential reading" prior to serious deliberation. It is also an area that Canada's contemporary mindset has virtually excluded from discussion, preferring to dismiss it as belonging to the cold war—too unpleasant for liberal Canadians to contemplate.

Just as there is a case against defence policies, there is a surprisingly strong case against arms control and disarmament, at least against investing too high expectations in such processes.[11] This argument ought not to be off limits. Certainly the question of Soviet motives in seeking negotiations deserves attention, and examination ought to heed the record of Soviet observance of treaties. All this should of course be balanced by a more optimistic view.

Over conflict resolution, the debate ought presumably to address such events as the Iran–Iraq war, the Middle East, Southern Africa, Central and South America, and other cockpits of war. Both sides of conflicts should be aired; solutions that reject violence ought to be welcomed. The war in Afghanistan called for analysis. How did it begin, how was it fought, how might it be ended? How too should the West and Canada react to such cruelty inflicted by one of the superpowers? Here the debate would enter into a crucial area of appropriate and effective democratic responses to totalitarian aggression—a key to peace during the remainder of the twentieth century.

This is apparently not the way that the Peace Institute has gone about its work. Its agenda seems to have been confined within limits permitted by the peace ideology. Many of the papers and articles published by the institute seem to be excellent. The series of *Background Papers* on subjects such as SDI, nuclear freeze, nuclear winter, conventional arms control, and the "no-first-use of nuclear weapons" are factual and well researched. The institute also published a quarterly journal, *Peace and Security*, distributed free to 3500 high schools and to all university and public libraries, opinion-formers, and all who expressed an interest. The first four issues presented articles on SDI (here referred to as Star Wars, presumably to appeal to the wider audience), Guatemala, East–West relations, apartheid, more about SDI, "The Nuclear World," "India and the Bomb," Grenada, New Zealand's defence policy, and peace education.

Many of these were also politically neutral and informative. And some were not.

The executive director seems to have interpreted his mandate to study his subject "from a Canadian perspective" within the optimistic mindset created over the past two decades, the Gwyns' "Canadian factor." Why else would the institute in its first two years have dealt extensively with issues that have some divisive potential in Canadian–U.S. relations—Central America, the Caribbean, Grenada, Guatemala, New Zealand's anti-defence policy—and neglected altogether such major issues of peace and war as Afghanistan, Angola, Ethiopia, international terrorism, the Middle East? Why else would the publications have pandered to the peace movement by emphasizing nuclear war dangers, including the theme of fear, and by commissioning constantly critical pieces dealing with possible Canadian participation in North American defence? The idea that it might be very much in Canada's interests, as well as the interests of peace, to play a role in defence was for a long period excluded. As though to fend off such criticism, in March 1987 the institute eventually published a *Points of View* paper by Lorne Green, director of nuclear and arms control policy in the Department of National Defence, called *Maintaining Peace with Freedom: Nuclear Deterrence and Arms Control*. It was a welcome speck of balance.

Pearson wrote in the introduction to the first issue of *Peace and Security* that the quarterly would carry articles "by invited authors on subjects which reflect our own research interests." Indeed it has. One example of this editorial policy appeared in the second issue of the quarterly.

The South African crisis is an appropriate subject for a journal dedicated to promoting, among other things, peace and conflict resolution. *Peace and Security*, however, seemed in this case more interested in promoting the intensification of violence. The editors commissioned Dan O'Meara, described as "a native of South Africa," to write on the subject. O'Meara, with two others, had written a book called *Struggle for South Africa*, sponsored by the Marxist-Leninist Center for African Studies at Eduardo Mondlane University in Mozambique.[12] The authors stated they were writing "from a Marxist perspective." The book had a preface by Mozambique's minister of information, and it was dedicated to the late Ruth First, of the South African Communist Party.

Considering that Marxists are ideologically opposed to conflict resolution and peace—excepting the peace of Communist victory—and are instructed to discard the truth whenever it is an impediment, it is an open question whether they have anything to contribute to a Canadian debate on peace and security. If they have, it is purely as the spokesmen of a warring faction—a viewpoint from the trenches. One might expect such a viewpoint to be introduced as such. Moreover, that it would be balanced in the same issue by an opposing statement: in this case, presumably, from the far right of White South African opinion. Two such extreme views would set the stage for discussion and for seeking conflict resolution.

Given his politics, O'Meara made the most of his opportunity. Introduced as a "researcher/journalist," he advocated that Canada "downgrade diplomatic links with South Africa" and recognize the Communist-controlled African National Congress, providing the latter with funding. The article contributed to the South African insurgency war, not to peace. And no opposing viewpoint was presented.

Pearson had used the first issue of *Points of View* to expose his readers to the notion described earlier: that the Russian people do not really want freedom or democracy. He also asked, "Must we assume that our [Western] values are better [than the Soviet]?" He went on: "Both sides in the cold war have exaggerated the conflict over values, in part, because both the USSR and the USA wish to be regarded as lamplighters in a world of darkness." We are thus gently encouraged toward the "moral equivalence" theory, in which the two superpowers are to be seen as equally to blame for the world's ills and the threat of war. More importantly, we are tempted to abandon or suspend moral judgements, on the grounds that we have no right to them. Because our own societies are not perfect (which society ever was?), we should close our eyes to Soviet imperfections.

In the second issue of *Peace and Security*, alongside the

O'Meara article, the executive director discussed security, comparing the "conventional" belief in defence and deterrence with what he called the "naive" vision of the mainstream peace movement. Canada had "occasional misgivings over particular policies of our allies, especially the US," we had been skeptical over Soviet involvement in "the world's trouble spots." In Pearson's view, "the conventional assumptions about Soviet objectives in Europe are now outdated, if indeed they were correct in 1949," and "Canadians should not accept" the notion that nuclear deterrence is stable. SDI was a danger—and no other interpretation was considered, not in Pearson's article, not in any material so far produced by the institute. Finally Pearson endorsed the peace ideology theme that nuclear weapons, not those who threaten to use them, are "the enemy."

The really significant aspect of the article lay not in the detail, but in the overall drift, which seemed designed to confine the debate about Canada's policy within very narrow limits. On the one hand, the peace movement's concept of defenceless neutrality was given legitimacy, being seen as slightly ahead of stuffy official opinion but very much part of the agenda. On the other hand, the door was seemingly slammed shut on any possible consideration that Canada might ever snap out of the apathetic condition in which Trudeau had left her—with hopelessly inadequate and outdated defences and no political philosophy on which to build a rational foreign and defence policy. Consequently, when in June 1987 Defence Minister Perrin Beatty unveiled his White Paper on defence, which contained both philosophy and a blueprint for action, Canadians who had been reading the institute's output were unprepared to make an informed contribution to the debate.

The November 1986 Edmonton conference where ambassador Roche gave his benediction was a quintessential festival of defencelessness. Called "The True North Strong and Free? A Public Inquiry into Canadian Defence Policy and Nuclear Arms," the event was sponsored by the Council of Canadians—a "new nationalist" group—and the Physicians for Social

Responsibility. The Peace and Security Institute and External's Peace Fund provided most of the money.

According to the promotional blurb, "the program provides a balanced point of view" about defence and nuclear arms. This "balance" was cosmetic. Spokesmen from External Affairs and the Department of National Defence were invited to speak before an audience at least 80 percent composed of committed peace activists. One member of the panel, Cynthia Cannizzo, did believe in deterrence and defence. But against these brave, outnumbered, isolated defenders of the conventional faith was ranged a whole regiment of peace apostles.

The apostles invited to speak included the Institute for Policy Studies' William Arkin, the Canadian Labour Congress' Shirley Carr, Gwynne Dyer—equipped with his latest National Film Board anti-defence film, the Veterans Against Nuclear Arms' Giff Gifford, the Physicians' Dorothy Goresky, the Canadian Peace Alliance's Robert Penner, Ploughshares' Ernie Regehr, the general for peace Leonard Johnson, and Toronto Disarmament Network's Wendy Wright. Geoffrey Pearson also spoke.

Penner, fresh from the Peace Alliance's convention one week before, presented arguments that would surely have satisfied the 40-plus percent pro-Moscow delegates at that earlier event. Faced with the risk of the end of the human race, he said Canadians must take risks themselves. The Canadian government should support Soviet peace proposals and "stand up like New Zealand" by telling the Americans we care not for their friendship because "we're going to end our support for the nuclear arms race."[13] Penner's words fully justified DaSylva's prediction in World Marxist Review fourteen months earlier that the alliance would concentrate on "transforming Canadian foreign policy." They were rapturously received by his audience.

The idea that the deterrent balance, the alliance system, and Canada's whole defence apparatus could simply be thrown overboard was the predominant theme of the conference. In answer to a question, Geoffrey Pearson said that "people can lead—can help governments take some risks," a remark that also earned applause.

The risks imagined seemed never to exceed US displeasure with consequent minor inconvenience. No mention was made of the destabilizing effects of such precipitate action: effects that at worst might include the nuclear war everyone wishes to avoid, and, at least, the abandonment by Canada of her democratic credentials. As usual in such gatherings, the international political aspects were ignored completely, the weapons, and now also the alliances, being the only threats to peace.

The frontal attack on NATO and NORAD came predictably enough from Gwynne Dyer. Developing his theme of neutrality, he ignored completely the possibility of non-nuclear war in Europe—the option that Soviet generals now prefer—and indulged in the wildest fantasies of Soviet respect for small nations' neutrality. Later, he showed his newest production, which he described as "counter-propaganda" against the Western alliance.

The National Film Board has produced Caldicott's *If You Love This Planet*, the women's film unit's *Speaking Our Peace*, and the Dyer series, all supportive of the peace ideology. It has yet to produce a foot of film for general release that gives the rational point of view. It has become a publicly funded anti-defence propaganda agency. According to the preliminary list of participants, one of the NFB's staff, Audrey Schirmer, attended the World Peace Council's October 1986 conference in Copenhagen, being registered as representing the National Film Board.

One of the most virulently anti-American speeches at Edmonton was delivered by the Veterans' Giff Gifford. "Is it our policy to be a silent collaborator in US violation of its commitments to the United Nations and to NATO in the Third World?" he asked. "In other words, is our military policy going to be to continue to be one of collaboration in the preparations for World War III?"

Although NATO had created a "stalemate" in Europe (which some observers might regard as better than Soviet aggression), Gifford believed that "the overall function of NATO now is to find ways of dismantling the stalemate." His most controversial recommendations took him perilously close to urging Canadian servicemen to disobey lawful orders. The bravery that he required from the Canadian Armed Forces was the bravery of one Maj. Helmut Priest and his uniformed colleagues in the West German army who organized an appeal against the placing of cruise and Pershing II missiles on West German soil. Gifford ended by saying:

> This too is not a change of role, but an emphasis on the kind of Canadian patriotism shown by such leaders as Sir Arthur Currie, Lieutenant-General A. G. L. McNaughton, Major-General Worthington, Lieutenant-General E. L. M. Burns, and Major-General Leonard Johnson.[14]

Though Johnson was present, he made no comment. What the other Canadians named might have said, had they still been among the living, we can only imagine.

One of the last speakers was Wendy Wright of the Toronto Disarmament Network. She told the conference about the Peace Voter Strategy adopted a week earlier by the alliance. This would confront candidates for the next federal election with an either/or question, or series of questions, concerning peace. In effect, the candidates would have to come out in favor of "peace" by endorsing the anti-defence agenda, or be publicly branded as warmongers. Wright thought a minority government might emerge from the next election, which "would be vulnerable to pressure." She assured her audience that "we are not just ridding the world of nuclear weapons but accepting a new way. We are changing the priorities of our society."

Speaking to parliamentarians attending the Plenary Session of the North Atlantic Assembly in Oslo on September 24, 1987, NATO's secretary general, Lord Carrington, reminded his audience that the likely treaty banning medium-range missiles

> ought to provide a clear refutation of the [NATO] Alliance's anti-nuclear lobby. Ever since the Alliance took its twin-track decision in 1979, the unilateral disarmers were very loud in telling us to avoid deployment of cruise and Pershing II. But,

unless I misheard, they were very quiet when it came to helping us remove the menace of the SS-20. In fact they contributed nothing at all to solving the problem. Indeed, if we had
followed the advice and policies of the campaigns for nuclear
disarmament, we should now be faced with no Western nuclear capability at all, but an increasing and formidable Soviet
nuclear armoury.[50]

So strong is the urge to self-deception, however, that Carrington's logic was lost on Canada's peace movement and its parliamentary supporters. Television news coverage of the treaty negotiations and signing in Washington in December 1987 included
scenes of peace activists claiming credit amid the popping of
champagne corks. In an interview with *Pacific Tribune*, Bob
Penner claimed that the peace movement, and not what he
called "the ultra-right's 'peace through strength' policies," could
claim credit for the pact.[16] In the House of Commons, Bill
Blaikie, member for Winnipeg–Birds Hill, asked the House to
"remember the role various peace movements have played in
coming to this particular point in human history."[17]

False claims to virtuous achievement may be unimportant, except when they encourage folly. Hardly had the wrong lessons
been learned from the medium-range missile treaty than the
movement began to apply the wrong pressures on strategic missile negotiations. A satisfactory agreement to cut strategic stock-
piles will obviously depend on the West showing the same cool
determination at this level as it did over the European weapons.
But this did not stop Simon Rosenblum, political affairs co-
ordinator for Project Ploughshares, appealing in the *Globe and
Mail* on October 27, 1987, for an end to flight-testing over
Canadian territory of US air-launched cruise missiles, and using
the progress toward a European missile treaty to support his argument. Since the type of cruise missile being tested over Canada
is an important component of the West's strategic deterrent, this
appeal amounted to a call for unilateral disarmament—precisely
what would destroy all Soviet incentive to negotiate seriously.

Rosenblum was adding to the domestic political pressures that had presumably caused John Turner, leader of the Liberal party, to execute a volte-face on October 1. Turner had never shown himself to be anti-defence and defeatist and had previously held out against members of his caucus who were. Presumably he calculated that his shaky hold on party leadership needed strengthening, and this could be done only be opposing cruise-testing and thus accommodating the Liberal left-wing.[18] He put domestic considerations above international stability and national security, as many other Western politicians have done, using the self-serving rationalizations of the peace lobby as justification. When we consider the pedigree of the peace lobby's themes of propaganda, we can see precisely what the Soviets mean by reflexive control.

It would seem that Douglas Roche was right when he attributed political power and influence to the Canadian peace movement. Unfortunately it is power and influence for peace *without* freedom.

CHAPTER XIV

PEACE EDUCATION

"All education is a battle to capture the minds of the young. The essential question, therefore, is what those minds are to be captured for."

The Times (London), lead editorial, September 25, 1984

Perhaps the greatest gift of European civilization to mankind is the academic mode of thinking and teaching, which stands in contrast to the ideological mode. The academic method looks for logical coherence, makes use of all available evidence, accepts criticism, and is ready to be proven wrong. The ideological mode has a dogmatic attitude toward knowledge. It does not seek the truth because the ideology is the truth, providing answers to all questions and explaining everything past, present and future. It requires, therefore, that arguments and data be selected and assimilated into the ideological framework, which is deemed infallible.

While the academic mode is abstract and dispassionate, avoiding emotional and moral pressure, and separating academic work from political activism, the ideological regards intellectual and political activity as inseparable. An ideology is sometimes argued formally and, within its own framework, deductively; alternatively it is thrust at audiences in an emotional, moralistic, and pejorative manner.[1]

The essential question referred to by *The Times* is whether the minds of Western youth should be captured by the academic mode, or by the ideological. Should we teach our children *how* to think, or *what* to think?

In the last two decades a well-funded, articulate minority of teachers, educationalists, school board trustees, and bureaucrats of the New Class have fostered various "progressive" methods and programs within Canada's schools. Some of these innovations have been decidedly ideological in character; as such, they have posed threats to academic standards and to democracy. Three of these "disciplines" are world (or global) studies, development studies, and peace studies. All three overlap, as explained by two leading Canadian proponents of peace education, Terrance Carson and Wytze Brouwer:

> Our current concern for global peace requires us to extend our thoughts and actions beyond interpersonal and communal relations to justice on a global scale. Real peace on earth can only be the product of international justice, global understanding, equitable access to the earth's resources, the obligation of technologically advanced nations to help developing nations in a lasting way, and the development of empathy between the different peoples of this world, whose fate is shared by all.[2]

Seemingly without exception, proponents of "peace education" are activists from the peace movement imbued with its peace ideology. From what some of their number have had to say, it becomes clear that they are committed to the ideological mode of education rather than the academic—that they wish not only to impose their own ideas on their pupils but also to insist that these youngsters participate in revolutionary politics. Here are some examples.

• Donald Craig, associate editor of *Ethics in Education*, writes in a special issue on peace education that "the schools' first priority is therefore to educate today's youth to understand and accept the [nuclear] danger and to cope with it as adults. Such coping must be political—only politics, or revolution, can affect the behaviour of government."[3]

• A report based on an interview with Toronto's City School's teachers Bob Morgan, Myra Novogrodsky, and John Pendergrast reads: "We're not just interested in the plurality of views, but think that some views are more persuasive and valid than others. We make clear that we have our biases. We also expect that students will often differ from our points of view. But we believe it right to make our biases visible. We are not neutral in the matter of nuclear armaments and war."[4]

• Jack Boulogne, teacher of, among other things, ethics, at Princess Margaret Secondary School, Surrey, BC, has this to say: "At my school over the past ten years I have pushed nuclear knowledge fairly hard, taking considerable risks about negative (mainly parental) feedback; and I've been able to get away with it." Two of Boulogne's "useful exercises" are "The Great Trial of Harry S. Truman," in which students act out parts in a bogus trial at which the US president is accused of murdering "Aiti Hitachi, a nine-year-old Japanese girl" killed by the Hiroshima bomb, and "The Great Nuclear War Dilemma," which requires students to contemplate 100 million casualties in the United States and Canada caused by a war that "our side has lost."[5]

• Peace activist Simon Dalby was guest editor for a special peace education issue of the Simon Fraser University publication, *Education and Culture*. The Canadian Institute for International Peace and Security provided the money, along with the Alma van Dusen Fund and the Peak Publication Society. On the Soviet threat, Dalby writes that the "military-industrial complex relies on it to squeeze ever larger appropriations from the federal budget, and to keep the arms race going." He goes on to describe the threat as being "consistently exaggerated and misinterpreted for political and economic gain by narrow interests in the U.S. and here in Canada."[6]

• Allan McKinnon, described as a college psychology instructor, insists that "we must empower our students." And as for teachers, "we cannot feign any apolitical, academic impartiality," and "we must be partisan. We must be unabashed advocates of Peace."[7]

• Douglas Ray, of the Faculty of Education, University of

Western Ontario, spoke at an Inter-University Workshop on Peace Education at Brock University in May 1984. He sees disarmament education as "intensely, explicitly political. It rejects the caution that counsels military preparation as a means of assuring peace." Also, "because it is necessary to correct intolerable injustices, education may help citizens reform governments or industries that oppress or despoil." Peace education, Ray believes, "is value centered, comprehensive, analytical, multi-disciplinary, and action-oriented." Teachers "must learn how to motivate, set the context, move to a new phase, de-emphasize, let tension build in appropriate circumstances."[8]

• Writing in the peace education special issue of *The History and Social Science Teacher* in 1985, Ken Osborne, professor in education at the University of Manitoba, advises that peace education should focus on a specific goal, "be it the establishment of a nuclear-free zone; the achievement of a nuclear freeze; the abandonment of some policy commitment such as the testing or installation of Cruise missiles; the adoption of disarmament measures, or whatever." The subject should also be linked to "simultaneous political action."[9]

• Terrance Carson and Wytze Brouwer consider that peace education must "involve the re-examination of educational methods" and implies "an examination of national and international structures." "Peace education . . . is a longer term project which aims both at developing awareness and at giving an orientation to action."[10]

These quotations, taken almost at random from recent Canadian publications, disclose a determined commitment to the ideological mode of teaching. The message is more important than the students. An examination of the materials provided in various provinces of Canada for peace education uncovers characteristics similar to those encountered in Western Europe and the United States, overlaid with specifically Canadian issues and concerns.

A 1984 British study by Caroline Cox and Roger Scruton noticed these features and analyzed them in a paper that is worth our attention. The study found that, throughout, peace studies tended to trivialize the issue of peace and war, to cloud it with emotional appeals, and to present it one-sidedly. Advocates exploited the emotive connotations of the word "peace" so as to beg serious and difficult questions. Even the label "peace studies" was misleading. One technique, apparently, is to preach one-sided disarmament and defencelessness to school children under the guise of encouraging considerate behavior—the latter being an objective that any decent school would pursue anyway, without describing it as a "study." Moreover, "peace teachers" brought the theme of terror into the schools, under the pretence of catering to fears of nuclear war.

Another feature observed by Cox and Scruton was the attempt to deceive pupils by misinformation and omissions over the difference between democracy and totalitarianism, and which is inherently the greater threat to peace. Consequently, peace education tended to undermine faith in the democratic system by blaming it for the dangers of war and all the ills of the Third World. It also indoctrinated pupils with the notions of "structural violence," being the supposed cause of inequality, forced on populations by tyrannical governments, and "reactive violence," in other words revolution, presented as the excusable response. Within this concept, the Stalinist "just war" theory legitimizing pro-Soviet "wars of national liberation" was sanctified.[11]

Carson and Brouwer are faculty members of the Department of Secondary Education at the University of Alberta, home of the International Institute for Peace Education. Two of the institute's financial backers are External Affairs and the Peace and Security Institute. Brouwer, a fellow of that institute, undertook a survey on the state of peace education in Canada in which he reiterates his opinion that human rights, social justice, underdevelopment, militarism, and even agricultural and ecological concerns are part of the subject. Like his colleagues in the peace education industry, he omits reference to the following vital issues as factors in peace studies:

• Various definitions of "peace," from God's "peace which passeth understanding," through the Western democratic view enshrined in the UN Charter, to the Communist concept of peace as the triumph of their system;

• Notions of "just war," from St. Augustine as well as Josef Stalin;

• The relationship between peace and individual freedom;

• The rare and imperilled privilege of living in a democracy as enjoyed by Canadians;

• How peace is maintained in society—police forces and citizen co-operation; and between states in an age of nuclear-armed totalitarianism—defence, deterrence, arms control, vigilence; and

• The political nature of the East–West conflict.

Of all these omissions, the last seems the most grave. Without an understanding of the essentially political differences between Marxism-Leninism and democracy, any discussion of peace and war in the East-West context is likely to be dangerously misdirected.

For an example of distortion of this issue, one need look no farther than the Christian Movement for Peace's "high school curriculum" series, *People Living for Justice*. In the issue titled *Militarism and Hope* there is a section called "What about the Russians?"

This begins with a "history" of the arms race, consisting of the usual carefully selected list of who-got-what-first, designed to blame the United States for setting the pace and excusing the USSR for trying to keep up. By selecting different topics, the list could demonstrate the exact opposite. Then there is the obligatory tear-jerker about the Soviet experience of war. No mention, of course, of Canada's experience. It would seem that the Soviets are expected to be proud of their war record, while we are supposed to be ashamed of ours. (When have the National Film Board or CBC last made films or programs that depict Canadians at war in a positive light?)

The core section deals with military interventions by the two great powers. "Generally," we are told, "the Russians have been very cautious about their foreign policy moves, but will indeed strike hard when they feel their 'buffer zone' or control over that 'buffer' is about to give way." The implication is that it is unfair to criticize Soviet behavior in Hungary, Angola, Czechoslovakia, East Germany, Poland, or Afghanistan; that it is improper to ask why, forty-two years after the end of World War II, the Soviets continue to occupy Eastern Europe and deny those peoples the political independence and individual freedoms promised by Stalin at Yalta. By omission and selection, the Christian Movement for Peace excuses the killing fields of Cambodia and the megamurders of Afghanistan, while encouraging our children to remain in ignorance of such behavior.

The movement, however, is not so forgiving about the United States. Here we find the true enemy of mankind, the appropriate focus of Christian scorn. "U.S. troops," we are told, "directly intervened" in such places as Guatemala (1954), the Congo (1960), Iran (1953), as well as Lebanon (1956), the Dominican Republic (1965), and Indo China.

The first three assertions are simply untrue: no US troops were involved; of the remainder, US troops quit the Lebanon and the Dominican Republic soon after intervening, leaving those countries independent. As for Vietnam and its adjacent countries, few would defend an involvement that ended so tragically for all concerned. But here too there is all the difference in the world between the US objective of resisting North Vietnamese aggression against its southern neighbor and the Soviet objective in Afghanistan, Angola, Ethiopia, and in Europe of imposing or consolidating totalitarian regimes obedient to Moscow. By excluding the political aspects from their document, the Christian Movement for Peace has engaged in a deception.[12]

In his survey, Brouwer lists and describes thirty sample peace education units for use in schools. He writes that "there is clearly a need to familiarize teachers with a greater variety of conflict resolution strategies," and he recommends three publications, one being *Militarism and Hope*.[13]

There are two main methods by which peace educators hope to infiltrate peace studies into schools, one being curriculum-driven, the other teacher-driven. A workshop at the Canadian Peace Alliance's second convention advised activists to advance on both routes. Concerning the first, the trick was to identify elements in the existing curriculum that were vulnerable to infiltration by peace material. "Citizenship" and "global issues" were mentioned as good entry points. Delegates were also advised to manipulate the student-controlled agenda, through unions or councils, and "current events." Where, as in Hamilton, there were student peace groups, these made good allies.

Teachers who were peace activists could advance the cause by getting themselves onto professional development committees—this was a "must." These committees set the programs for teacher development and conventions and could influence curriculum development. Activists should have a pool of readily available speakers to be called upon as opportunity allowed. By ensuring that peace education was a regular subject at professional events, the activists could condition their colleagues into acceptance.

Still, there was the problem of the unsympathetic school board or department of education. Here it was necessary to sell the idea. This called for careful preparation. A four-part sequence was recommended. First, cobble together "evidence" from available studies that "prove" that school children have grave concerns about nuclear war. Physicians for Social Responsibility or their psychologist opposite numbers were recommended sources. Second, work on "social needs"—by persuading trustees or politicians of the link between "the arms race" and "development," and, in the case of conservatives, some financial economy that might appeal to minds obsessed with the bottom line. Third, enlist support from parents, students, and churches—particularly those already active in the peace movement.

With the groundwork done, phase four would set the whole in motion. The obstructive board or department, already influenced by the "guns or butter" ploy, would come under pressure from teachers and sympathetic trustees arguing that something must be done to ease the pupils' concerns. To do nothing would be uncaring, callous. At the same moment, it would receive letters and delegations from the grassroots—actually a committed minority, but seemingly a representative cross-section—pressing for peace education. Both teachers and grassroots would quote from material supplied by the physicians group, the quasirational argument necessary to support every emotional and covertly political operation of this kind.

Delegates attending the workshop were told how such an operation had just succeeded in Quebec, on a province-wide scale. Here the Quebec Teachers Union, CEQ, managed to persuade the provincial ministry of education to help it prepare peace education materials. Thus the operation had government support from the outset and was well funded by taxpayers and union. Initially, some hard-left CEQ members objected to a cooperative venture, fearing compromise. They were persuaded when assured that the materials would reflect their extreme views. When the materials were ready to be issued, a last-minute objection was raised by one of the Catholic school commissions. The thrust was seen as too political and lacking a spiritual dimension. The commission blocked the program.

Immediately, CEQ ran a "propaganda blitz," using TV, radio, newspapers, and press kits. The objectors were depicted as being reactionary and against peace. It was as though they had been threatened with excommunication from the community of good liberal, utopian Canadians. They capitulated inside a week. Apparently the Word of God had fallen before the pagan magic of "peace."[14]

This example may provide a clue to the mystery of why so many otherwise sensible Canadian individuals and institutions provide support for so anti-educational and potentially anti-democratic a concept as the political indoctrination of school children through "peace studies." The peace ideology has evidently succeeded in mesmerizing Canadians, creating that situation feared by Edmund Burke: "For the triumph of evil all that is necessary is that good men should do nothing."

The peace educators have received support from the peace movement's network and from an intimidated public sector. With this help they have set out to perform at the national level the conversion and infilitration techniques advised by the Peace Alliance for the individual school.

In October 1983 the *Globe and Mail* published an article about children living in fear of the bomb. It described the nightmares of seven-and-a-half-year-old Micah, relating to a nuclear war. His parents, described as "well-educated government employees," discussed current affairs over dinner and participated in peace demonstrations with the child. Mum was completing her master's degree in environmental studies and Dad had his master's in sociology. The journalist did not consider a possible link between the child's upbringing and his nightmares, although he quoted Frank Sommers, then president of the physicians' group, as saying that "children are extremely sensitive to their environment."[15]

One year later the *New York Times* quoted Robert Coles, an author and child psychiatrist who teaches at the Harvard Medical School, as saying that he believed fears of nuclear war were largely confined to children of liberal, affluent parents, themselves concerned about nuclear war. "My heart is with the freeze," Coles added, "so that has gotten me into a jam." Coles went on to say that "much of the research that's been done on this subject is just based on questionnaires given to kids. To find out what the impact is you have to spend days and months doing interviews with the kids, their families and their schools . . . I'm afraid this is an issue where there has been political use made of research."[16]

These warnings did not prevent Ambassador Roche and Geoffrey Pearson pouring public monies into a research project called "Canadian Children's Concerns About Their Future." Prof. K.

Ross Parker of McMaster University, assisted by peace activists Susan Goldberg and Brock Macdonald, oversaw the project, which was based on a questionnaire addressed to 7567 Canadian school children in grades seven through twelve. The results showed that, of the children questioned, 51.7 percent listed the war and peace issue as one of their three major worries, 44 percent went for lack of employment, and 36 percent, human relations issues.

This is the document, appropriately bound in a mushroom-cloud cover, that is now available to the peace education lobby to use as quasi-rational "evidence" of the need to calm pupils' fears. Two facts will be conveniently omitted from the presentations to school boards and departments of education. One, that the 51.7 percent figure is a monument to the effectiveness of the peace movement's theme of nuclear terror propaganda, rather than a reflection of any indigenous concerns; two, that the result of any peace education program must inevitably be to magnify the very concerns that have been used to justify the course.

Concern over a lack of employment, on the other hand, has not been artificially stimulated. Education has broader goals than merely fitting pupils for employment, but this prosaic aspect is nonetheless important. Trustees, politicians, civil servants and parents might serve pupils' interests well if they paid heed to this figure. Political indoctrination—teaching kids *what* rather than *how* to think—is subversive of true education and potentially damaging to young people's employment prospects.

Consequently it was extraordinary to hear Stephen Lewis, Canada's ambassador to the UN, saying that the educational system ought to be turning out peace activists. "It is a calamity that peace education is not automatically part of every curriculum," he went on.[17] Lewis was speaking in April 1986 at a McGill University conference, partly funded by the Peace Institute, which was mainly devoted to peace education. His views were rejected by Claude Ryan, education minister for Quebec. Ryan had the courage to say that the first priority of schools was to teach the basics; schools could promote peace by helping to eliminate "prejudices of all types." Yet a few months later, as will be outlined shortly, Ryan's ministry was co-operating in a peace education program more radical and more political than anything previously seen in Canada.

In British Columbia various Vancouver-based peace education lobbies received money from the Peace Institute to produce a guide to postsecondary peace and war studies in Canada, a curriculum guide, postsecondary educational modules—whatever they might be—and "school materials." Smaller grants went for similar projects elsewhere in the country. Even the National Film Board, which already has one hand in the taxpayer's pocket, received $8,000 to turn out a "multi-media kit for schools." For enhanced effectiveness, one wonders, in terrorizing our kids? The importance of such materials in the infiltration and conversion game has been made clear by the New Westminster Public Education for Peace Society, whose endeavors were admired by delegates to the alliance convention.

In addition to producing a well-packaged peace education curriculum called "Conflict and Change," the society has produced a twenty-three-minute video "covering all aspects of the implementation of a peace education program in the public school system, including the needs assessment and rationale for the program, the role of the school board, teacher and community reaction, and student response." The flyer about the video contains endorsements by three educators, all peace education activists.

Ready-made curriculum material and a glossy presentation that shows only the supposedly positive aspects can rather easily persuade parents and authorities that peace education is already an established study, one that deserves a place in their children's schools. Moreover, the educators who speak so frankly about their political agendas when addressing the like-minded at conferences or in specialist literature adopt a very different style when dealing with outsiders. Here the tone is moderate. Political indoctrination is denied, and it is claimed that all sides to every question will be heard. In Toronto in the mid-1980s we even have the subject renamed "critical issues studies" in the long-established left-wing tradition of semantic deception.

A clue as to how supposedly "balanced" material will actually be taught in the classroom is often to be found in the recommended viewing and reading lists. The National Film Board's anti-defence films feature large, and most if not all the literature is from the peace movement mainstream. For an example, see *Bibliography on Materials on Peace Education* offered by the Stewart Resources Centre of the Saskatchewan Teachers' Federation, or Toronto's Parents for Peace *Information Kit*. The latter recommends films such as *If You Love This Planet, War without Winners*, and *Nuclear Countdown*. The booklist includes works by Helen Caldicott, the Institute for Policy Studies and several of its fellows, and Schell's *Fate of the Earth*. Nothing in any of them about the political differences that divide East from West, or about democracy, or about Afghanistan.

Political indoctrination for "peace" is combined with propaganda against US business in a publication of the Federation of Women Teachers' Associations of Ontario called *Peace 1*. The author, Margaret Arnott, provides a "peanut game" in which children obtain treats according to their luck as dependants of Third World workers. They draw cards that describe their fate. Examples: "Your family's small farm produced very little this year because you could not afford fertilizer. Companies from America made record profits. Take *no* treat" and "Your father works at an iron mine. He and the other miners have been asking the company to raise their wages, which no longer cover the costs of bare necessities. The company says it will not because it would cut its profits; in fact, it will move away if the miners don't keep quiet. Take only *one* treat."[18]

In Quebec a Marxist or neo-Marxist teaching policy has been adopted within the "peace" program, although one may hope that teachers will have sufficient professional and ethical standards to reject its worst aspects.

Although the CEQ was the driving force, the blame must be shared by the provincial government, which co-operated in this travesty of education, and by la Fédération québécoise des directeurs d'école, l'Association des directeurs d'école de Montréal, la Commission des écoles catholiques de Montréal, l'Association des cadres scolaires du Québec, la Fédération des comités de parents de la province de Québec, l'Association des directeurs généraux des commissions scolaires, and la Fédération des commissions scolaires catholiques du Québec—all of which endorsed the material.

The CEQ, in common with many other Canadian labor organizations, has published a policy document on peace and disarmament. This calls for consciousness-raising among youth and public in order to generate opposition to defence, nuclear deterrence, NATO and NORAD policy, and cruise missile testing, and to drum up support for the freeze, Canada as a nuclear free zone, the peace movement, and a general state of alarm. While the CEQ may be entitled to these policies, the teachers who compose it are bound by their vocational ethics to avoid forcing political opinions upon their pupils, even if they personally hold those opinions dear.

The earlier *Cahiers pédagogiques* issued by CEQ were the exclusive responsibility of the union and therefore open to criticism from without. One such, *la Jeunesse s'engager au-delà des mots*, introduces its section on peace with the statement: "Daily confronted by the fear and sense of helplessness before the enormous war machine, we forget the power of unity, solidarity, of common action . . . The solution . . . is a collective opposition to the militaristic policies of governments."[19] One of the consequences of war, according to this text, is "L'accumulation de richesses," presumably by warmongering capitalists. There is a section praising the Sandinista government of Nicaragua.

In a preliminary draft of his survey, Wytze Brouwer agreed that "the units present a particular political orientation urging students to accept a particular point of view rather than leaving them 'free' to arrive at their own conclusions."[20] He also reported that CEQ was developing a new text in consultation with others, including the education ministry, "which will ensure the presentation of issues in a manner that recognizes the right of students to develop their own points of view." The result, un-happily, is the new program that was forced through against weak opposition by the church, and which bears the stamp of approval of the minister for education, Claude Ryan—he who had opposed political indoctrination at the McGill conference. The key document is a *Cahier pédagogique*, *"Eduquer à la paix: c'est contribuer à bâtir la paix,"* *Paix sans frontières*.

This teaching workbook commands that at the secondary level pupils are to be indoctrinated in the beliefs that violence "is an indicator of the quality of the human environment," stemming from negligence, brutality, greed, and misused power—the theory of structural violence. At preschool and elementary level, pupils are warned that "they copy the violence seen on television in their behavior," and they are required to promote community action, such as blacklisting violent programs, "taking positive action so that the media bar all violent programs from the air," and telling their parents to provide "recreational activities" instead of violent TV. Elementary and secondary grades are drilled into accepting that, by Canada's "tolerance for the power of some of its allies," the country undermines its "diplomatic peace missions."[21] Not a word is said about the power of some potential aggressors, that make the countervailing power a necessity. The lessons then become indoctrinations against any Canadian military spending and defence manufacture. Dr. Goebbels would have been proud of the sly, vindictive methods employed.

The section "War and Peace around the World" begins with the perplexing statement: "At the international level, many conflicts are now raging in the context of a race for conventional weapons and the threat of a nuclear war." Teachers are told that "it is important that the pupils have enough time to express their feelings of fear, worry and anxiety" about nuclear war. Translated into practice, this presumably means, "get them into a state of panic as a preliminary to brainwashing them." Secondary grades study the causes of war, choosing from such titles as "liberation war," which provides the opportunity for the teacher to legitimize the concept of "reactive violence." There follows a frontal attack against the concept of deterrence, which is dismissed out of hand.

Under the heading "Nuclear Weapons," children are coerced into political action. Elementary classes are to send messages of peace to the government; secondary grades can send letters, petitions, or follow the suggested methods of protest listed on the back of the document—form a peace group or join an existing one, distribute peace literature, make and exhibit posters for peace, circulate a petition demanding that Canada become a nuclear free zone, participate in a worldwide referendum on peace and disarmament. Secondary classes are to sing the song "*Assez*," after which the teacher "asks them to demonstrate, in an individual and collective gesture, how they have 'had enough' of living with wars and the nuclear threat."

On the subject of "peace and development," the usual statistics are given, as always out of context and one-sidedly, with the added threat that "if we do not choose to reduce military budgets . . . international tensions will increase between East and West, as well as between North and South, and the arms race will escalate, which will certainly lead to nuclear war." At best, this is an irresponsibly wild and implausible assertion; at worst, it is a deliberate lie.

The final section, "What Can I Do for Peace?," returns to political activities as a substitute for education. The brainwashed and ignorant pupils created by this anti-educational program are to be ordered by their teachers to "invest their newly acquired knowledge [*sic*] in a program of action." The product of this lesson in propaganda technique is that "each pupil retains one means of action and plans accordingly," taking into account the project goal, the target audience, the means to be used, any deadline, and human and material resources required. A new generation of Goebbels-clones is in the works.

Jumping smartly onto this bandwagon of their own creation, CEQ supplemented the ministry's document with one of its own. This carried over both the title and the Peace Without Frontiers logo, so that the union's document could easily be confused with that issued by the ministry. CEQ provides material excusing Soviet and Polish leadership behavior in Poland, a section alleging that "patriotism, militarism and sexism are all linked," attacks on NATO and NORAD, a teaching plan where students make charts demonstrating US guilt for leading in technological development—all from biassed information provided—and an exercise where pupils draw maps showing the likely effects of a nuclear attack on their home towns.

In the "What Is to Be Done?" pages the union goes further than the ministry. Pupils are to be coerced into endorsing all the peace movement's demands, including no-first-use of nuclear weapons, the nuclear free zone, and a nuclear test ban. "If there is no committee in the school for peace, one should be set up." A questionnaire is provided, together with "correct" answers.[22]

CEQ certainly knows all the answers. It was the establishment of NATO that restarted the arms race already begun by the US development of the atomic bomb. The race was accelerated by the Reagan Administration, of course, and taken to its extreme by Star Wars. For good measure, the point is made that alliances cause wars. The "historical" essay provided to make these assertions is an insult to the reader's intelligence and a monument to CEQ's hostility to democracy.

These Quebec materials have been discussed at some length because that province is looked upon as the pace-setter in peace education in Canada, and we can expect peace lobbies elsewhere to urge governments and school boards to follow the same path. It is the road to serfdom.

Of course we want our schools to produce young Canadians who desire peace and who work for it. The political intolerance and the brainwashing of youth that are inseparable from "peace education" as we know it are, however, small acts of war. They condition young people for the "permanent struggle" of Marxism-Leninism or any other totalitarian vice. Knowledge and the power to reason are two assets in the creation of real peace. These emerge only from educational systems dedicated to the academic mode.

At the university level, the subject of peace and war can be studied within strategic studies, international politics, and the history of international relations and of war. Philosophy, logic, theology, economics, and sociology are also relevant. Departments of war studies have existed for decades in some universities, and these have always devoted a large part of their effort to promoting peace. At Kings College, London, England, for instance, the war studies department is especially strong on ethics, and the pacifist viewpoint is well represented in the faculty.

There is no intrinsic reason why such departments should not be called war and peace studies or, indeed, peace studies. However, experience seems to show that whenever the latter title is adopted the department becomes politically biassed and drifts away from the academic toward the ideological mode. Bradford University in England established what has become that country's major postgraduate school of peace studies in 1973. In their survey, Caroline Cox and Roger Scruton showed that the school had acquired all the biasses and anti-educational characteristics that a one-sided approach inevitably attracts.

There is, nevertheless, one important distinction between peace education in schools and in universities. As Professor Hilborn has pointed out, at the higher level such programs "at least have the virtue of being optional."[23]

CHAPTER XV

NEW THINKING

"One will readily agree that any army which does not train to use all
the weapons, all the means and methods of warfare that the enemy
possesses, or may possess, is behaving in an unwise or even criminal
manner. This applies to politics even more than it does to the art of
war . . . Unless we learn to apply all the methods of struggle, we may
suffer grave and sometimes even decisive defeat."

Lenin[1]

Prof. Jacques Ellul has written that Lenin was convinced that
the extreme use of all means would, as a matter of course, lead to
the establishment of socialist society. The end—utopian
communism—thus became a truism that was easily forgotten.
That is why Lenin designed a strategy and a tactic on the political plane. There as elsewhere he permitted the means to assume
first place; but that led him, on the one hand, to modify Marx's
doctrine and, on the other, to give the doctrine itself a level of
importance secondary to the means or tactics of achieving it.[2]

The major impact of Mikhail Gorbachev upon Soviet society
has been his quest for new means. Under Brezhnev, means had
become static, part of the fixed fabric of Soviet life. The status
quo benefited the party functionaries, but it did not advance the
cause of socialism. Lying derailed astride the track, the engine of
revolution blocked the progress it was supposed to achieve. Perestroika attempts to get the engine back on the rails, headed in
the correct direction with a full head of steam. Glasnost is essential, because unless the crew and the passengers realize what has
happened, they cannot be expected to push and shove effec-

tively. When Gorbachev talks of democracy, he means mass involvement at grassroots level, a sense of participation in the revolutionary process; his use of the word does not embrace the essence of its meaning in the West: free political choice.

The search for new means extends to global politics. The frantic and probably doomed efforts to get the Soviet economy working efficiently are marketed abroad like snake oil. Western journalists report ambitions as though they were achievements and Leninist "democracy" as if it were the real thing. At the same time the apparatus of international persuasion and coercion, co-ordinated by the International Department, the Propaganda Department, and the KGB, has launched a major offensive to weaken the non-Communist states, isolate the United States, and dismantle the Atlantic Alliance and its strategy of nuclear deterrence. The French sovietologist Françoise Thom has described some of Gorbachev's new methods: a renewed Soviet grip on the Communist states and attempted rapprochement with Communist China; the extension of the tactics of "front" organizations to international relations, by creating anti-American groupings at the regional level; the covert control of social democratic parties by Communist parties; and the division of Western societies between "peace" and "war" factions.[3]

Gorbachev's evident intention is to persuade the West that Soviet Communism no longer harbors global ambitions. He tells us what we want to hear: that the USSR, though "socialist," is really no different from other great powers; that deals can be struck on the basis of spheres of interest; and that the spectre that has been haunting the world for seventy years, in spite of what Marx and Engels might have written, was always a figment of our imagination. One of the conduits for these messages is his book, *Perestroika*.

Although this propaganda masterwork is available to Soviet readers, the relatively small run of the Russian-language version (300,000, against three million copies of Gorbachev's speech of November 2, 1987) suggests that the book is intended primarily for Western readers, few of whom have been trained to decipher Marxist-Leninist doubletalk.

Indeed, the US organization MediaWatch has pointed out that, whereas the US edition begins: "The purpose of this book is to talk without intermediaries to the citizens of the whole world," going on about common sense and the future of our planet, the edition in Hungarian starts: "In our work and worries, we are motivated by those Leninist ideals and noble endeavours and goals which mobilized the workers of Russia seven decades ago." Perestroika, in this version, is "a continuation of the October Revolution."[4]

The crudity of the appeal to Western sentiment in the second part of the book inspired Harvard professor Richard Pipes to write that the work "aims at a very low level, one that Soviet experts must have decided represents the common Western denominator of ignorance and wishful thinking. Not the least depressing feature of this work, hailed by the *New York Times* as the 'international publishing event of the year,' is what it reveals of the Soviet establishment's contempt for the West."[5]

The deceptive and psychological strategies adopted by Gorbachev undoubtedly owe much to two individuals of exceptional experience and talent. Anatoliy Dobrynin was Soviet ambassador to the United States for twenty-four years; Alexander Yakovlev, a former exchange student at Columbia University, was ambassador to Canada for ten years. Between them, these men understand the social and political structures of the democracies intimately, especially our vulnerabilities. Yakovlev is a professional propagandist of outstanding brilliance, and he evidently impressed Gorbachev during the latter's visit to Canada in 1983. Both ambassadors were recalled to Moscow to serve in key appointments under Gorbachev: Dobrynin to replace Boris Ponomarev as head of the International Department; Yakovlev as secretary for propaganda.

Judging from policies subsequently adopted, and from the tone of Gorbachev's book, it would seem that what these two men told the new secretary general went something like this: "The West is weak and divided, lacking political vision, religious or philosophical conviction, racked by guilts, and concerned only with material well-being. Although the peace offensive did not have the short-term results hoped for, in that the cruise and Pershing II missiles were deployed, it did succeed in a wider, political sense in that it persuaded many people that *nuclear weapons, rather than any country, were the major threat to mankind.* That was a great achievement. But in spite of this, mistrust of communism and the Soviet Union still remained powerful.

"For this, general secretary, the USSR has only itself to blame. In spite of all our advice to the effect that 'realistic' forces in the West (progressives and liberals) were only too anxious to deceive themselves and be deceived concerning Soviet policies, intentions, and military strength, and to fall in with almost any proposals Moscow might offer, your predecessors' adventures in Africa, Asia, Latin America, and, most importantly, Afghanistan have forced glimpses of reality upon unwilling eyes so that even the most stupid and cowardly could not deny the threat that we pose to their very existence. Our propaganda has been saying one thing; our actions, another.

"Bring the two into line, comrade secretary general, and you will have the West eating out of your hand. They are *tired* of resisting us; many are looking for a way out. Offer them 'peace' and they will accept. Most important, recognize that the climate of opinion created in the West by our peace offensive makes it increasingly difficult for politicians to endorse nuclear weapons and deterrence policy. Jump in with an offer that appeals to public sentiment, and governments will have to say yes."

Gorbachev must also have received advice from his military experts. Foremost among these would have been Marshal of the Soviet Union N. V. Ogarkov, who had been arguing for several years that a war in Europe could be won and won quickly *without* nuclear weapons, provided the West did not or could not resort to their use.[6] This highly professional advice matched the political realization that nuclear war offered only mutual destruction. Whilst nuclear weapons served the Western doctrine of deterrence perfectly, by making war too dangerous, they were worthless as a *means* of aggression. Although the Soviet achievement of parity or superiority in strategic systems provided security against unprovoked US attack, this was a limited benefit because the Politburo had known for years that such an attack was highly improbable. Parity had not unlocked the door of opportunity that had been slammed shut in 1945. New means were therefore needed on the international level: means that were *usable*.

Central in the new pack of ideas was "peace." By a series of dazzling proposals, statements, and negotiations, the Soviet Union seized the initiative and set the agenda. The West, unable to respond outside the narrow limits imposed by the "peace culture," was seen as uncertain, divided, and fearful. Gorbachev was destroying the West's deterrence structure, stone by stone, and being applauded by the West as he did so. The world, Europe in particular, was being made safe for conventional aggression. Even the inclusion in this arms control process of conventional force cuts is a means to the same end; for these may remove the US presence from Europe and, with that, eliminate "extended deterrence" as a credible doctrine. The product could be a West Europe dependent on the USSR for its security, and the consequence of that would be a choice between gradual surrender and war. The new way of thinking required of Western Europe is to choose the former.

To project these psychological bombshells into the Western camp, the subversive apparatus was revamped. The new head of the International Department, Dobrynin, received continued support from the veteran Vadim Zagladin—he who had launched the campaign of nuclearphobia back in 1970—and a new first deputy chief, Georgiy Korniyenko, a high-calibre diplomat. In addition, Lieut.-Gen. Viktor Starodubov, formerly Soviet commissioner at the Standing Consultative Commission (on arms control), was transferred to the International Department, presumably to handle the psychological conditioning of Western opinion-formers on the subject of arms control.

New leadership has been supplied for the two principal organizations responsible for executing International Department policy over "peace." In the World Peace Council, Romesh Chandra, who had run the front as its president since 1977, was moved sideways and effectively downward. The new head is

Johannes Pakaslahti, a Moscow-line Finnish Communist with the soft touch of the polished propagandist. He is the secretary general, a post re-established for the occasion. In the Soviet Peace Committee, the abrasive, crudely ideological chairman, Yuri Zhukov, was ousted in favor of another smoothie, KGB agent Genrith Borovik. A new group, the International Fund for the Survival of Humanity, has also been formed with offices in Stockholm, Washington, and Moscow.[7] This will likely act as a transmission belt rather than a straightforward front.

New thinking in the exploitation of the universal desire for peace has led to several interesting new means. It was apparently appreciated that the political potential of Western peace movements greatly exceeded their instrumental value as lobbies against particular NATO weapons systems. With Gorbachev taking the lead in arms control proposals, the pre-propaganda of the previous six years of peace offensive could be used both to gain advantage in all negotiations and to divide Western societies into two warring camps—those who supported "peace" and those who opposed—a formulation offering better results than the exhausted Marxian division between exploited and exploiting classes. But it was also appreciated that the rigid ideological line previously adhered to by the Peace Committee and the World Peace Council—that Western weapons were evil, while Soviet weapons were sublime—would not sell in the West beyond the narrow confines of the hard-core Communists.

Gorbachev's "return to Lenin" reinstates tactical flexibility to pride of place among means. Even ideology can be bent, so long as this promises success. So all manner of compromises and deceptions were brought into play.

To the Soviet audience, Gorbachev promises there will be no change in the historically determined march to global communism, as he did on Moscow television on November 2, 1987: "In October 1917 we departed the old world and irreversibly rejected it. We are travelling to a new world, the world of communism. We shall never deviate from this path."

At the same time, but on different channels, he tells the outside world that the Soviet leaders see communism as "the inevitable evolution of the world. Let the West think that capitalism is the highest achievement of civilization. It's their prerogative to think so. We simply do not agree with this. And let history decide who is right."[8] By omitting the fact that the party is committed to proving history right and to hastening the process by all means, Gorbachev leaves his Western readers with the comforting impression that there is no threat.

For the domestic audience, Gorbachev does nothing to change the indoctrination of hatred of the West, of constant suspicion and fear, that is necessary to maintain discipline and support for the warfare state. For the West, he redoubles the efforts of the previous seven years to redefine the "enemy." By loudly proclaiming himself as the champion of peace, he makes it socially unacceptable in the democracies for anyone to doubt his sincerity, to question Soviet motives, or to be anti-Communist. Then he begins a second redefinition of the enemy, although in truth it was one attempted by Ponomarev many years earlier: rather than regarding the weapons as the enemy, ought not good people in the West see the opponents of peace as the evil threat? Whereas Ponomarev's statements had no credibility outside Communist ranks, Gorbachev's every word is golden. New thinking defines NATO's armed forces, Westerners who believe in democracy, defence, and deterrence, and anyone who resists vocally or spiritually or physically as "enemies of the people." Inevitably, the chief defender of the West, the United States, features large in this demonology.

While the Soviet Peace Committee continues to uphold the objective truth internally, insisting on the moral purity of Soviet weapons and the evil of Western, to the outside audience total flexibility is practised. Borovik has encouraged meetings with prominent Westerners of all political views, especially conservatively minded people, and permits polite criticism of Soviet policies and an even-handed condemnation of all weapons. He tells them what they want to hear: that the Soviets share the Western concept of peace.

Pakaslahti has converted the World Peace Council into a front catering almost exclusively to Western European and

North American audiences. In a determined and skilful effort to repair credibility and create an appearance of nonalignment, the council actively courts the nonaligned segment of the Western peace movements, especially Thompson's European Nuclear Disarmament movement, groups that were anathema two years earlier. East European peace groups, controlled by their governments, are encouraged to host visits by such Western activists, presumably to compromise and deceive them. The Council's journals, *Peace Courier*, *Disarmament Forum*, and *New Perspectives*, now look like Western publications and, being composed almost entirely of articles by Western peace activists, read the same way. Reports from Canada and other countries appear regularly. While no criticism of Soviet weapons and policies appears in these publications, stark ideological statements are avoided; almost nothing written in Moscow appears at all. Two years earlier, Pakaslahti would have been expelled from the party for writing that "neither an anti-American nor anti-Soviet peace movement is necessary," yet these were his words in the new-look *Peace Courier*.[9]

The new policy was well illustrated in the second issue of *Peace Courier* for 1988. A special double-page "interview" featured the de facto head of the Canadian Peace Alliance, Robert Penner. His questioner was the Canadian Communist Gordon Flowers. The content was what you might expect.[10] Penner knows perfectly well that *Peace Courier* is a World Peace Council publication and that the council belongs to Moscow. The question that Flowers did not ask was why Penner agreed to the interview.

Gorbachev's desire to convert Western conservatives and moderates was well illustrated by two events. A Soviet-sponsored international forum, "For a Nuclear Free World, for the Survival of Humanity," was staged in Moscow in February 1987. Although this was a project of the Soviet Peace Committee, efforts were made to suggest that it was called "on the initiative of Soviet cultural figures." Yevgeniy Velikhov, chairman of Soviet Scientists Against the Nuclear Threat, later declared that the meeting had been arranged "on the initiative of a group of scientists,"[11] as if one foreigner could be summoned to Moscow by *any* nongovernmental group, let alone one thousand. Invited guests included lifelong critics of the Soviet Union. Gorbachev himself addressed the gathering. And International Department chief Dobrynin went out of his way to flatter the Generals for Peace and Disarmament, giving them a special welcome.

The second example of the campaign to deceive Western moderates occurred in Washington, DC, in December 1987. During his summit visit to sign the European missile treaty, Gorbachev hosted several private meetings with groups of US intellectuals, activists, businessmen, and publishers. Robert Bernstein of Random House, Katherine Graham of the *Washington Post*, Ted Turner of Turner Broadcasting, and Laurence Tisch, CBS, were in the last category. Others invited included Stephen Cohen, the *Nation's* Soviet columnist, John Kenneth Galbraith, Billy Graham, George Kennan, Bernard Lown, founder of the physicians' group, and Gene La Rocque, director of the Center for Defense Information.

La Rocque told a reporter that he had "a nice chat with Mr. Gorbachev and Raisa Gorbachev. Mr. Gorbachev indicated he knew . . . exactly who I was [and] thanked me for all the initiatives I had taken last year."[12] Indeed he might. There is no record of Gorbachev having met Michael Myerson, his official "peace" apostle in the United States, long-term Communist, and head of the US Peace Council. It would never do for the leader of the supposedly non-Communist Soviet Union to be seen associating with "subversives."

Prime Minister Thatcher's courageous statements to Gorbachev and others that nuclear weapons keep the peace and should therefore stay in military inventories for as long as political threats remain have been almost unique within the Western Alliance.[13] Even President Reagan seems to have succumbed to Gorbachev's "charm offensive," going on record as saying that, whereas Moscow used to seek world domination, Soviet leaders "no longer feel that way." Small wonder that ordinary citizens, with limited access to information beyond media reports, have often felt confused or deceived.

A discussion bulletin issued by the Communist Party of Canada in preparation for its 1988 congress insisted that the "policy of nuclear deterrence must be compelled to give way to a policy of total nuclear disarmament." Lest there be any confusion about Moscow's orders, the statement continued: "The Canadian government *must be compelled to come out for the total elimination of nuclear weapons.*"[14]

At the end of a recent article on Soviet psychological policies, Roger Beaumont concluded:

> The Soviets' hard-headed, rigorous, numerical, historically based approach to doctrine and strategy formulation should be kept in view in considering the recent apparent changes in policy manifested in *glasnost.* Both veteran Sovietologists and defectors have raised a warning against optimism. Both have seen variants of it before and accept Gorbachev's *defensas* of Marxist-Leninist-Pavlovian ideology and protestations that it is undilutable at the heart. *Soviet psychologists have discovered that a few phased signals alter perception of an object more than the actual change in the nature of the object.*[15]

The ideology of peace that had been created to provide the faithful of the Canadian peace movement with an all-embracing creed had never been acceptable beyond the circle of adherents. Various aspects, such as the notion that nuclear weapons were the enemy, had been adopted quite widely, but the package as a whole failed to capture the multitude of Canadian minds. The weak links in the cycle of beliefs were the "no evil" theme, which denied the evidence of seventy years and the bloodshed of Afghanistan in order to remove the Soviet threat, and the peace movement's disdain for freedom and human rights.

Gorbachev's charm offensive has gone a long way to melt Canadians' resistance to these peace movement themes, and therefore to make the peace ideology package more widely acceptable. "A few phased signals" from Moscow have changed perceptions throughout the West. The "no evil" theme has been the prime message carried by these signals. Gorbachev has told us what we want to hear. This is not to say that a majority of Canadians is willing to surrender democratic freedoms; however, in the perceived absence of a threat, resistance to communism can be abandoned without placing those freedoms at risk.

Field Marshal Montgomery defined leadership as "the will to dominate, together with the personality that inspires confidence." Gorbachev is the living embodiment of this description. To a considerable extent, he has used his personality to impose his will upon the West. While at the personal level it is appropriate to admire this performance, politically it should ring alarm bells. Gorbachev also benefits from the fear engendered by the peace offensive.

Specialists in terrorism studies have identified what they term the Stockholm syndrome. According to this widely accepted theory, hostages tend in time to identify their own hopes of survival with the well-being of their captors. They fear that the police chief, while doing his best to locate and rescue them, will botch the operation, and the hostage lives will be forfeit. The "enemy" is redefined. If the bandit leader promises to release the hostages, he is seen as a savior. For police chief read Reagan; for bandit leader read Gorbachev. Add the charisma, and it becomes clear why Western Europeans in 1987 identified Gorbachev rather than Reagan with "peace."

A January 1988 opinion poll sponsored by the Canadian Institute for International Peace and Security, at taxpayers' expense, showed that Canadians, like Western Europeans, had suffered psychological injuries. A majority considered that Gorbachev was doing more for peace than President Reagan, that the two superpowers were morally equivalent, and other conclusions had been drawn as intended by Yakovlev.[16] Geoffrey Pearson rushed to print, throwing doubt on the threat assessment that had appeared in the Defence White Paper and advocating annual reassessments, a reaction that was, of course, precisely that anticipated by Yakovlev.[17] No defence effort can be sustained unless there is continuity; the proposal would undercut the long-overdue attempt to modernize Canada's Armed Forces.

According to *Toronto Star* reporter Val Sears, the same poll persuaded the Liberal party that "what Canadians want is a less warlike defence policy, particularly in the Arctic." Apparently accepting the poll results at face value, Liberal leader John Turner was reported as producing "the bones of a Liberal defence position that would eliminate nuclear submarines and demilitarize the Arctic."[18] Round Two to Yakovlev; reflexive control wins again?

Sears quotes Pearson in support of Arctic demilitarization. He also quotes John Lamb, of the Canadian Centre for Arms Control and Disarmament, dismissing the idea as a "thinly veiled [Soviet] effort to hive off Danish and Norwegian support for NATO," and Ron Purver of the Peace and Security Institute saying that it was "quite impractical." Nowhere in the article did Sears remind readers that the Soviet Union has the massive base on the Kola Peninsula—by far the largest fixed nuclear installation in the Arctic—and that they have no intention of including it in their proposed "zone of peace."

Fortunately for the nation's future, Canadians have demonstrated remarkable sense in the face of an eight-year bombardment with "peace" nonsense. Opinion polls, including the one from the Peace and Security Institute, confirm steady majority support for Canadian participation in NATO and for a strong Canadian military. The institute's poll, in spite of its bewildering confusion of responses from a public under psychological attack, also showed that 58 percent of the Canadians questioned agreed that "the Soviet military threat is constantly growing and represents a real, immediate threat to the West."[19] It would seem that the Soviets may have been more successful in influencing soft-headed policy élites and the media than ordinary hard-headed Canadians.

It is an open question how successful the Gorbachev-Yakovlev offensive will be in dividing Western societies into warring factions, with the "peace" factions acting as revolutionary vanguards in the Soviet cause. In West Germany the opposition Social Democratic Party has committed itself to the goal of a "security partnership" with Warsaw Pact countries, which would probably amount in practice to assimilation by the pact. In government, such a party might destroy NATO; in opposition, it might form the nucleus of a pro-Soviet "peace" faction. In Canada Geoffrey Pearson wishes to encourage a debate between "those who believe that deterrence and a balance of forces is the guarantee of peace, and those who believe that it leads to war."[20] There is no sinister political twist to that formulation, but it distorts the situation out of all recognition.

The true debate is between those who believe that deterrence, defence, and diplomacy offer the best policy for preserving peace and our freedoms, and those so fearful, or so uncaring about freedom and human rights, or both, that they prefer to submit *rather than live with a small measure of uncertainty.*

It is the first group that deserves to be on the high moral ground, being the forces of both peace and freedom. Access to this lofty zone, however, requires more than the expression of pious platitudes. It calls for intellectual as well as political effort, particularly in the rejection of the dangerous utopian illusion that nuclear weapons can be abolished. It is necessary that the genuinely new thinking of the atomic age be understood and championed: that nuclear weapons have for the first time in history provided mankind with the means of preventing war, of using technology to deter rather than fight. While the forces of peace and freedom welcome arms control treaties that improve stability, they are not fixated with arms control as an end in itself.

What will it take to persuade the likes of this author that the Soviet Union no longer threatens the West?

The simplest and most satisfactory answer would be the outright rejection by all Politburo members, proclaimed throughout the USSR and repeated in texts and teachings, of the doctrine of historical determinism as unscientific and false, and confirmation that it no longer underpins party ideology.

Since no senior Communist can possibly agree to this and remain a Communist, such an answer could only come *after* the party is overthrown. Therefore it is likely to come later rather than sooner, although we cannot be sure.

From a party that wishes to introduce real political reforms while clinging to the essential ideological tenets that provide a cloak of legitimacy, these might be important *first* steps:[21]

• To announce that antagonism between nations or between groups on the basis of class is outmoded, and that consequently the whole notion of a struggle between capitalism and socialism is obsolete.

• To repudiate such errors and crimes as the collectivization of agriculture in the 1920s and 1930s; to allow the administration of justice in the USSR to be independent of party and government; to release all political prisoners; to permit religious freedom and to abolish the hideous abuse of psychiatry as a means of repression and punishment.

• To repeal the article in the Soviet Constitution that obliges the USSR to support "the struggle of peoples for national liberation," and withdraw Soviet troops *and support* from Afghanistan, Angola, Ethiopia, and so on.

• To revise relationships between the USSR and the central and Eastern European states to permit the Yalta Agreement to be implemented and free elections held, while maintaining security through a defensively oriented Warsaw Pact and a Finland type of bilateral relationship.

• To abolish the International Department and all its front and subversive organizations, and sever links between Moscow and nonruling Communist parties throughout the world.

• To permit citizens of the USSR to emigrate if they want to, and if they have somewhere to go. In this respect, Vladimir Bukovsky has suggested removing an article from the Soviet Penal Code that makes it a crime no different from military desertion in the face of the enemy for a civilian to leave the USSR without authorization. Bukovsky considers this implies a state of "war" between Soviet citizens and the rest of the world.[22]

To be convincing, these reforms would have to be carried out, not just talked about in communications to the West. The ending of antagonism, for instance, would be reflected in domestic and foreign propaganda. The Communist International, forerunner of the International Department, was "abolished" during World War II, but only to deceive the West; this time we would have to be sure that its duties had not been transferred to another agency.

The West is uncertain of its role and its future, yet has managed its affairs quite well. Eastern societies and economies are in crisis, yet the leaders proclaim that the future belongs to communism. The one area where the East outshines the West is confrontation, the exploitation of the social and political asymmetries between the two systems to Soviet advantage, by the unspoken threat of military force and the covert and overt manipulation of Western opinion—Lenin's persuasion and compulsion.

Yakovlev told Spanish journalists that sometimes the Soviet leaders are told "You are now going towards liberalization; you are going towards a Western type of democracy." His reply was forthright: "Nothing of the kind. We are moving away from it. We think and even hope that in certain respects you will have to follow our example."[23] Are we to subject the entire world to the appalling Soviet experience, simply by a massive failure of imagination leading, when the truth emerges, to a failure of will?

Canadians of good will, old-style peace activists among them, can contribute to peace and freedom by facing realities and protecting democracy during the forthcoming period of Soviet adjustment or collapse. Those who find themselves in contact with

Soviet citizens might suggest the measures listed as pathways to real peace.

Alternatively, Canadians may close their eyes to the truth and indulge in the hypocrisy and moral posturing that has done so much to weaken the moral fibre and physical strength of the nation, and the West generally. The grassroots seem confused but generally ready to support the first option; as for the élites, many have shown a dismal drift to self-deception that could lead us to the abyss.

Peace *with freedom*, anyone?

NOTES

Introduction

1 Charter of the United Nations, San Francisco, 26 June 1945, preamble, lines 13–14.
2 See *The Economist*, 12 December 1987, pp. 15–16.
3 Quoted in *Canadian Tribune*, 16 November 1987, special supplement, p. 15.
4 S. A. Tiuškevič, *Vojna i sovremennost* (Moscow: Nauka, 1986), p. 126; quoted in Françoise Thom, "Moscow's 'New Thinking' as an Instrument of Foreign Policy," *Mackenzie Paper* No. 4 (Toronto, December 1987).
5 Thom, cited, passim.
6 Mikhail Gorbachev, *Perestroika: New Thinking for Our Country and the World* (New York: Harper & Row, 1987), p. 130.
7 Ibid.
8 V. I. Lenin, *Collected Works*, vol. 29 (Moscow: Progress Publishers, 1972), p. 153.
9 G. F. Kennan, *Russia and the West Under Lenin and Stalin* (1961), p. 184, quoted in Alex de Jonge, *Stalin and the Shaping of the Soviet Union* (London: Collins, 1986).

Chapter 1

1 Karl Marx and Frederich Engels, "Manifesto of the Communist Party," Lewis S. Fever (ed.), *Marx and Engels: Basic Writings on Politics and Philosophy* (New York: Doubleday, 1959), p. 6.
2 See Ju. Ja. Kiršin, V. M. Popov, R. A. Savuškin, *Političeskoe soderžanie sovremennykn vojn* (Moscow: Nauka, 1987), p. 267, quoted in Thom, cited.
3 UN Document A/4880. Letter from J. J. McCloy and V. A. Zorin, 20 September 1961.
4 Earl Mountbatten of Burma, speech in Strasbourg, 11 May 1979.

Chapter II

1   Gennady Pisarevsky, "Socialism and Human Rights," Associated Press Novosti, 16 September 1985.

2   See Ronald Duncan and Colin Wilson (eds.), *Marx Refuted* (Bath: Ashgrove Press, 1987); Klaus Bockmuehl, *The Challenge of Marxism: A Christian Response* (Downers Grove, Ill.: InterVarsity Press, 1980).

3   Quoted in T. Logvinova, "V Usluzhenii Monopolii," *Kommunist Kirgizstana* 11, 1985.

4   See P. H. Vigor, *The Soviet View of War, Peace and Neutrality* (London: Routledge and Kegal Paul, 1975).

5   V. I. Lenin, "The Proletarian Revolution and the Renegade Kautsky," 1917, *Collected Works* (trans. George Hanna), (London: Lawrence and Wishart, 1963).

6   Tiuškevič, cited, p. 13.

7   K. T. Fann, "Marxism-Leninism, World Peace, and World Revolution," in John Somerville (ed.), *Soviet Marxism and Nuclear War; an International Debate* (Westport: Greenwood Press, 1981), p. 75.

8   *Kommunist* 2, 1979.

9   In *Questions of Philosophy* (Moscow), October 1980.

10 See David Holloway, *The Soviet Union and the Arms Race* (New Haven and London: Yale University Press, 1983), pp. 15–28.

11 Ibid., p. 19.

12 Ibid., pp. 23–28, 81–108.

13 For a fuller argument, see Robin Brown, "Arms Control: Has the West Lost its Way?" Institute for European Defence and Strategic Studies, *Occasional Paper* No. 28, 1987.

14 Tiuškevič, cited, p. 7.

15 Kiršin, cited, p. 265.

16 See Richard Pipes, *Survival is not Enough: Soviet Realities and America's Future* (New York: Simon and Shuster, 1984), pp.29–33.

17 Michael Voslensky, *Nomenklatura: The Soviet Ruling Class* (New York: Doubleday, 1984), pp. 326–327.

18 Ibid.

19 For a discussion, see Jacques Ellul, *Propaganda: the Formation of Men's Attitudes* (New York: Alfred Knopf, 1965; Vintage, 1973), pp. 232–258.

20 See, for instance, de Jonge, cited pp. 120–125, 135–141; Vladimir Bukovski, *To Build a Castle: My Life as a Dissenter* (New York: Viking, 1978), passim.

21 See Françoise Thom, cited.

22 Oliver North's private army being a recent example.

23 De Jonge, pp. 135–136.

24 In a 5 July 1985 letter to the Union of Concerned Scientists, Gorbachev denied that the USSR was developing a large-scale ABM system or laying the foundations for one.
25 Quoted in *Washington Times*, 1 December 1987, p. 1; see also Robert Fulford, "The Kafkaesque reality of glasnost," *Financial Times of Canada*, 30 May 1988.
26 V. I. Lenin, *Collected Works*, vol. 26 (Moscow: Progress Publishers, 1977), p. 386; J. A. Emerson Vermaat and Hans Bax, "The Soviet Concept of 'Peace,'" *Strategic Review*, Fall 1983.
27 Tiuškevič, cited, pp. 203, 210.

Chapter III

1 Quoted in Tiuškevič, cited, p. 72.
2 V. I. Lenin, Speech at the 8th Soviet Congress, 22 December 1920, *Collected Works*, vol. 31, (Moscow: Progress Publishers, 1966).
3 Kiršin, cited, p. 265.
4 See Roger Beaumont, "Soviet Psychological Warfare and Propaganda," in *Signal, Journal of the Armed Forces Communications and Electronics Association*, vol. 42, no. 3, 1987.
5 See Randall Heather, "Terrorism, 'Active Measures,' and SDI," *Mackenzie Paper* no. 3 (Toronto, September 1987).
6 See, for instance, *Globe and Mail*, 21 August 1987, pp. 1–2; *Dallas Morning News*, 12 February 1988, p. D1; William C. Triplett, II, "Crimes Against the Alliance," *Policy Review*, Spring 1988.
7 Kim Philby recruited Britons as Soviet spies by asking if they would help him work for peace. See Nigel West, *Mole Hunt* (London: Weidenfeld & Nicolson, 1987), p. 2.
8 See Derek Nelson, "Nicaragua: The Pilgrims' Progress," *Mackenzie Paper* No. 5 (Toronto, January 1988).
9 Susan Labin, "The Techniques of Soviet Propaganda" (US Congress, Senate, Committee of the Judiciary). Revised edition. 90th Congress, 1967, Document no. 34.
10 Ibid.
11 Peter Kenez, *The Birth of the Propaganda State: Soviet Methods of Mass Mobilization, 1917–1929* (New York: Cambridge University Press, 1986).
12 Stefan T. Possany, "Communist Psychological Warfare," Walter F. Hahn and John C. Neff (eds.), *American Strategy in the Nuclear Age* (New York: Anchor Books, 1960).
13 De Jonge, cited, p. 139.

14   M. Ionov, "On the Methods of Influencing an Opponent's Decision," *Voyennaya mysl'* (Military Thought) 12 (December 1971), p. 58.

15   V. A. Lefevr and G. L. Smolyan, *Algebra of Conflict* (Moscow: 1968 JPRS Translation 52700, March 1971), pp. 33–34.

16   V. I. Lenin, *Collected Works*, vol. 45 (Moscow: Izdatel'stvo Politicheskoy Literatury, 1964), p. 34.

17   Theses, 6th Congress of the Comintern, 1928.

18   Quoted in *Rude Pravo* (Prague), 5 March 1961.

19   A. S. Milovidov and V. G. Kozlov (eds.), *The Philosophical Heritage of V. I. Lenin and Problems of Contemporary War* (Moscow: Voyenizdat, 1972).

20   *Kommunist* 12 (1983), p. 26. (Unsigned editorial.)

21   Quoted in John J. Dziak, *Chekisty: A History of the KGB* (Lexington: D.C. Heath, 1987), p. 43.

Chapter IV

1   Gary Moffatt, *A History of the Peace Movement in Canada* (mimeograph; c. December, 1982), p. 8.

2   Ernie Regehr, *Making a Killing: Canada's Arms Industry* (Toronto: McClelland and Stewart, 1975).

3   Ernie Regehr and Murray Thomson, *A Time to Disarm* (Project Ploughshares, 1978).

4   Church Monograph No. 1: "Concern for Peace Expressed by Canadian Churches, Submissions to the Standing Committee on External Affairs and National Defence, Ottawa, February 16, 1982," in Robert Matthews and Cranford Pratt (eds.), *Church and State: The Christian Churches and Canadian Foreign Policy* (Toronto: Canadian Institute for International Affairs, n.d.), p. 52.

5   See *The Military Balance, 1982–1983* (London: International Institute for Strategic Studies, 1982); Robert Jastrow and James Frelk, *How the Soviets Emasculated America's Deterrent* (Washington, DC: George Marshall Institute, n.d.); Joyce E. Larson and William C. Bodie, *The Intelligent Layperson's Guide to the Nuclear Freeze Debate* (New York: National Strategy Information Center, 1983); Robert W. Kagan, "Why Arms Control Failed," *Policy Review*, Winter 1984; George F. Will, "Why Arms Control is Harmful," *Newsweek*, 18 June 1984.

6   Matthews, cited, pp. 52–56.

7   "A Statement On Canada's Nuclear Weapons Policies, Presented to the Prime Minister, December 14, 1982," in Matthews, cited, pp. 71–73.

8   See William Johnson, "Churches' Critique is Moralistic Rubbish," *Ottawa Citizen*, 19 February 1988.

9   Hans Kohn, *The Age of Nationalism* (New York: Harper, 1962), p. 63, quoted in James E. Dougherty and Robert Pfaltzgraff, Jr. (eds.), *Shattering Europe's Defense Consensus* (New York: Pergamon-Brassey's, 1985).

10   C. S. Lewis, *The Screwtape Letters: Letters from a Senior to a Junior Devil* (London: Collins, 1942), pp. 42–43.

11   *Saturday Night*, April 1978.

12   Alan Whitehorn, "The New Democratic Party in Convention," in George Perlin (ed.), *Party Democracy in Canada* (Toronto: Prentice Hall, 1987).

13   Thomas P. Socknat, *Witness Against War: Pacifism in Canada 1900–1945* (Toronto: University of Toronto Press, 1987).

14   James M. Minifie, *Peacemaker or Powdermonkey* (Toronto: McClelland and Stewart, 1960).

15   Norman Z. Alcock, *The Bridge of Reason* (Oakville: John Wilkes Press, 1961).

16   Moffatt, cited; Ernie Regehr and Simon Rosenblum, "The Canadian Peace Movement," in Regehr and Rosenblum (eds.), *Canada and the Nuclear Arms Race* (Toronto: Lorimer, 1983).

17   Moffatt, cited, p. 35.

18   *Communist Viewpoint*, May/June 1972.

19   Quoted in Moffatt, cited, p. 60.

20   Harry G. Gelber, "Australia, the Peace Movement and the International Balance," *Australian Outlook*, vol. 40, no. 1, April 1986.

21   Saul D. Alinsky, *Rules for Radicals* (New York: Random House, 1971), p. 36.

22   Operation Dismantle, "Concept of a Global Referendum on Disarmament" (handout, c. early 1982).

23   Ibid.

24   *Congressional Record*, 16 May 1978: E-2592–93; *New Perspectives*, May/June 1973, p. 2; *Peace Courier*, July/August 1983; *Disarmament Forum*, August 1983; *Daily World*, 9 July 1983.

25   Reported in *Telegram* (Toronto), 6 February 1968.

26   *Globe and Mail*, 19 June 1984.

Chapter V

1   Richard F. Staar (ed.), *1987 Yearbook on International Communist Affairs* (Stanford: Hoover Institution Press, 1987), p. 58.

2   See James L. Tyson, *Target America: The Influence of Communist Propaganda on U.S. Media* (Chicago: Regnery, 1981), pp. 8–18; John Barron, "The KGB's Magical War for 'Peace,'" in Ernist W. Lefever and E.

Stephen Hunt (eds.), *The Apocalyptic Premise* (Washington, DC: Ethics and Public Policy Center, 1982), p. 119–120.

3   See *Soviet Influence Activities: A Report on Active Measures and Propaganda, 1986–87* (Washington, DC: U.S. Department of State, August 1987).

4   *The Road to Socialism in Canada: The Program of the Communist Party of Canada* (Toronto: Progress Books, 1985), p. 45. Originally adopted as the program of the party at the 21st Convention, 1971, and first published in 1972.

5   Ivan Avakumovic, *The Communist Party in Canada: A History* (Toronto: McClelland and Stewart, 1975); Norman Penner, *Canadian Communism: The Stalin Years and Beyond* (Toronto: Methuen, 1988).

6   Ibid.

7   See Clive Rose, *Campaigns Against Western Defence* (London: Macmillan, 1985), pp. 20–94.

8   Herbert Romerstein, *The World Peace Council and Soviet "Active Measures"* (n.p.: Hale Foundation, n.d. [available 1982]), p. 8.

9   Ibid., p. 9.

10   Quoted in Moffatt, cited, p. 23.

11   *Canadian Tribune*, 20 September 1982, p. 3.

12   Quotations from Rogers Cablevision tape of proceedings.

Chapter VI

1   See Martin Ceadel, *Pacifism in Britain, 1914–1945: The Defining of a Faith* (Oxford: Clarendon, 1980), pp. 87–108; Guenter Lewy, *Peace and Revolution: The Moral Crisis of American Pacifism* (Grand Rapids, Michigan: William B. Eerdmans, 1988).

2   Arthur Koestler, "On Disbelieving Atrocities," *New York Times Magazine*, January 1944.

3   *l'Humanité*, 15 September 1979.

4   Brian Crozier, Drew Middleton, Jeremy Murray-Brown, *This War Called Peace* (London: Sherwood Press, 1984), pp. 197–199.

5   William Kashtan, "Imperialism: The Source of the War Danger," *Communist Viewpoint*, March 1985, p. 9.

6   Truong Nhu Tang, "The Myth of Liberation," *New York Review of Books*, 21 October 1982, p. 33; see also Doan Van Toai and David Chanoff, *The Vietnamese Gulag* (New York: Simon and Schuster, 1986); and Nguyen Van Canh, *Vietnam Under Communism, 1975–1982* (Stanford: Hoover Institution Press, 1983).

7   Truong Nhu Tang, cited.

8   Quoted in Peter Collier and David Horowitz, "Goodbye to All That," *Washington Post Magazine*, 17 March 1985.
9   Collier and Horowitz, cited.
10 Ibid.
11 Freya Stark, *Dust in the Lion's Paw* (London: Murray, 1961), p. 205.
12 Claude Malhuret, "Soviet Terror in Afghanistan," *Foreign Affairs*, Winter 1983–84.
13 *Soviet News and Views* 9–10 (Ottawa: Press Office of the USSR Embassy, May 1987), p. 6.
14 *Peace Magazine*, August/September 1986, p. 26.
15 V. I. Lenin, "Left-Wing Communism: An Infantile Disorder," 1920, *Collected Works*, vol. 31 (Moscow: Progress, 1961).
16 Jeane Kirkpatrick (ed.), *The Strategy of Deception* (New York: Farrar, Straus, 1963).

Chapter VII

1   Jacques Ellul, cited.
2   Victor Zagladin, *Mezhdunarodnye kommunisticheskoye dvizhenyg; ocherki strategie i taktiki* (Moscow, 1970), p. 114, quoted in Count Hans Huyn, "Countering Subversion, Neutralism and Pacifism," paper given at Leeds Castle, England, July 1982.
3   *Communist Viewpoint*, July/August 1971.
4   The events are carefully documented in Sherri L. Wasserman, *The Neutron Bomb Controversy: A Study in Alliance Politics* (New York: Praeger, 1983). The *Times* article was 12 July 1977.
5   Rose, cited, p. 109.
6   See Rose, Barron, Romerstein, cited; Rael Jean Isaac and Erich Isaac, "The Counterfeit Peacemakers," and Vladimir Bukovski, "The Soviet Role in the Peace Movement," in Lefever and Hunt, cited.
7   A collection of Ponomarev's speeches given between 1977 and 1983 is published in Boris Ponomarev, *Against the Threat of Another World War* (Moscow: Progress, 1983). The quote from the Paris speech is on p. 94.
8   Ibid.
9   Ponomarev, cited, pp. 120–138.
10 *Programme of Action* (Helsinki: World Peace Council, [issued very early, 1981]).
11 Ibid.
12 John Clews, *Communist Propaganda Techniques* (New York: Praeger, 1964).
13 *Programme of Action*, p. 3.

14   Barron, cited, p. 134.

15   See Russell Seitz, "In from the Cold: 'Nuclear Winter' Melts Down," *The National Interest* 5 (Fall 1986), pp. 3–17.

16   Quoted in *Toronto Star*, 10 April 1982, pp. 1A–2A.

17   *Globe and Mail*, 13 June 1984, p. 11.

18   *Globe and Mail*, 18 December 1984, p. 7.

19   David Macfarlane, "In the Shadow of the Cruise," *Saturday Night*, December 1984, pp. 19–28.

20   *Newsweek*, 18 June 1984.

21   Quoted in Ceadel, cited, p. 138.

22   *Press Release*, Prime Minister's Office, Ottawa, 10 May 1983.

23   *Canadian Dimension*, July/August 1982.

24   Salvador de Madariaga, quoted in Julian Lewis, "The Lessons of the 'Peace Offensive,'" *Encounter*, July/August 1985.

25   Ponomarev, p. 15.

26   Ibid., p. 98.

27   Quoted in *The Ottawa Citizen*, 19 May 1983.

28   *Communist Focus* 14, December 1983.

29   Judith Timson, "A Death in the Family," *Saturday Night*, October 1984, p. 32.

30   Quoted *Pravda*, 14 March 1946; see "Letters to the Editor," *Financial Post*, 18 January 1988.

31   Northern Friends Peace Board, *Report of the visit of the delegation to the Soviet Peace Committee* (Horsford, Leeds: NFPB, 1982), p. 1.

32   Andrew Brewin, "The Chance for Canada to become an Arms dropout," *Globe and Mail*, 6 August 1982.

33   *Kingston Whig Standard*, 29 September 1984.

34   Geoffrey Pearson, "East–West Relations: Values, Interests and Perceptions," *Points of View* 1, March 1986.

35   In Regehr and Rosenblum, cited, pp. 63–84.

36   Simon Rosenblum, *Misguided Missiles* (Toronto: Lorimer, 1985).

37   See G. P. Armstrong, *Soviet Arms Transfers to the Third World* (Ottawa: Department of National Defence, June 1986), D STRAT A Staff Note 8604; *Washington Times*, 13 March 1988.

38   Ronald Babin, Eric Shragge, and Jean-Guy Vaillancourt, "Directions for the Canadian Peace Movement," in Shragge, Babin and Vaillancourt (eds.), *Roots of Peace* (Toronto: Between the Lines, 1986), p. 175.

39   Communiqué issued by Direct Action, 17 October 1982, claiming responsibility for the bombing of the Litton Systems plant near Toronto.

40   V. I. Lenin, *Collected Works*, vol. 26 (Moscow: Progress, 1964), p. 501.

41   *Kommunist* 15, 1971.

42   Ponomarev, cited, p. 134.

43   Ibid., p. 137.

44   Reported in *New York Times*, 27 July 1982, p. 10.

45   See Randall Heather, cited.

46   Abraham H. Miller, "The Evolution of Terrorism," *Conflict Quarterly*, vol. V, no. 4 (Fall 1985), pp. 5–16.

47   Peter M. Sandman and JoAnn Valenti, "Scared stiff—or scared into action?" *Bulletin of the Atomic Scientists*, January 1986.

48   Heather, cited.

49   Kiršin, cited, p. 265.

50   Christine Peringer (compilation), *How We Work For Peace* (Dundas: Peace Research Institute, 1987), pp. 365–382.

51   Karl Liebknecht, *Militarism and Anti-Militarism* (1907). English translation. (Cambridge: Rivers Press, 1973).

52   Ponomarev, cited, p. 34.

Chapter VIII

1   T. James Stark, "Disarmament is the Only Defence," *Maclean's*, 12 December 1980, p. 6.

2   *The Three Shadows.* A Reflection by Clarke MacDonald at the Church of the Transfiguration, Good Friday, 1981. (Mimeograph.)

3   Peace Magazine, February/March 1987, p. 39.

4   Brewin, cited.

5   *Globe and Mail*, 11 February 1985.

6   In a letter dated 18 November 1986 addressed to students' council presidents of Canadian schools on behalf of a project sponsored by James Stark, "Paix/Peace 2000."

7   *The Toronto Star*, 26 July 1986.

8   See Vigor, cited.

9   *Globe and Mail*, 10 October 1987.

10   Isaac and Isaac, cited.

11   Ibid.; see also "The KGB's Role in Vermont's Nuclear Freeze Referendum," *Human Events*, 30 October 1982; "Soviet Involvement in the Freeze," *Washington Report*, June 1983; John Rees, "Reds and the Peace Movement," *Review of the News*, 8 December 1982; Romerstein, cited.

12   See John R. Pottenger, "Liberation Theology: Its Methodological Foundation for Violence," in David C. Rapoport and Yonah Alexander (eds.), *The Morality of Terrorism: Religious and Secular Justifications* (New York: Pergamon, 1982).

Chapter IX

1   David Easton, *A Systems Analysis of Political Life* (New York: John Wiley, 1965), p. 290.

2   Jacques Ellul, *The Betrayal of the West* (New York: Seabury Press, 1978).

3   See, for instance, *Peace Magazine*, February/March 1987, pp. 21–23 and 24–26; June/July 1987, p. 31; October/November 1987, p. 29.

4   Arthur Koestler, "Anatomy of a Myth," in *The Yogi and the Commissar* (London: Jonathan Cape, 1945), pp. 132–133.

5   Alison Acker, "Webs of Bright Wool: Women in the Peace Movement," *This Magazine*, June 1984.

6   Quoted in Henry F. Cooper, "US-Soviet Defence and Space Treaty Negotiations—Important Difficulties Still to be Overcome," *NATO Review* 6, December 1987.

7   "SDI: The Soviet Program," *Current Policy* 717 (Washington, DC: US Department of State, 1985); "Soviet Defense Monopoly," *Colorado Springs Gazette*, 6 March 1985; Thomas H. Krebs, "BMD: Soviet Countermeasure Strategies," *Defence Science 2003 +*, August/September 1985; Sayre Stevens, "The Soviet Factor in SDI," *Orbis*, Winter 1986; *Globe and Mail*, 17 June 1986; "While Opposing Reagan's SDI, Moscow Pushes its own Star Wars," Heritage *Backgrounder*, No. 540, 21 October 1986; *US News and World Report*, 27 October 1986; *Manchester Guardian Weekly*, 2 November 1986; *Washington Times*, 7 November 1986 and 16 November 1987; *Defense Daily*, 1 December 1986; *Military Technology*, No. 11, 1986; *New York City Tribune*, 4 August 1987; Robert K. Ackerman, "Soviet Military Advances," *Signal: Journal of the Armed Forces Communications and Electronic Association*, November 1987; "New Evidence Points to Soviet ABM Breakout," *Washington Times*, 10 March 1988; "Red Shield Rising," *Wall Street Journal*, 15 March 1988.

8   Charles Glickham, "The Soviet Union's Response to SDI: Military Press Coverage," *Radio Liberty Research* RL 49/86, 31 January 1986.

9   See Dean Godson, *SDI: Has America Told Her Story To The World?* (New York: Pergamon-Brassey's, 1987).

10 "World Dialogue on the Prevention of Nuclear War, for Disarmament and Peace," Toronto, November 23–25, 1984. Handout.

11 Letter of invitation from Toronto Disarmament Network, 5 November 1984, concerning second annual conference 1–2 December.

12 Quoted in *Globe and Mail*, 6 April 1985.

13 Artem Melikyan reporting on Radio Moscow (TASS) in English 0842 GMT, 6 April 1985.

14 *Peace Magazine*, May 1985, p. 6.

15 *Peace Magazine*, May 1985, p. 6.

16 *Peace Magazine*, June 1985, p. 5.

17 Robert Penner, "The Canadian Peace Movement Since 1982," *The Name of the Chamber Was Peace* (Toronto: Science for Peace, 1988), p. 51.

Chapter X

1   Penner, cited, p. 52.
2   Ellul, *Propaganda*, p. 29.
3   *Canadian Dimension*, March 1986, p. 29.
4   See *Human Events*, Isaac and Isaac, Rees, Rose, Romerstein, all cited.
5   Ibid.
6   Romerstein, p. 34.
7   J. A. Emerson Vermaat, "Moscow Fronts and the European Peace Movement," *Problems of Communism*, November/December 1982, p. 54.
8   Ibid., p. 55.
9   The full text is quoted in "Moscow and the Peace offensive," *Heritage Backgrounder* No. 184, 14 May 1982, p. 20.
10 Barron, pp. 232–236; Romerstein, pp. 28–30; Rose, pp. 156–187.
11 Viktor Suvorov, *Soviet Military Intelligence* (London: Hamish Hamilton, 1984). Grafton edition, p. 136.
12 *Edmonton Journal*, 8 November 1986.
13 *Agents of Deception*, CTV, 4 May 1986.
14 Jonathan Ross, "The Peace Movement and the Radical Left," Part IV, *Our Canada*, 1 November 1982, p. 9.
15 Ibid.
16 Ibid; see also *Canadian Tribune*, 30 April 1979, 28 September 1987, 8 June 1988.
17 See brochure, Veterans Against Nuclear Arms, Toronto Branch, issued 1986.
18 Private information.
19 Reported *Globe and Mail*, 30 September 1987; see also *Vancouver Sun*, 15 April 1988.
20 Ponomarev, cited, pp. 218–219.
21 Gerhard Wettig, "The Peace Movement in Western Europe: Manipulation of Popular Perceptions," *Contemporary Soviet Propaganda and Disinformation* (Washington, DC: US Department of State, 1987), p. 167.
22 *Agents of Deception*, cited.
23 Shultz and Godson, cited, pp. 116–120.
24 *Globe and Mail*, 9 April 1985, quoted by Bert Keser, *Canadian Dimension*, March 1986, p. 29.
25 Keser, p. 29.
26 *The Daily Peacenik* convention newsletter, issued November 1985.
27 "Genocide in Afghanistan," *Town Hall Journal* (Los Angeles), 15 April 1985, p. 89.

28   *Peace Magazine*, February 1986, p. 27.
29   *Now* magazine, 14–20 November 1985.
30   *Canadian Dimension*, March 1986, p. 27.
31   Ibid., p. 26.
32   Interview, 1 November 1986.
33   *Canadian Dimension*, March 1986, p. 29.
34   Ibid., p. 26.
35   William Kashtan, "The Present Stage of the Fight for Peace, Jobs and Canadian Independence and the Developing Mass Movements," *Communist Viewpoint*, March 1986, p. 10.
36   *Canadian Dimension*, May 1986.

Chapter XI

1   *Cominform Journal*, 29 November 1949.
2   Quoted in Vera Tolz, "Soviet Press Treatment of Terrorism," Radio Liberty Research, RL 161/86, 17 April 1986.
3   *Pravda*, 25 July 1985.
4   *Agents of Deception*, cited.
5   Ponomarev, p. 218.
6   On Generals for Peace, see *Chronicle* (London), November 1984, p. 12; J. A. Emerson Vermaat, "The Strange Phenomenon of the 'Generals for Peace,'" *Strategic Review*, Spring 1985; Rose, pp. 74–76, 293–294.
7   Leonard V. Johnson, *A General for Peace* (Toronto: James Lorimer, 1987), pp. 97, 109–110.
8   Ibid., p. 97.
9   See "Institute for Policy Studies," *Institution Analysis* No. 2, Heritage Foundation, May 1977; *Wall Street Journal*, 5 February 1982, p. 26; Rael Jean Isaac and Erich Isaac, *The Coercive Utopians* (Chicago: Regnery, 1983), pp. 108–118; Scott Steven Powell, *Covert Cadre: Inside the Institute for Policy Studies* (New York: Hannaford, 1988).
10   *Observer* (London), 13 January 1985.
11   William Arkin, "Canada's Agreements with the US and her role in Strategic Defence Initiative." Address at "The True North Strong and Free?" Conference, Edmonton, November 1986 (from official tapes).
12   Isaac and Isaac, *The Coercive Utopians*, pp. 121–124; see also Michael Johns, "The Admiral Who Jumped Ship," *Policy Review*, Spring 1988, pp. 58–64.
13   Vermaat, "Generals for Peace."
14   "True North Strong and Free?" tapes, cited.
15   "Militarism in America," *The Defense Monitor*, vol. XV, no. 3, 1986.

16   Irving Louis Horowitz, "The Doctors and the Bomb," *Chronicles*, March 1986, pp. 26–32; Loren R. Graham, "Scientists, human rights, and the Soviet Union," *Bulletin of the Atomic Scientists*, April 1986, pp. 1718; Milan Korcok, "Controversy exploding around physicians-for-peace movements," *Canadian Medical Association Journal*, 15 August 1986; John Hersey, "Asymmetry," *The New Yorker*, 7 September 1987; Jack Rosenblatt, "Soviet Propaganda and the Physicians' Peace Movement," *Mackenzie Paper* No. 6, May 1988.

17   *Peace Magazine*, August/September 1986, pp. 20–21.

18   Korcok, cited.

19   Ibid.

20   Ibid. Concerning Soviet abuse of psychiatry, see Sidney Bloch and Peter Reddaway, *Soviet Psychiatric Abuse* (London: Gollancz, 1984).

21   *New Times* (Moscow), no. 19, 1981.

22   Alun Chalfont, "SDI: The Case for the Defence," Institute for European Defence and Strategic Studies, *Occasional Paper* no. 12, 1985, pp. 31–35; Steven P. Adragna, *On Guard for Victory: Military Doctrine and Ballistic Missile Defense in the USSR* (New York: Pergamon-Brassey's, 1987); "The War Against 'Star Wars,'" *Commentary*, December 1984.

23   Quoted in *Peace Magazine*, August/September 1986, p. 19.

24   *Peace Magazine*, October/November 1986, pp. 21–23.

Chapter XII

1   Ponomarev, cited, p. 164.

2   V. Matveev, "Disarmament: An Ideal, A Practical Orientation," *The Democratic Journalist* (Prague) 12 (1984), p. 4.

3   E. P. Thompson, *Protest and Survive* (Harmondsworth: Penguin, 1980), p. 45.

4   David Langille, "Strategies for the Canadian Peace Movement," Parts 1 and 2, *Canadian Dimension*, March/April and May/June 1985.

5   Nicholas Prychodko, "The Growing Peace Movement in Canada," *Communist Viewpoint*, October 1982.

6   *World Marxist Review*, September 1985.

7   Ibid.

8   Marv Gandall, "Foreign Affairs: the CLC Abroad," *This Magazine*, February 1986; letter to the editor from the Coordinating Committee, Ottawa Disarmament Coalition, *This Magazine*, June/July 1986.

9   Letter to the editor from Michael Murphy, *This Magazine*, June/July, 1986.

10   *Peace Magazine*, December 1986/January 1987, p. 46.

11   *Canadian Dimension*, December 1984.
12   *Peace Magazine*, September 1985, p. 7.
13   *Hansard*, 1985, p. 4910.
14   Penner, cited, p. 50.
15   Ellul, *Propaganda*, p. 29.
16   *Globe and Mail*, 2 November 1987.
17   *Toronto Sun*, 3 June 1987.
18   See David Regan, "The New Republics: Municipal Intervention in Defence," Institute for European Defence and Strategic Studies, *Occasional Paper* no. 30, 1987.
19   See Thom, cited, pp. 30–31.

Chapter XIII

1   Quoted in David Somerville, *Trudeau Revealed: His Actions and His Words* (Richmond Hill, Ont.: BMG Publishing, 1978), p. 205.
2   Quoted in Associated Press, Paris, 16 June 1980.
3   Quoted in *Our Canada*, 1 October 1982.
4   Richard and Sandra Gwyn, "The Politics of Peace," *Saturday Night*, May 1984, pp. 19–32.
5   *Toronto Star*, 9 December 1987.
6   Ibid.
7   Penner, cited, p. 51.
8   *Globe and Mail*, 12 December 1986.
9   Quoted in *Pacific Tribune*, 13 April 1988, p. 5.
10   *Globe and Mail*, 24 July 1986.
11   Robin Brown; George Will; Robert Kagan, all cited; Malcolm Wallop and Angelo Codevilla, *The Arms Control Delusion* (San Francisco: Institute for Contemporary Studies, 1987).
12   Dan O'Meara, with Bob Davies and Sipho Dlamini, *The Struggle for South Africa: A Reference Guide to Movements, Organizations and Institutions* (2 vols.) (London: Zed Books, 1984).
13   Conference tapes.
14   Ibid.
15   Lord Carrington, "Alliance Challenges and Opportunities," *NATO Review*, October 1987.
16   *Pacific Tribune*, 16 December 1987, p. 9.
17   *Hansard*, 1987, p. 11620.
18   Reported in *Globe and Mail*, *Toronto Star*, 2 October, 1987.

Chapter XIV

1   The formulation was originated by Baroness Cox and offered at a workshop at the University of New Brunswick in April 1986.

2   Terrance R. Carson and Wytze Brouwer, "Dimensions of Peace Education," *Curriculum Praxis Occasional Paper* No. 3, Faculty of Education, University of Alberta, 1985, p. 10.

3   *Ethics in Education*, vol. 3, no. 10, June 1984, p. 1.

4   "If at first you don't succeed," *Ethics in Education*, cited.

5   "Films, A Trial, a Dilemma," *Ethics in Education*, cited.

6   Simon Dalby, "The Soviet Threat and Peace Education," *Issues in Education and Culture*, July 1986, p. 34.

7   Allan McKinnon, "Psychological and Political Realities in Peace Education at the Post Secondary Level," *Issues in Education and Culture*, cited, p. 44.

8   Douglas Ray, "Peace Education in Canada," *Approaches to Peace Education* (Dundas: Peace Research Institute, 1986), pp. 773–778.

9   Ken Osborne, "Peace Education and the Schools: What Can We Learn from History?" *The History and Social Science Teacher*, Spring 1985, pp. 33–41.

10 Carson and Brouwer, cited.

11 Caroline Cox and Roger Scruton, "Peace Studies: A Critical Survey," Institute for European Defence and Strategic Studies *Occasional Paper* No. 7, 1984; see also John Marks, *"Peace Studies" in Our Schools: Propaganda for Defencelessness* (London: Women and Families for Defence, 1984); Roger Scruton, "World Studies: Education or Indoctrination?" Institute for European Defence and Strategic Studies *Occasional Paper* No. 15, 1985.

12 Alyson Huntley, Jim Morin, Marsha Sfeir, *Militarism and Hope* (Iowa: Wm. C. Brown, 1983). Canadian edition.

13 Wytze Brouwer, *A Survey of Peace Education in Canada* (Ottawa: Canadian Institute for International Peace and Security, [issued Fall 1986]), p. 23.

14 From notes taken at the workshop.

15 *Globe and Mail*, 27 October 1983.

16 *New York Times*, 16 October 1984, p. 16; see also Joseph Adelson and Chester E. Finn, Jr. "Terrorizing Children," *Commentary*, April 1985.

17 *Globe and Mail*, 22 April 1986.

18 Margaret Arnott, "Peace," FWTAO Curriculum Insert, 1987/88, no. 2 (for grades 5 to 8), "Peace 1".

19 "La Jeunesse s'engager au-delà des mots," *Cahier pédagogique*. Issued by Centrale de l'enseignement du Québec, June 1985, p. 206.
20 Brouwer, cited, preliminary report dated April 1986, p. 7.
21 "Eduquer à la paix: C'est contribuer à bâtir la paix," *Cahier pédagogique, Paix sans frontières*. Issued by the Quebec Ministry of Education in conjunction with CEQ, 1986, passim.
22 "Eduquer à la paix: C'est contribuer à bâtir la paix," *Cahier pédagogique Niveau collegial, Paix sans frontieres*. Issued by CEQ, October 1986.
23 *The Idler* (Toronto), February 1985, p. 22.

Chapter XV

1   V. I. Lenin, "Left-Wing Communism—An Infantile Disorder" (1920), *Collected Works*, vol. 31 (Moscow: Progress, 1966), p. 96.
2   Ellul, *Propaganda*, p. 195.
3   Françoise Thom, cited, passim.
4   Edmund Levin, "Word for Word, Perestroika Reads Better in Russian," *Wall Street Journal*, 8 February 1988; *Daily News Digest*, 10 February 1988.
5   *Wall Street Journal*, 2 December 1987, quoted in Melvin J. Lasky, "The Cycles of Western Fantasy," *Encounter*, February 1988, p. 6.
6   See Mary C. Fitzgerald, "Marshal Ogarkov on the Modern Theatre Operation," *Conflict Quarterly*, Summer 1986, pp. 39–58.
7   *Washington Post, New York Times*, 16 January 1988.
8   Gorbachev, cited, p. 151.
9   Johannes Pakaslahti, "Growing Optimism in the Peace Movement," *Peace Courier*, No. 8/87, p. 12.
10 "Canada's Peace Alliance: Moving onto High Ground," *Peace Courier*, No. 2/88, pp. 4–5.
11 *Izvestiya*, 17 February 1987.
12 *Washington Times*, 9 November 1987.
13 *Globe and Mail*, 31 March 1987; *Time*, 13 April 1987.
14 CPC 27th Convention, 1988, *Discussion Bulletin no. 1*, January 1988, p. 6. (Emphasis added.)
15 Beaumont, cited.
16 Don Munton, "Peace and Security in the 1980s: The View of Canadians," *Working Paper, CIIPS*, January 1988; digested in *Peace and Security*, Winter 1987/88, pp. 2–3.
17 Geoffrey Pearson, "Review of Peace and Security Issues in 1987 and the Canadian Response," *CIIPS Paper*, January 1988.
18 Val Sears, "Turner defence policy targets public mood," *Toronto Star*, 17 February 1988.

19 Munton, cited, p. 51.
20 Pearson, "Review," pp. 24–25.
21 Some of these ideas originate with Vladimir Bukovsky. See *Encounter*, January 1988, p. 22; see also G. P. Armstrong, D STRAT A *Staff Note*, 87/11, Ottawa, July 1987.
22 *Encounter*, January 1988.
23 Quoted in ibid., p. 24.

INDEX